The Biblical and Historical Background
of the
Jewish Holy Days

THE BIBLICAL
and
HISTORICAL BACKGROUND
of the
JEWISH HOLY DAYS

BY
ABRAHAM P. BLOCH

KTAV PUBLISHING HOUSE, INC
NEW YORK
1978

Library of Congress Cataloging in Publication Data

Bloch, Abraham P
   The Biblical and historical background of the Jewish
holy days.

   Bibliography: p.
   Includes index.
   1. Fasts and feasts—Judaism. I. Title.
BM690.B53   296.4'3   77-10687
ISBN 0-87068-338-1

Manufactured in the United States of America

To the Memory of my Parents,
Rabbi Chaim Yitzchak and Chana Bloch,
this book is affectionately dedicated.

Contents

PREFACE xi
1. THE SABBATH 1
   A Marah Tradition—Departure from Noachism—
   Sabbath and Parental Honor—The Sabbath in Post-
   Sinaitic texts—*Shamor* and *Zachor*—The Date of the
   First Sabbath—Friday Eve—The Sabbath and
   Bodily Purity.
2. ROSH HASHANAH 13
   In the Pre-Synagogue Era—After the Establishment
   of the Synagogue—The Name of the Holiday—A
   Day of Judgment—The Timing of the Day of Judg-
   ment.
3. YOM KIPPUR 27
   Early History—In the Second Temple—In the Post-
   Temple Era—Prayer—Charity—Penitence.
4. SUKKOT 39
   Symbolism of the Sukkah—A Symbol of Home-
   lessness—Date of Sukkot—A Festival of National
   Independence—*Ezrach* and *Ger*—Hoshana Rabba—
   Simchat Torah.
5. CHANUKAH 49
   Introduction—Initial Opposition—I Maccabees—II
   Maccabees—Miracle of Fire—Chanukah and Sukkot
   Josephus—Festival of Lights—*Megillat Antiochus*
   —Simon the Just—Kindling of Lights—Talmudic
   Sources—Rabban Gamliel II—Rabbinic Chanukah
   —Vernacular Term—Summation.
6. PURIM 79
   Rabbinic Identification of Ahasuerus—Date of Mor-
   decai—Rabbinic Views—Survey of Rabbinic Pas-
   sages—The Feast of Ahasuerus in Homiletics—The

Timing of Haman's Decree—Opposition to Purim —Introduction of *Mikra Megillah*—The Septuagint —The Prophets' Decree—Canonization of Book of Esther—Summation.

7. PASSOVER 101

    I. *Chag HaPesach*—Rite of Circumcision—Passover Pageantry—

    II. *Chag HaMatzot*—Matzot: Symbol of Redemption—Definition of *Etzem*—Objectives of Passover—

    III. From Joshua to Rabbi Gamliel II—Passover Pageantry in the Temple—The Babylonian Interlude—The Seder Service—Triumph of Rabbinic Judaism—The Seder in the First Century B.C.E.—The Seder of the First Century C.E. —The Seder Outside of Jerusalem—

    IV. The Seder in the Post-Temple era—The Dictum of Rabbi Gamliel—Evolution of the Haggadah— The Four Cups of Wine—

    V. The Evolution of the Four Sons—Anti-Rabbinic Movements—*Chacham:* A Hellenist— *Rasha:* A Judeo-Christian—*Tipesh,* A Saducee —One Who Does Not Ask Questions.

8. LAG B'OMER 167
A Precedent for a Celebration of Hitler's Downfall— In the Talmudic Period—Geonic Revision—Emergence of Lag B'Omer.

9. SHAVUOT 179
An Appendage of Passover—The Length of Festivals —Passover and Shavuot—The Date of the Giving of the Law—Falasha Date of Shavuot.

10. THE SECOND FESTIVAL DAY OF THE DIASPORA. 191
Introduction—Intercalation—The First Commonwealth—The Early Diaspora, 586–538 B.C.E.— Extent of the Diaspora in the Sixth Century B.C.E.— The Persian Era—The Hellenistic Era—The Kindling of Flares—Substitution of Messengers—The Need for an Additional Festival Day.

11. THE FESTIVAL OF THE FIFTEENTH OF AV 215
Ancient Origin—Agricultural and Matrimonial Holiday—The Wood-Offering Ritual.

12. THE FAST OF ESTHER 221
    Replacement of the Festival of Nikanor—Early
    Sources—Abolition of *Megillat Taanit*—Effects of
    Abolition of *Megillat Taanit*—Introduction of the
    Fast of Esther.
13. THE FAST OF THE SEVENTEENTH OF TAMMUZ .. 231
    Four Commemorative Fasts—Change from the
    Ninth to the Seventeenth of Tammuz—Date of the
    Capture of Jerusalem by the Romans—Suspension
    of the *Tamid*—The "Period of Stress"—Summation.
14. THE FAST OF TISHA B'AV 245
    A Day Predestined for Disaster—Shabtai Tzvi and
    Tisha B'Av.
15. HOLOCAUST DAY 253
    In Search of a Date—Suggested Dates—Alternate
    Suggestions.
    BIBLIOGRAPHY 259
    INDEX 263

Preface

THE DEVELOPMENT OF Judaism began at its birth on Mount Sinai. Moses was not only the giver of the law but also its chief interpreter. His appointment of a judiciary, empowered to interpret the law, led to the creation of a growing body of oral tradition to supplement the written text.

The process of legal development was slowed during the era of the prophets, who were preachers rather than teachers. Their appearance was timed to respond to the challenge of pervasive idolatry and its moral corruption, which had eroded the fabric of the law.

The conclusion of the prophetic period coincided with the eradication of paganism in Judea. The process of interpreting the ancient law was thereupon resumed with great vigor by a rabbinic leadership which came to the fore as the influence of the increasingly politicized priestly caste was on the wane.

The task undertaken by the rabbis was many-faceted. In addition to academic juridical development, there was a need for integrating the moral insight of the prophets into the law in order to prevent internal subversion. It was also imperative to build a defense against external threats through the forging of a spiritual force to bring hope and unity to fragmentized Jewry, scattered throughout the world.

Holidays and fasts hold a unique place in the religious code of Judaism. They form an integral part of the body of ritual and social laws through which Jews have traditionally related to God and to society. They have also been instrumental in producing a sharply focused awareness of historic links to the past. More importantly, their morale-lifting effect upon the average Jew has been crucial to his survival in an increasingly hostile environment.

Our talmudic sages invested the sacred days with symbolic ceremonials to counteract the demoralization which was inflicted by traumatic experiences. These therapeutic measures were part of the great achievement of the ancient rabbis.

The framework of rabbinic Judaism was completed by the end of the talmudic era. Post-talmudic scholarship elaborated upon this legacy and added a few floors to the structure, leaving its design and character unchanged. In tracing the history of the development of the biblical holidays, we must look to the Talmud and other sources of that period for information on the progress of that process.

There are a few notable exceptions. The transformation of the Sabbath is indicated in the Pentateuch, which provides the necessary sources. Our brief discussion of its development is mainly confined within that circumscribed context. The evolution of the post-talmudic holidays must, of necessity, be looked for in contemporary sources.

Abraham P. Bloch

1

The Sabbath

A MARAH TRADITION

SEMITIC TRADITION, PRIOR to the Torah, did not prescribe an official day of rest. The verse in Genesis proclaiming the Sabbath a holy day (2:3) was not followed by a provision for enforced rest, nor did it prescribe a ritual observance. Indeed, the last day of the week was not yet designated as the Sabbath but merely as "the seventh day." It was not until the Jews were admonished not to gather manna on that day that the name Sabbath was introduced for the first time, to indicate its new character as a day of rest (Exod. 16:13–29).

According to one rabbinic source, the earliest instructions pertaining to the observance of the Sabbath were given in Marah, three days after the Jews had crossed the Red Sea (*Sanhedrin* 56b). The laws alleged to have been expounded in Marah included the seven Noachite laws, the Sabbath, honor of parents, and *Dinim* (Litigations).

The basis for this statement is obscure. Rabbi Judah cites the Deuteronomic version of the Decalogue, where the Sabbath and parental-honor commandments contain an appended reference to a prior command—"As the Lord thy God commanded thee" (*Sanhedrin* 56b, Deut. 5:12, 16). The occasion of the prior command, according to Rabbi Judah, was the pause at Marah. We may assume that Rabbi Judah used the Deuteronomic text merely as corroborating support of an old rabbinic tradition, but the real reason must be found elsewhere. The second Decalogue

1

does not designate Marah as the point of origin of the two commandments. Furthermore, if the second Decalogue refers to Marah, why was this reference omitted in the first Decalogue, which was proclaimed shortly after Marah? However, even if we are to consider the Deuteronomic text as the sole basis for the tradition of an early version of the two commandments, we may still wonder what theological or historical point the rabbis sought to convey by including the Noachite laws in the Marah tradition.

It seems to me that the Marah tradition offers a clue to the content and number of the commandments of the Tablets of the Law. Did the Sinaitic covenant, which marked the birth of Judaism, represent a break with Noachism (or Semitism), or was it merely a new, advanced stage of development? If the latter, what distinguishing feature did Judaism introduce to indicate its departure from Noachism? Why did the Tablets contain ten commandments?

The Marah tradition makes it clear that Judaism did not reject its Noachic roots. The preliminary instruction—leading, according to the rabbis, to the Sinaitic covenant—began with a restatement of the seven Noachite laws. Of these only the belief in God is a positive injunction. The remainder are negative injunctions, admonishing against the commission of various crimes. There is no mention of man's moral, ethical, and social obligations to his fellow man. Indeed, this is characteristic of all ancient Semitic codes.

DEPARTURE FROM NOACHISM

Judaism's distinctive innovation is its development of new concepts of socio-ethical human relations and obligations. It was the psalmist who succinctly defined it in his admonition: "Remove thyself from evil and do good" (Ps. 34:15). Noachism was concerned only with the "removal from evil." Judaism included "do good" within its philosophic and juridical framework.

The biblical allegation that "there [in Marah] he made for them a statute and an ordinance" (Exod. 15:25) indicated to the rabbis that Marah was the location of a substantial pre-Sinaitic theological and juridic exposition. The Judaic character of the new revelation is reflected in the phraseology of the succeeding verse: "If thou wilt hearken to the voice of the Lord thy God, and wilt do that which is right in his eyes, and wilt give ear to his commandments, and keep all his statutes . . ." (Exod. 15:26). The admonition to "do that which is right" (*yashar* may also be translated "fair," "equitable," or "ethical"), in addition to the compliance with laws and statutes, is Judaism's point of departure from Noachism. The Judaic elements of the Marah tradition were inherent in the Sabbath and parental-honor laws which supplemented the seven Noachic laws.

That the rabbis regarded the Marah laws as a preparatory stage to the Sinaitic covenant is evident from a *Mechilta* comment on the text in Exodus 15:26: " 'If thou wilt hearken to the voice of God thy Lord'—the reference is to the Ten Commandments, which were proclaimed from mouth to mouth in a loud voice." It may be said, therefore, that the Marah tradition was formalized by the Decalogue, which in effect comprises the seven Noachite laws and the three supplementary laws added to them in Marah. The commandment against bearing false testimony properly comes under the heading of *Dinim*.

SABBATH AND PARENTAL HONOR

Why were the Sabbath and parental honor singled out as symbols of the socio-ethical elements of Judaism? The primary function of the Sabbath was to restrict the self-proclaimed right of primitive man to exact unlimited servitude from his children, slaves, and beasts of burden. Ancient society generally granted to the head of the family absolute control over dependent children and slaves. Their very lives and existence were at the sufferance of the master. The aged and the ailing also constituted a pitiful segment of society because they could not look to it for assistance and support. This situation was tolerated even within the context of the Noachite civilization. The Sabbath and parental-honor laws stressed man's social obligations to the most helpless elements of the population—the elderly ("honor thy parents"), the young, the slave, the stranger, and even the beast of burden (the Sabbath). The right of litigation gave them a recourse to law to protect them from neglect. Human dignity became an inalienable right painfully acquired with the exodus. The proclamation of monotheism on Mount Sinai begins with a reference to the God who took the Hebrews out of Egypt, not with a cosmogonic declaration of the God who created the universe. Judaism thus indelibly left its mark as a champion of human rights.

The objective of the Sabbath was spelled out in the original version of the Decalogue: "Remember the Sabbath to keep it holy . . . thou shalt not do any manner of work, thou, nor thy son, nor thy daughter, nor thy man servant, nor thy maid servant, nor thy cattle, nor thy stranger . . . " (Exod. 20:8–11). The socio-ethical purpose of the Sabbath was even more clearly indicated in the motivation expressed in a subsequent passage: "on the seventh day thou shalt rest, in order that thy ox and thy ass may have rest, and the son of the hand-maid, and the stranger may be refreshed" (Exod. 23:12).

The main theme of the first tablet is the proclamation of monotheism, stressing man's obligation to God (*bein adam lamakom*). The commandments of the Sabbath and parental honor were included in the same tablet, even though they were primarily social laws (*bein adam lachavero*), as an indication that the declaration of human rights, inherent in these two commandments, emanates from the new concept of Judaic theology.

THE SABBATH IN POST-SINAITIC TEXTS

A subtle change in the social classification and goals of the Sabbath and parental honor is perceptible, however, soon after the proclamation of the Decalogue. This change is reflected in the substitution of the verb *shamor* ("observe") in subsequent Sabbath injunctions in place of *zachor* ("remember"). The reference to a day of rest for the sake of one's children and slaves was no longer repeated after its last mention in Exodus 23:12 (with the exception of the Deuteronomic version of the

Decalogue, which is basically a copy of the original version). A new rationalization declared that the purpose of the Sabbath is to contribute to the awareness of holiness. There is also a subtle introduction of the term "fear" of mother and father, an expression normally reserved for man's attitude to God.

The change seems to indicate a shift in emphasis from the sociological aspects of the Sabbath and parental honor to the theological, an intent to use these two laws as religious tools to bolster monotheism, while their primary social objectives remain unchanged.

In the earliest biblical passage where the change is manifest, primacy is given to the theme of God's election of Israel and the latter's special obligation to God. The Lord sanctified the Sabbath and gave it to Israel as a token of its assumption of holiness. The importance of the Sabbath is enhanced by a special covenant, confirming the Sabbath for all time (Exod. 31:12–17).

SHAMOR AND ZACHOR

The change from zachor to shamor is significant. The etymological root of shamor means "to engrave" (Mandelkorn, Concordance, s.v. Shamor). Ancient documents and legal statements of great importance were engraved in order to preserve them for posterity. "To engrave," therefore, came to mean "to preserve." The "preservation" of a religious law carried with it an obligation to take active steps to assure its perpetuation through transmission from generation to generation.

The Bible uses the verb shamor in a small, select number of fundamental laws, whose preservation is of supreme importance. It was originally used in connection with the Abrahamitic covenant (Gen. 17:9), which became the basis upon which the relationship between God and the Jewish people rested. Thereafter, the verb shamor was used in conjunction with every law which was made the subject of a covenant.

The rite of circumcision, the visible sign of the Abrahamitic covenant (Gen. 17:2), was in itself made a covenanted commandment (Gen. 17:13). The Jews were therefore enjoined to "preserve" it (zot briti asher tishmaru—Gen. 17:10). The exodus from Egypt fulfilled God's promise which was incorporated into the Abrahamitic covenant (Gen. 15:16). This fact called for a special effort to preserve the Passover ritual (*ushmartem hayom haze*—Exod. 12:17).

The Kohanim were in charge of the sacrificial rituals by means of which man worshipped God. The priesthood was granted to them by a special covenant (Num. 25:13). They were therefore under injunction to "preserve" the priesthood   (*ve-shamru et khunatam*—Num. 3:10).

The category of laws known as *chukim* (lit. "engraved" laws, i.e., laws to be preserved) generally refers to rituals whose rationale is unknown, but which must be accepted as an expression of faith. Such rituals, intimately associated with divine worship, are an affirmation of the practitioner's adherence to the covenant. They must therefore be "preserved" (*et chukotai tishmoru*—Lev. 19:19).

When the Sabbath was given the new role of a testimonial of the supremacy of God, the creator of heaven and earth, it was transformed into a covenanted institution (Exod. 31:16). Thereafter the Jews were ordered to "preserve" it (*ushmartem et haShabbat*—Exod. 31:14).

The shift in the emphasis of the Sabbath was apparently brought about as a result of the vacillation of the Jewish people and the ease with which they had relapsed into idolatry. The fact that the new aspect of the Sabbath was initially recorded in the Bible immediately preceding the incident of the golden calf points to an obvious causal relationship.

The Sabbath was to become, henceforth, the principal reminder of God and the paramount preserver of the faith. A similar role was assigned to parents and elders, who were entrusted with the prime responsibility of transmitting the creed to succeeding generations. Prior to the establishment of schools and the emergence of professional teachers, the duty of teaching the faith devolved exclusively upon parents. The biblical injunction "and thou shalt teach them diligently" (Deut. 6:7) was addressed to parents. The injunction "Honor thy father and thy mother" was originally an expression of Judaic ethics. In its expanded role, as a means for preserving the faith, "honor" became synonymous with reverence, contributing to the child's receptive mood. What was now expected of the child was more than respect or honor. As the custodian of the faith, the parent became the representative of God. The younger generation was therefore instructed to "fear" one's mother and father (Lev. 19:3), even as one must learn to "fear" God. We may parenthetically note that the word "mother" precedes "father" in the verse in Leviticus, reversing the sequence in the parental-honor commandment of the Decalogue. In the role of the parents as teachers, nature has given the mother earlier access to the mind of the child. The broader objective of the veneration of the aged is spelled out in the injunction: "Thou shalt rise up before the hoary head, and honor the face of the old man, and thou shalt fear thy God . . ." (Lev. 19:32).

The relation of the Sabbath and parental honor to monotheism sheds light on the sequence of some of the biblical verses. Thus the instructions of Moses to the entire congregation of Israel, following, according to tradition, his descent from Mount Sinai in the aftermath of the golden calf episode, began with a restatement of the law of the Sabbath (Exod. 35:2).

The passage commanding the attainment of holiness begins with the triple injunctions of respect for parents, the observance of the Sabbath, and the prohibition of idolatry (Lev. 19:2–4). The affinity of the Sabbath to holiness is expressed in Exodus: "Verily, you shall keep my Sabbaths, for it is a sign between me and you throughout your generations, that you may know that I am the Lord who sanctifies you" (31:13). The same relationship is reflected in the sequence of two verses in Leviticus: "Profane not thy daughter, to make her a harlot. . . . You shall keep my Sabbaths and reverence my sanctuary" (19:29–30).

The Deuteronomic version of the Decalogue reflects the new scope and mission of the Sabbath, which evolved after its promulgation on Mount Sinai. The socio-ethical objectives are retained, but the new aspect is incorporated through the substitution of *shamor* for *zachor*. This indicates the connection between the Sabbath and the Abrahamitic covenant. The linking of the Sabbath to the exodus is a similar expression of affirmation of the covenant, which included the divine promise of redemption from Egyptian slavery.

The new theological importance of the Sabbath and honor of parents is apparently underscored by the addition in the Deuteronomic version of the Decalogue, at the conclusion of these two commandments, of the phrase "as the Lord thy God has commanded thee." The fulfillment of these commandments must be a conscious response to the divine will and not merely an expression of a humane impulse.

The new interpretation of the Sabbath and parental honor makes them truly an integral part of the theme of the first tablet. It is the second tablet which deals exclusively with social obligations and restrictions, binding on all, even if they are not members of the covenant. Indeed the name of the Lord does not even appear in it.

THE DATE OF THE FIRST SABBATH

Two talmudic traditions assign different dates to the first Sabbath observed by the Jewish people. One source (*Sanhedrin* 56b) states that the Jews received instruction in the law of Sabbath while they paused at Marah. According to Ibn Ezra, the Jews spent only one day in Marah, the day of the Sabbath (Exod. 15:27). Marah was three days distance from the Red Sea, which the Jews had crossed on the twenty-first of Nisan. It follows that the first Sabbath was observed on the twenty-fourth of Nisan.

Other talmudic sources (*Shabbat* 118b, *Seder Olam*, chap. 5) consider Iyar 22 to be the date of the first Sabbath (see Tosafot, *Kaasher Tzivcha*; *Shabbat* 87b). This tradition is based on an implication of the verse "And the people rested on the seventh day" (Exod. 16:30), the first biblical reference to the observance of the Sabbath.

The two dates are not necessarily inconsistent. The author of *Seder Olam* mentions both dates, implying that the observance of the Sabbath was voluntary beginning with the earlier date but compulsory after the second date.

FRIDAY EVE

The biblical text makes it amply clear that the observance of the Sabbath preceded the giving of the Law on Mount Sinai (Exod. 16:25–30). It is generally assumed that the Sabbath, from its very inception, began on Friday evening. Rabbi Pinchas Horowitz, an eighteenth-century sage, suggested that prior to the giving of the law the Sabbath began on Saturday morning (*Hamakneh, Kiddushin* 37b). This opinion is based on the assumption that prior to Mount Sinai the night constituted the conclusion of the preceding day rather than the beginning of the following day. This opinion was apparently concurred in by the famous twelfth-century exegete, Rashbam. He derived this inference from the verse in Genesis (1:5): "And there was evening and there was morning, one day." There seems to be a reasonable conclusion that the "day" was finished by sunrise of the second day rather than on the preceding evening. However, there is evidence to the contrary.

The account of the mannah includes an injunction against the collection of mannah on the Sabbath. For that reason it did not come down on the Sabbath. The mannah fell at night so that it should not melt in the heat of the day. The fact that no mannah fell on Friday nights seems to indicate that even at that early period the night was already considered part of the following Sabbath day.

Ibn Ezra vehemently attacked the view that the night was part of the preceding day (Exod. 16:26). He wrote at length on the subject in a special pamphlet entitled *Iggeret Shabbat*.

THE SABBATH AND BODILY PURITY

Among the Sabbath restrictions which are common to the Falashas, Karaites, and Samaritans is the prohibition of marital relations on the Sabbath. All nonrabbinic sects share some basic principles. They all stress the laws of impurity because the Bible stresses these laws and discusses them at length. They all emphasize the sanctity of the Sabbath and its numerous restrictive laws because the Bible repeatedly emphasizes the same subject. They all interpret the Bible with a strict literalness because they have no oral law and tradition to supplement the written text.

The prohibition of sexual relations on the Sabbath is not spelled out in the Bible. The Talmud sanctions such practice. The common restriction of cohabitation on the Sabbath, followed by all nonrabbinic sects despite many divergencies in other areas, may possibly be traced to the Book of Jubilees, the earliest source to mention such a restriction. The rationale of this prohibition may lie in a link between marital relations and the laws of impurity.

The Karaite code, *Eshkol HaKofer*, associates sexual activities with an impurity of the body which is claimed to be inconsistent with the sanctity of the Sabbath. The author supports his statement with the biblical provision for the segregation of the sexes three days prior to the Sabbath when the law was given on Mount Sinai (Exod. 19:15), so that the people might preserve their purity and sanctity.

It is of interest to note that the Talmud relates that the *Chasidim HaRishonim* (early pietists) engaged in marital relations only on Wednesdays so that their wives might not bring about "a desecration of the Sabbath" (*Niddah* 38a). The Amoraim labored hard to explain this practice and in the end were forced to amend the passage to read as follows: "The *Chasidim HaRishonim* engaged in marital relations from Wednesday on" (*Niddah* 38b). The amendment hardly improves on the original and sheds little light on the reason for the practice. One is tempted to suggest a substitute amendment: "The *Chasidim HaRishonim* engaged in marital relations only until Wednesday." The *Chasidim HaRishonim* were the pious men of the pre-talmudic era. They too might have prohibited marital relations on the Sabbath and extended the prohibition to include a three-day period prior to the Sabbath. This might have been based on the rule that emission of sperm in a woman within three days after sexual relations renders her impure (*Shabbat* 86a). This law was derived from the restriction imposed for three days prior to the giving of the law.

The Talmud's view of the joys of the Sabbath is devoid of the harsh solemnity attributed to it by nonrabbinic sects. Some historians identify the *Chasidim HaRishonim* with the Essenes, an early nonrabbinic sect. That may explain their restricted practice. Incidentally, the New England Puritans strictly prohibited sexual relations on the Christian Sabbath.

2

Rosh HaShanah

IN THE PRE-SYNAGOGUE ERA

ROSH HASHANAH IS the second most sacred day in the Jewish religious calendar. Yet its solemnity is hardly evident to a casual reader of the pertinent biblical texts. The first reference to Rosh Hashanah is in Leviticus (23:24): "In the seventh month, in the first day of the month, shall be a day of rest [*shabaton*] unto you, a memorial proclaimed with a blast [of the shofar], a holy convocation." Another passage dealing with Rosh Hashanah is in Numbers (29:1): "And in the seventh month, on the first day of the month, you shall have a holy convocation: you shall do no manner of work, it is a day of the blast [of the shofar] unto you."

The attributes which we have come to associate with the first of Tishri, those of a New Year and a Day of Judgment, are not spelled out in the preceding verses. The English translation of *shabaton*, "a solemn day of rest," falls short of accuracy. *Shabaton* is mentioned in the Bible in conjunction with the Sabbath (Exod. 16:23) and Yom Kippur (Lev. 16:3) as well as the first day of Sukkot and Shmini Atzeret (Lev. 23:39), where the term carries no implication of solemnity.

There was nothing unusual about the sacrificial rites of the first of Tishri, inasmuch as similar rites were conducted on all festivals. The only distinct ritual, unique to Rosh Hashanah, was the blast of the shofar. The average Jew of antiquity was probably unimpressed by this ritual because the Sanctuary regularly resounded to the blasts of trumpets when the

13

additional offering (Musaf) was sacrificed on the Sabbath and festivals (Num. 10:10).

Indeed nonrabbinic sects, such as the Samaritans, Sadducees, Falashas, and Karaites, did not regard the first of Tishri either as a New Year or as a Day of Judgment. The same is true of Philo the Alexandrian (1st cent.), the outstanding religious philosopher of Hellenistic Jewry, Josephus, the prominent Jewish historian of the first century, and the author of the Book of Jubilees.

It was due to the profound insight of rabbinic Judaism and its research into the intent and spirit of the Bible that the holiday of the first of Tishri was invested with a moralistic tone of universalist import. Even Philo noted the universalist message of this holiday, addressed to all of mankind. He viewed the shofar, an instrument used to direct men at war, as an appeal to end all conflicts plaguing man and nature. However, he failed to grasp the sweeping moral perception of rabbinic Judaism, which regards the sound of the shofar as a call for the eradication of evil instincts and the reaching out for perfection through devotion to God and charity to man.

Ancient Jews, particularly prior to the Babylonian diaspora (6th cent. B.C.E.), were hardly aware of the significance of the first of Tishri. They may even have considered that day a minor holiday. The only imposing holidays were the Pilgrimage Festivals, at which times the entire nation was enjoined to assemble at Jerusalem. Reunions of such magnitude strengthened national solidarity and reinforced religious consciousness.

Rosh Hashanah, on the other hand, was mainly observed in the privacy of one's home. In the absence of synagogues and a prescribed order of prayers, what form did the religious observance of the first of Tishri take? The sacrificial rite of the holiday was confined to the Temple, and most of the people did not witness it. The same was true of the blowing of the shofar, which was done by the Kohanim in conjunction with the ritual of the Musaf (additional) offering.

The commandment to hear the sound of the shofar was,

indeed, not restricted to the Temple (*Rosh Hashanah* 33a). It is most unlikely, however, that in ancient times this ritual was observed outside Jerusalem. Most people lacked the required skill, and there were no synagogues where a skilled individual could blow the shofar in public.

One must also take into account the fact that up to the time of the Babylonian exile, monotheism had waged a losing battle against idolatry, and ignorance of the Bible was commonplace.

The assumption that the shofar ritual was not practiced outside Jerusalem appears to be corroborated by several ancient sources. When Zerubbabel came to Palestine from Babylonia in 521 B.C.E., he restored the sacrificial rites on the first of Tishri (Ezra 3:6). The Temple had not yet been rebuilt, and the offerings were brought upon an altar specially erected for that purpose. There is no mention of the blowing of a shofar. Apparently this practice had been suspended prior to the reconstruction of the Temple.

Ezra came to Jerusalem in 458 B.C.E. to discover a community rife with intermarriage and weakened by assimilation. He assembled the people on the first of Tishri and read to them passages from the Pentateuch. The assembly burst out crying in a mood of contrition and penitence. Ezra comforted them: "This day is holy unto the Lord your God, mourn not, nor weep" (Neh. 8:9). The people were unaware of the nature of the day. He told them to go home "to eat the fat, and drink the sweet, and send portions" to the poor. On the second day (possibly the second day of Rosh HaShanah; according to the Talmud [Jer. *Eruvin*, chap. 3], the holiday was celebrated on two days in Palestine since the time of the former prophets), the people were instructed to prepare for the festival of Sukkot. Once again, there was no mention of the blowing of the shofar on either day. Apparently this was omitted because the rite of the shofar had been performed in the Temple by the Kohanim.

The apocryphal Esdras (3rd cent. B.C.E.) seems to imply that the festivities ordered by Ezra on the first of Tishri were not due to the festive character of the day. It states that the people went to their homes "to eat and drink and make merry . . . because they understood the words wherein they were instructed" (I Esd. 9:54–55). In other words, the people celebrated because they rejoiced in their ability to comprehend the lesson which Ezra had taught them.

For some obscure reason, Josephus reported that the date of the assembly before Ezra was the first day of Sukkot. He, too, appears to imply that joyous celebrations were not part of the observance of the first of Tishri (*Antiquities* 9. 5) This is in contradiction to the rabbinic emphasis on the joyous character of Rosh HaShanah, despite its solemnity (*Chulin* 83a). Occasionally, the Talmud refers to the *Yom tov shel Rosh Hashanah* (*Rosh HaShanah* 29b, *Erachin* 13a).

Philo the Alexandrian explicitly stated that the Temple was the location where the shofar was blown. "Then came the opening of the sacred month, when it is customary to sound the shofar in the Temple at the same time that the sacrifices are brought there" (*Treatise On the Ten Festivals*, The Eighth Festival).

In his description of the various festivals, Josephus noted: "In the seventh month . . . they . . . sacrificed a bull, a ram, and seven lambs and a kid of the goat for sins" (*Antiquities* 3. 10). Amazingly, he omitted to mention the shofar, which he apparently considered merely incidental to the sacrifices.

AFTER THE ESTABLISHMENT OF THE SYNAGOGUE

The growing significance of the rite of the shofar began with the establishment of the synagogue in the period of the Second Temple. The synagogue, essentially a Pharisaic institution, most likely registered a spurt of growth following the triumph of Pharisaism upon the death of King Jannai in 76 B.C.E. In Egypt, where the Sadducees had no influence, synagogues are known to have existed by 250 B.C.E.

The sounding of the shofar on the first of Tishri was unquestionably among the early rituals introduced into the synagogue, in addition to a prescribed order of prayers and the reading of the Pentateuch. Even in the environs of Jerusalem, people no longer depended upon the Temple rite of the shofar because the practice had spread to the synagogues in their own locations (*Rosh HaShanah* 29b).

It seems that in the initial period, the task of blowing the shofar in the synagogue was entrusted to Kohanim, since they had also been in charge of this ritual in the Temple. In a talmudic account of a public fast for rain in the second century C.E., selections of Rosh HaShanah prayers that precede the sounding of the shofar were recited, and following that the Kohanim were requested to blow the shofar (*Taanit* 15a). It is quite clear that this must have been the general procedure on Rosh HaShanah. In time, as the practice of blowing the shofar became more widespread, many Israelites acquired the skill of shofar blowing. Others brought the shofar to an expert on Rosh HaShanah to get instructions (*Rosh HaShanah* 29b).

The peak in the widespread practice of shofar blowing was reached after the destruction of the Temple in the year 70, when the synagogue became the primary institution of Jewish religious life. The talmudic rabbis of the Temple era left few dicta pertaining to the rite and qualifications of the shofar. The entire matter seems to have been left to the jurisdiction of the Kohanim. The earliest rabbi to discuss a legal question with regard to the sounding of the shofar was Rabban Yochanan b. Zacai, the great religious leader who left besieged Jerusalem to found the academy of Yavneh. He decreed that the shofar be sounded at Yavneh on Rosh HaShanah even on the Sabbath, just as it had been done in Jerusalem (*Rosh HaShanah* 29b). The process of religious continuity was thus dramatically demonstrated.

It was left to Rabban Gamliel, the first *nasi* of Hillel's genealogy after the destruction of the Temple, to institute the practice which assured the centrality of the shofar in the synagogal Rosh HaShanah service. The rabbis of the post-Temple era had emphasized the individual obligation of every Jew to blow the shofar. However, Rabban Gamliel ruled that despite this obligation, one person may be delegated to sound the shofar on behalf of the entire congregation (*Rosh HaShanah*

33b). Thus the ancient practice prevailing in the Temple was restored in the synagogue.

Incidentally, the gigantic task of adjusting Jewish religious life to conditions created by the destruction of the Temple fell to Rabban Gamliel (head of Yavneh, 80–110). It was his influence which was decisive in the change of the historical emphasis of the Passover Seder service (see chap. 7), and he was likewise responsible for the centrality of the shofar on Rosh HaShanah.

It is in the second century that we find the greatest number of rabbis involved in legal discussions pertaining to the shofar. This preoccupation attests to the fact that the preeminence of the rite of the shofar had become widespread by the second century.

THE NAME OF THE HOLIDAY

The biblical name of the holiday of the first of Tishri is Yom Teruah ("day of the blast of the shofar"). As late as the first century C.E. Philo called this day the "holiday of the shofar." There is no reference in the Pentateuch to a New Year. Such a designation would be in contradiction to the chronological date of the holiday: "In the seventh month, on the first day of the month . . ." (Lev. 23:24, Num. 29:1). Following the Exodus from Egypt, the month of Nisan was proclaimed to be the first month of the year (Exod. 12:1). (According to *Targum Jonathan b. Uziel* on I Kings 8:2, Tishri was the first month of the year prior to the exodus.) Nisan thus came to mark the beginning of the year. As late as the first century C.E., Josephus wrote: "In the month of Xanticus, which is by us called Nisan, and is the beginning of the year . . ." (*Antiquities* 3. 10). Yet there is evidence in the Pentateuch that Tishri, the start of the fall season, was an agricultural or farmers' new year. Thus we read about "the feast of the ingathering [Sukkot] at the end of the year" (Exod. 23:16). A similar reference is found in Exodus 34:22—"and the feast of the ingathering at the turn of the year."

An ancient farmers' calendar, unearthed at Gezer, marks the succession of the months with regard to the various tasks which a farmer has to perform in the course of the year. It opens with the fall season, which obviously was the beginning of the agricultural year. The task indicated for the first month is "ingathering," the identical chore mentioned in the Bible for the month of Tishri.

The spring festival of Passover (Exod. 34:18) has its counterpart in the fall festival of Sukkot. The seasonal aspects of these festivals were highlighted along with their historical facets. The first of Tishri apparently was designated a religious holiday to mark the beginning of the seasonal year, an appropriate time for a period of judgment. According to the author of Jubilees, the first of Tishri merely marks the beginning of the fall season. He does not admit to its being a day of judgment (6:23).

The name Rosh HaShanah was attached to the first of Tishri after the return of the Babylonian diaspora to Palestine. Babylonian Jewry had adopted the Babylonian names of the months, and this innovation was retained by the Jewish repatriates in Palestine (Jer. *Rosh HaShanah*, chap. 1). In the course of time, the practice of identifying months by their numerical order was abandoned, and the use of names was substituted. "The first day of the seventh month" faded from usage, and "the first day of Tishri" came into vogue. The identification of the first of Tishri with Rosh HaShanah was brought about by several factors. Tishri was the first month in the Babylonian calendar, and Jews gradually also came to view it as such. A more important factor was the rabbinic interpretation of the religious implications of the holiday as a day of judgment set on the anniversary of the creation of the world.

The gradual shift to a popular acceptance of Tishri as the beginning of the year is indicated in talmudic halachic decisions. An early law, established at a time when Nisan was still regarded as the beginning of the year, stated: "A house leased 'for the duration of this year,' its lease expires on the first of Nisan, even if the lease had been executed on the first of Adar [a month earlier]" (Tosefta, *Rosh HaShanah*, chap. 1). The juridical principle that the qualifying phrase "this year," when used in bilateral legal transactions, is to be construed to mean up to the month of Nisan, remained in force even when many people no longer regarded Nisan as the beginning of a new year.

A contrary construction of the phrase "this year" was adopted in the case of unilateral transactions, where the true intent of the principal was crucial. It was therefore ruled that "if one takes a vow to abstain from accepting favors from another individual . . . 'for the duration of this year' . . . the year expires on the first of Tishri" (*Rosh HaShanah* 12b). Subsequent rabbis explained that in interpreting the intent of the person who made the vow, we must take into consideration the layman's understanding of the phrase "this year." It is obvious that to the common people of the second century, Tishri marked the beginning of a new year.

The Hebrew term Rosh HaShanah appears for the first time in Ezekiel (40:1): "In the five and twentieth year of our captivity, in the beginning of the year [*rosh-hashanah*], in the tenth of the month . . ." Obviously, Ezekiel did not refer to the first of Tishri but to Yom Kippur. According to the Talmud, Ezekiel was describing a jubilee year, which goes into effect on Yom Kippur. It is also likely that Ezekiel used the term broadly, similar to the Pentateuchal *m'reishit hashanah* (Deut. 11:12), "in the early part of the year."

The Babylonians celebrated their New Year on the first of Tishri, and they called this festival Rish Shattin. This did not influence the development of the Hebrew Rosh HaShanah. In the first place, their holiday was thoroughly pagan in character. In the second place, we find no trace of the name Rosh HaShanah (the equivalent of Rish Shattin) for a period of five hundred years after the restoration of the Jewish community in Palestine. It was not until the fourth century, when the name Rosh HaShanah was well established, that some Babylonian sages used an Aramaic rendition, Reish Shata (*Rosh HaShanah* 32b, *Baba Batra* 147a). The same was true of Yoma d'Kippura and Pischa, Aramaic names of Passover and Yom Kippur.

The Talmud mentions four Rosh HaShanah days in the year: Nisan 1, for Kings (for the purpose of reckoning of years since the ascent of a king); Elul 1, for the tithing of animals; Tishri 1, for the civil calendar; Shevat 1, for the trees (*Rosh HaShanah* 2a). Of these four days, only the first of Tishri became universally known as Rosh HaShanah.

The earliest rabbi to use the name Rosh HaShanah was

Rabban Gamliel (1st cent.). However, his reference was to the new year of trees (*Rosh HaShanah* 15a). Others whose dicta included the name Rosh HaShanah were his younger colleagues of the second century, Rabbi Joshua (*Rosh HaShanah* 6a) and Rabbi Akiva (*Rosh HaShanah* 16a).

A DAY OF JUDGMENT

The rabbinic tradition which declared Rosh HaShanah a day of judgment has its origin in scriptural texts and in the admonitions and proclamations of the prophets and psalmists. The rite of the shofar was another revealing indication of the judgment aspect of the holiday.

The first historical occasion associated with the sounds of the shofar was the Sinaitic revelation (Exod. 19:16). The opening of the jubilee year, a momentous event in the life of the people, was also announced by the sound of the shofar. The Decalogue established a Judaic social and religious order. The jubilee year renewed one's social order by proclaiming freedom from poverty and bondage. Rosh HaShanah offered an opportunity to set one's religious life in order by liberating him from sin and transgression.

Isaiah explicitly associated the sound of the shofar with an admonition against sin. "Cry aloud, spare not, lift up your voice like a shofar, and declare unto my people their transgression, and to the house of Jacob their sin" (58:1). The ingathering of the Jewish people and its ultimate return to God will be announced by a prolonged blast of the shofar. "And it will come to pass in that day that a great shofar shall be blown, and they shall come that were lost in the land of Assyria, and they that were dispersed in the land of Egypt, and they shall worship the Lord in the holy mountain in Jerusalem" (27:13). The prophet Zechariah prophesied that God will restore to Israel the land which was unlawfully taken away by other nations, who will pass in judgment before him. This event will be heralded by a blast of the shofar (9:14).

The forty-seventh chapter of Psalms proclaims the triumph of God as he surveys, from his holy throne (of judgment), the nations of the earth. "God is gone up admist the sound of the shofar" (v. 6). The link between the shofar and justice is asserted again in the eighty-ninth chapter. "Righteousness and justice are the foundation of your throne, mercy and truth go before you. Happy are the people that understand the sounds of the shofar" (vv. 15–16). In a comment on this verse, the rabbis elucidated: "Happy is the people that understands how to conciliate their creator with the blast of the shofar" (*Pesikta Rabba*). The eighty-first chapter warns the Jewish people of the dire consequences of betrayal of the faith and assures them of God's protection when they turn to him. "Blow the shofar at the new moon [of Tishri]" (v. 4).

These biblical pronouncements had little impact upon pre-talmudic Jewry, most of whom were ignorant of scriptural messages. However, the prophetic heritage helped shape the rabbinic perception of Rosh HaShanah.

Tne rabbis also laid much stress on the allusion to the judgment aspect of Rosh HaShanah in Deuteronomy: "The eyes of the Lord your God are always upon it [the land], from the beginning of the year unto the end of the year." This sentence precedes a passage which speaks of the judgment of God, his protection of the righteous and punishment of the wicked (11:13–18).

Another factor which might have contributed to the rabbinic perception of the first of Tishri was the term *zichron* ("remembrance") used in connection with the holiday of Rosh HaShanah (Lev. 23:24). Why was it designated a holiday of remembrance? Who is to remember? Is it the Jews who are enjoined to remember that day, or is it a promise that God will "remember" (or judge) the Jews on that day? This appears to be the opinion in *Breishit Rabba* (56:13): "They take a shofar and are remembered by God."

The term *zikaron* was also used in connection with the festival of Passover. The meaning of that *zikaron* was explicitly spelled out: "And this day shall be unto you a remembrance . . ." (Exod. 12:14). It is the Jews who must remember the Passover's message of freedom. On the other hand, the *zikaron* used in conjunction with the census in the desert, which was taken by means of an individual contribution of half a shekel, clearly implied that it is God who will remember this act of charity. "That it may be a remembrance for the children of Israel before the Lord, to make atonement for your souls" (Exod. 30:16). It is significant that a *zikaron* by God was linked to atonement.

In view of the ambivalence of the *zikaron* of the shofar, we may find it helpful to compare it to the *zikaron* mentioned in connection with the blowing of the trumpets (*chatzotzrot*). "And on the days of your gladness, and in your new moons, you shall blow with the trumpets . . . and they shall be a remembrance before God" (Num. 10:10). The *zikaron* is thus defined as a remembrance by God. The blast of the shofar in the Temple was accompanied by blasts of the trumpets. The rabbinic interpretation of Rosh HaShanah as a day of judgment is thus substantiated by the phrase *zichron teruah*. We must add, however, that in its halachic application, the *zichron* of Rosh HaShanah was also interpreted to mean an inclusion of the name of the holiday in the prayers (*Eruvin* 40a) so that the people may remember the day.

Oddly, the nonrabbinic Qumram sect appears to have agreed with the rabbinic definition of *zichron* as a judgment of God. In describing the military strategy of the Sons of Light, prominence is given to their trumpets and the symbolic inscriptions on each of them. A paraphrased version of Numbers 10:10, *uvemoadeichem . . . lezikaron*, was said to have been inscribed on one of the trumpets. The inscription read: *Zikaron Nakam B'Moed El*—"God will remember to exact vengeance in the appointed season" (*War of the Sons of Light and the Sons of Darkness*).

On the other hand, the first of Tishri is known in the Falasha tradition as the Commemoration of Abraham. The *zichron* of Rosh HaShanah is accordingly interpreted as an injunction to the Jewish people to remember the virtues of Abraham (Leslau, *Falasha Anthology*.

The rabbinic consensus that Rosh HaShanah is a day of judgment generated much controversy and discussion of the scope and character of the judgment. The earliest opinion is attributed to the school of Rabbi Ishmael (2nd cent.). "At four seasons judgment is passed on the world, on Passover with regard to crops, on Shavuot with regard to fruit, on Sukkot with regard to rain. Man is judged on Rosh HaShanah, and the verdict is sealed on Yom Kippur" (*Rosh HaShanah* 16a). This view seems to coordinate the *zikaron* of the festivals (Num. 10:10) with the *zichron* of the shofar (Lev. 23:24).

The tradition of four separate periods of judgment was later disputed by Rabbi Meir, who insisted that all judgments are passed on Rosh HaShanah (*Rosh HaShanah* 16a). Rabbi Nathan adopted the opposite view, asserting that man is judged every day (*Rosh HaShanah* 16b). He was undoubtedly motivated by the philosophic doctrine of divine intervention in the affairs of man every moment of his life.

The universality of the day of judgment, pointed out by Philo, is given equal stress in the Talmud. "At New Year all creatures pass before him like sheep, as it is stated: 'He that fashions the heart of them all, that considers all their doings' " (*Rosh HaShanah* 16a).

The different stages of divine judgment were further refined in the third century by Rabbi Yochanan. "Three books are opened on Rosh HaShanah, one for the wicked, one for the righteous, and one for the in-between. The righteous are immediately inscribed in the book of life, the wicked in the book of death, and the verdict of the in-between is suspended until Yom Kippur" (*Rosh HaShanah* 16b).

THE TIMING OF THE DAY OF JUDGMENT

The talmudic assertion that Adam was created on Rosh HaShanah (*Sanhedrin* 38b) provided the rationale for the timing of a day of judgment on the first of Tishri. The author of this statement was a second-century Tanna, Rabbi Eliezer. Although Rabbi Joshua disagreed with him and declared that Adam was created in the month of Nisan, it was the former view which prevailed and gained the acceptance of world Jewry. This tradition facilitated the rapid spread throughout the Jewish world of the belief that Rosh HaShanah was a day of judgment. It was logical to assume that man should be judged on the anniversary of his creation. It also influenced the belief that all of mankind is judged on that day.

The rationale of the timing of the day of judgment was given a homiletical touch in the third century. Adam sinned on the first day of his creation, and God forgave him on the same day. Adam was then informed: "Just as you stood before me in judgment on this day and came out free, so your children, who will stand before me in judgment on this day, will be set free" (*Vayikra Rabba* 29:1).

The tradition that the near-sacrifice of Isaac took place on the tenth of Tishri (*Pirke d'Rabbi Eliezer*) provided another rationale for the judgment period of Tishri. "The offspring of Isaac will someday transgress my will, and I will judge them on Rosh HaShanah. Should they appeal to my leniency, I will recall the binding of Isaac and let them blow then the horn of this ram [which was substituted for Isaac]" (*Tanchuma, Vayero* 22:13).

3

Yom Kippur

EARLY HISTORY

YOM KIPPUR, a sacred day of spiritual catharsis and divine forgiveness, is unique to Judaism. The steps leading to self-purification and atonement are carefully spelled out in the Pentateuch—affliction of one's soul, abstention from work, sacrificial rites, and the recitation of a confessional by the high priest (Lev. 16:1–34). The purpose of the solemn rituals is to induce man to purge evil from his life and appear pure in the sight of the Lord. (Lev. 16:30).

Sacrificial rituals of atonement were not an exclusive feature of Yom Kippur. The sacrificing of a goat for a sin-offering was mandatory on the first day of each month and all festivals (Num. 28:11–31, 29:1–39). The object of the sin-offering on Passover, Shavuot, and Rosh HaShanah is "to make atonement for you." However, while the theme of atonement is merely incidental on the previously mentioned occasions, as a reminder of the need for soul-searching even on the festive days of the year, it is all-pervasive and the sole raison d'etre of the solemn day of Yom Kippur.

The biblical name for the fast of the tenth of Tishri is Yom HaKippurim (Lev. 23:27). This name was generally retained in the Talmud. However, occasionally it was informally referred to as the Day of the Fast or the Great Fast (Jer. *Peah*). At times, its name was shortened to the Day. The Aramaic version of this name, Yoma, was given to the talmudic tractate which ex-

27

pounds the laws and ceremonies of Yom Kippur. Philo the Alexandrian (1st cent.) called the tenth of Tishri the Fast (*Treatise on the Ten Festivals*, the Ninth Festival). Josephus merely speaks of "the tenth day of the same lunar month," without identifying it by any name (*Antiquities* 3. 10). However, in describing Pompey's invasion of Jerusalem (63 B.C.E.), he records that the event took place "on the day of the fast" (*Antiquities* 14. 4). The same is true of his description of the sack of Jerusalem by Herod and Sossius (*Antiquities* 14.16), which occurred "on the solemnity of the fast." There is no doubt that he referred to Yom Kippur. Through some scribe's error it was indicated in both instances that the fast was in the third month of the year (Sivan).

Due to the prominence of Yom Kippur, there was no need to identify it by name, and a mere reference to "the fast" was sufficient. Even in the Acts of Apostles of the New Testament, most likely written by a contemporary of Josephus, Yom Kippur is referred to simply as "the fast" (27:9).

In post-talmudic times, Yom Kippur became known as Yom HaNora ("awesome day"). This designation is based on the comment of a post-talmudic midrash on Joel 2:11: " 'For great is the day of the Lord'—that is Rosh HaShanah. 'And highly awesome . . .'—that is Yom Kippur" (*Pesikta Chadata*). Malachi, the last of the prophets (5th cent. B.C.E.), seems to call the day when the Messiah will appear, the "awesome day" (3:23).

Another popular post-talmudic name of Yom Kippur is Yom HaDin ("judgment day"). In the Talmud, however, it is the day of resurrection which is referred to as the Yom HaDin (*Rosh HaShanah* 16b).

No explanation is given in the Bible for the timing of Yom Kippur. Since it is neither an agricultural nor a commemorative day, one wonders why it falls at that particular time of the year. The earliest rabbinic work of history, *Seder Olam Rabba* (2nd cent.), attributes the date of Yom Kippur to the fact that Moses brought down the second tablets of the law on the tenth of Tishri, bearing a message of divine forgiveness (chap. 6). The short interval between Rosh HaShanah and Yom Kippur lent a solemnity to the entire period, which became known as the Ten Days of Penitence (*Rosh HaShanah* 18a).

Philo linked the timing of Yom Kippur to the ingathering of the harvest and the influx of material wealth which coincided with that season of the year. The fast, he asserted, was designed to warn people against placing their trust in wealth, which may dissipate. One must put his reliance on God (*Treatise on the Ten Festivals*, the Ninth Festival).

Due to the conciseness of biblical style, the legal definitions and implications of the several elements of the Yom Kippur ritual are couched in vague terminology. The symbolic meaning of the sacrificial offerings is not indicated, nor are the definition of "affliction" and the substance of the high priest's confession spelled out. Oral tradition undoubtedly amplified the written word. Some of this tradition formed the basis for the explicit answers provided in the Talmud.

In the ancient world, the offering of sacrifices was a natural means of communication with heaven. The rationale of the rite varied from place to place. It meant sharing one's wealth with God. It was also a self-sacrificing gesture of piety, with the animal substituting for its owner. The killing of the sin-offering of Yom Kippur symbolized the destruction of evil and the purification of one's soul.

Abstinence from food was explained by the rabbis as a means of obtaining a spirituality totally divorced from bodily desires and passions. To Philo, the fast was a lesson in self-restraint. He also noted that a fast compels man to experience the misery of hunger and helps him to develop an empathy for the deprived and the needy.

Regardless of the rationale adopted by ancient Jewry, the symbolism of the Yom Kippur sacrificial rite must have appeared obscure to the average individual of limited sophistication. One could hardly expect that the rites would induce in such people a process of self-cleansing and spiritual regeneration. Even among the educated people of means, there were some men who deliberately perverted the symbolism of the ritual and stripped it of its social and religious significance.

The prophet Isaiah (8th cent. B.C.E.), seeking to restore the pristine purity of the Mosaic law, inveighed against the corruption of its spirit. "To what purpose is the multitude of

your sacrifices unto me? says the Lord. . . . The blood of
bullocks and of lambs or of goats [prominent features of the
ritual of Yom Kippur and other festivals] I do not desire. When
you come to appear before me [on the Pilgrimage Festivals], who
has requested you to trample my courts . . . . wash and cleanse
yourself, put away the evil of your doings from before my eyes.
Cease to do evil" (Isa. 1:11–12, 16). Isaiah did not object to
sacrificial rites but rather to the cynicism of some of the
worshippers.

The atonement ceremonies conducted in the Solomonic
Temple conformed to the instructions specified in the Pentateuch. The high priest placed his hands on the bullock and
confessed his sins and those of his household. Subsequently a
second confession was made for the Kohanim. Thereafter two
goats were brought before him. One was chosen by lot to be
sacrificed, the other was reserved for the Azazel ceremony, to be
sent off into the desert with the symbolic load of the sins of the
people. The high priest then entered the Holy of Holies, where
he placed some incense. This was followed by the sprinkling of
the blood of the bullock on the external curtain facing the ark.
Next in order came the sacrifice of the goat, and the sprinkling of
blood in the Holy of Holies and on the altar of incense. The high
priest then placed his hands on the goat of Azazel and confessed
"all the iniquities of the Israelites." Several more rituals were
then performed, and the service was concluded with the
lighting of the candelabra and the offering of incense.

Despite the rich pageantry, the resplendent vestments of the
high priests, the music, songs, and blare of trumpets, the impact
of Yom Kippur on pre-exilic Jewry was not profound. Since it
was not one of the Pilgrimage Festivals, Yom Kippur did not
attract overflow crowds to Jerusalem. Talmudic descriptions of
crowded conditions on Yom Kippur day do not apply to the
Solomonic Temple. In fact, they mention the presence of
Babylonian (or Alexandrian) Jews (*Yoma* 66a), thus making it
clear that they were discussing conditions in the Second
Temple.

In addition, one must always bear in mind that the entire
period of the First Commonwealth was interspersed with lapses

into idolatry, laxity in religious observances, and widespread ignorance of the laws. In these circumstances, Yom Kippur must have lost much of its solemnity.

It is quite evident that Yom Kippur did not attain, in the period of the Solomonic Temple, the transcendency which it was to acquire in the era of the Second Temple. There is no mention of Yom Kippur in the biblical description of Solomon's dedication of the Temple, which took place in the week preceding Sukkot (II Chron. 7:8–10). According to the Talmud, the dedicatory festivities were not suspended on Yom Kippur (*Moed Katan* 9a).

As late as 458 B.C.E., when Ezra came to Jerusalem, the Jewish community was unaware of the date of Rosh HaShanah. Ezra proceeded to instruct the people in the laws of Sukkot (Neh. 8:9, 14). Oddly, he failed to mention Yom Kippur. One may possibly explain this omission by the fact that the Yom Kippur rituals were mainly performed by the Kohanim in the Temple. However, this episode illustrates the depth of Jewish assimilation of Judea in that period.

Josephus always took note of Jewish holidays whenever Jerusalem was attacked on one of the Pilgrimage Festivals (*Wars* 2. 12, 14). The mention of these festivals was germane to his assertion that multitudinous crowds thronged Jerusalem at such times. However, he did not always stress the fact that an attack had taken place on Yom Kippur, an omission which no later Jewish historian would have been guilty of. Thus in 66 C.E. the Roman general Cestius opened hostilities against Jerusalem when he camped on Mount Scopus on the ninth of Tishri. On the next day, Yom Kippur, he sent his soldiers to attack Jewish villages and seize their corn. He entered Jerusalem on the thirteenth of Tishri (*Wars* 2, 19). The attack marked the opening of the Roman campaign against Judea and the outbreak of the Jewish rebellion against Rome. It was, to all intents and purposes, the "Yom Kippur War of 66." Josephus failed to take note of this fact.

IN THE SECOND TEMPLE

The Yom Kippur pageantry in the Second Temple is well documented in the Talmud. Some of the information was based on eyewitness reports, and much of it was reconstructed in later generations from interpretations of biblical texts.

In addition to the biblical rituals, the Talmud describes some functions not mentioned in the Bible. One of these was the recitation of a short prayer by the high priest when he left the Sanctuary (*Yoma* 53a). The following was the text of his prayer: "May it be your will. . . that no exile shall come upon us. . . and if exile shall come upon us . . . may we be exiled to a place of Torah. . . . May it be your will . . . that this year be a year when prices are low, a year of plenty . . . a year of rain . . . and that your people Israel may not need one another's help . . . and that they do not rise to rule over one another" (Jer. *Yoma* 5). The references to a "place of Torah," or academy, and to internal strife appear to point to the first century as the date of this prayer.

Despite the prescribed text of the prayer, individual high priests composed their own prayers to meet the exigencies of their times. Thus Simon the Just is said to have prayed that the Almighty would spare the Temple from destruction (Jer. *Yoma* 5).

Another innovation was the public reading by the high priest of portions of the Torah pertaining to Yom Kippur. The procedure is described as follows: The *chazan* handed the Torah to the head of the synagogue (*reish hakneset*), who turned it over to the deputy high priest, who in turn transferred it to the high priest (*Yoma* 68a). The reference to a *chazan* and *reish hakneset* indicates the growing influence of the rabbinic leadership in the first century and its ability to introduce new ceremonies into the Temple.

The Talmud also preserves the text of the high priest's three confessions on Yom Kippur (*Yoma* 35b, 41b, 66a). These texts may have been used also in the Solomonic Temple because they are based in part on a verse of Psalms (106:6).

The post-talmudic confessional *Al Chet*, which is preceded in our liturgy by the introductory paragraph *Tavo l'fonecha tefilatenu* ("May our prayers come before you"), is based on the confessional of Nehemiah (1:6): "I confess the sins of the children of Israel which we have sinned against you: yea, I and my father's house have sinned." This confessional was widely known in the Temple era. The Qumran sect's *Manual of Discipline* records the confession which initiates must repeat after the priest: "We have acted perversely, we have transgressed, we have sinned, we have done wickedly, ourselves and our fathers before us . . ." It is practically a copy of Nehemiah's confession.

Rabbi Ishmael described another Yom Kippur ritual performed in the Temple. A thread of crimson wool was tied to the door of the Sanctuary. When the Azazel goat reached the wilderness and the rite was completed, the thread used to turn white. It was a providential sign that the sins of Israel had been forgiven (*Yoma* 68b). It is likely that this quaint ritual was also performed in the Solomonic Temple, even though there is no mention of it in the Bible. Isaiah seems to have alluded to it in his criticism of those who offer sacrifices but fail to mend their ways. He urged them to turn to God and promised that "though your sins be as scarlet, they shall be as white as snow" (1:18).

The Talmud devotes much space to the high priest's preparatory period of seven days in anticipation of Yom Kippur. This, too, came into practice in the latter part of the Temple era. Rabbinic leaders impressed upon the high priest the urgency of following the proper procedure so as to make sure that he did not adopt Sadducean customs (*Yoma* 19b). Special efforts were made to keep the high priest awake during the night of Yom Kippur. Pious men in many places followed the example of the high priest and continued to do so even after the destruction of the Temple (*Yoma* 19b).

The custom of immersion on Yom Kippur was also introduced in the Second Temple period. We are told that the high priest used to immerse himself five times (*Yoma* 19b). From this derived the post-talmudic custom of immersion on the eve of Yom Kippur.

The impact of the high priest's Temple performance on Yom Kippur was profound, particularly after the triumph of the Pharisees, when the solemn service attracted large crowds. Even the Qumran sectarians warned their followers not to fall under the priestly spell. They registered their displeasure in the Commentary on the Book of Habakkuk, stating that "the wicked priest . . . on the occasion of the Sabbath of Atonement appeared to them [the Sectarians] in full splendor in order to confuse them and trip them up on the day of the fast, the day of their sabbatical rest."

IN THE POST-TEMPLE ERA

With the destruction of the Temple in the year 70, the rabbinic leadership was faced with the momentous task of restructuring the religious service of the fast day so that its solemnity could survive even without the Temple pageantry. In fact, due to their genius, the moral effectiveness of Yom Kippur was greatly enhanced, for the focal point of its observance was shifted from Jerusalem to every town and hamlet, wherever synagogues existed. The change also helped to win back to the fold the small segment of Jews who had become alienated due to their bias against sacrificial rites.

The initial shock to the rabbinic leadership as a result of the destruction of the Temple is reflected in the following passage: "Now that we have no prophet or Kohen or sacrifice, who shall atone for us? The only thing left to us is prayer" (*Tanchuma, Vayishlach* 10). Prayer was a natural substitute for the sacrificial offerings. Did not the prophet Hosea declare: "Let us render for bullocks the offering of our lips" (14:3)? Yet the recitation of prayers by rote can be as sterile an exercise as the offering of sacrifices without a comprehension of its moral imperatives. Subsequently, the rabbis added two more keys to salvation, essential to winning God's mercies on Yom Kippur. Said Rabbi Eliezer: "Three elements avert a harsh decree, they are—prayer, charity, and penitence" (Jer. *Taanit*, chap. 2). Although Rabbi Eliezer's statement did not originally address itself to Yom Kippur, rabbinic Judaism made it the very foundation of the Day of Atonement.

PRAYER

Institutionalized public prayers were not known to early Judaism prior to the establishment of the synagogue. However, individual praying, as a means of communicating with God, was always a feature of Jewish religious life. Abraham prayed for the health of Abimelech (Gen. 20:17). Moses prayed for the welfare of the people (Num. 21:7). Hannah prayed for a child (I Sam. 1:10). Prayer, it was said, leads to forgiveness (I Kings 8:30). Solomon dedicated the Temple as a house of worship where people of all creeds might come and pray (I Kings 38:41). Esther requested Mordecai "to gather together all Jews . . . and fast for me" (Esther 4:16). This is the first reference to a communal prayer.

In the course of time a practice of individual prayers, in conjunction with a sacrificial offering, was instituted in the Temple. This practice was predicted by Isaiah: "Their burnt offerings and their sacrifices shall be acceptable upon my altar; for my house shall be called a house of prayer for all peoples" (56:7).

The chanting of psalms in the Temple was an act of praying. Josephus described the custom of praying at the time when a sacrifice is offered "for the common welfare of all, and after that our own" (*Against Apion* 2.24). We have already mentioned the high priest's prayer in the Temple on the day of Yom Kippur.

While individual prayers were sporadic in the First Temple, they became a permanent feature in the Second Temple. The establishment of the synagogue in the Temple era gave rise to communal services outside the Temple. Philo's description of the Yom Kippur service may be typical of the Jews of the first century throughout the diaspora. "Everyone is at this time occupied in prayers and supplications . . . . they devote their entire leisure to nothing else from morning till evening, except to most acceptable prayers by which they endeavor to gain the favor of God, entreating pardon for their sins" (*Treatise on Ten Festivals*, The Ninth Festival).

The establishment of institutions of prayer, coexisting with the Temple, was a fortunate development. In the words of a later rabbinic maxim, "God precedes the cure to the illness." The synagogue was ready to fill the void when the Temple vanished behind fire and smoke.

CHARITY

The second rabbinic key to salvation is charity. The social importance of charity is frequently stressed in the Bible. Rabbinic Judaism made it a fundamental attribute of piety. Rabbi Eleazar said: "A man who gives charity in secret is greater than Moses" (*Baba Batra* 9a). The following quotations illustrate the rabbinic emphasis on charity. "Whoever turns away from charity is considered as if he were serving idols" (*Baba Batra* 10a). "Great is charity in that it brings the redemption nearer" (*Baba Batra* 10a). "Charity delivers from death" (*Baba Batra* 10a). "Jerusalem will be redeemed only through charity" (*Shabbat* 139a).

When Ezra met with the Jews of Jerusalem in 458 B.C.E. on the day of Rosh HaShanah, he ordered them to celebrate the festival by giving charity to the poor (Neh. 8:9). It was, therefore, logical to assign to charity an important role in the observance of Yom Kippur.

PENITENCE

The third rabbinic key to salvation is penitence. There were some religious philosophers in antiquity who rejected penitence as an injustice to the righteous. Why should man be given an opportunity to wipe away his sins and escape punishment? Jonah was reluctant to bring about the penitence of the Ninevites. His reluctance brought on God's reproof.

The classic statement on penitence was pronounced by Ezekiel. "As I live, says the Lord, I have no pleasure in the death of the wicked, but that the wicked turn from his way and live" (33:11). Hosea declared: "Return O Israel, unto the Lord your God. . . . Take with you words [of remorse] and return to God, and the offerings of our lips will take the place of the bullock" (14:2–3). When the offering of the bullock was no longer available after the destruction of the Temple, penitence became one of its prime substitutes.

It took some time for the rabbis to define the exact theological relationship of penitence to the day of Yom Kippur in effecting divine forgiveness. According to Rabbi Judah HaNasi, Yom Kippur atones for most transgressions even without penitence (*Keritot* 7a). It was Rabbi Eleazer b. Azaryah (2nd cent.) who offered a legalistic classification of the effectiveness of penitence. "Penitence effects an immediate pardon for a transgression of a positive commandment. It only suspends judgment in case of a violation of a negative injunction, which is then atoned for on Yom Kippur" (*Yoma* 86a). Penitence has its limitations where serious and grave offenses had been committed. It is also ineffective in the event that another person had been aggrieved or damaged. The damage must be made good and conciliation achieved to demonstrate the sincerity of one's penitence.

The rabbinic three keys to salvation emphasized the social aspects of Yom Kippur. Whereas the previous sacrificial motif of the fast was mainly God-directed, the rabbinic orientation gave concrete emphasis to the prophetic admonitions that man's protestations of piety are not acceptable to God if his sense of social justice is faulty. To obtain divine forgiveness, one must not only make peace with God but also with man. The attainment of peace, individual and communal, thus became a prime objective of Yom Kippur. It is in this spirit that Rabbi Eleazar declared: "Great is peace, for even if Israel is worshiping idols, if they keep the peace and are united, they will be spared the judgment of the Almighty" (*Pesikta Rabbati*).

Despite the new preeminence of prayer, charity, and penitence and their centrality in the theology of Yom Kippur, the memory of the *Avoda* (sacrificial rites in the Temple) continued to claim a dominant place in the post-Temple Yom Kippur service. A detailed account of the sacrificial rite was incorporated into the Yom Kippur liturgy. In view of the rabbinic hopes of an eventual restoration of the Temple, the leadership felt the need for retaining the biblical rituals, even if but in verbal form.

Rabbis Meir, Judah, and Jose devoted more time to the discussion of the laws of sacrificial rituals than most sages of the first post-Temple generation. Like Ezekiel in Babylonia, who saw a vision of the Temple services, these rabbis got involved in the details of sacrificial rites. Ezekiel sought to allay the fears of Babylonian Jews that the Temple might never be restored. The rabbis who lived through the Hadrianic persecutions tried to offer similar assurances.

Post-talmudic Judaism intensified the solemnity of Yom Kippur and added new customs, many of which have become an integral part of modern Orthodox observance. Among the best known of these customs are visitation of ancestral graves, the lighting of memorial lamps, *Kaparot*, and the chanting of *Kol Nidre*.

4

Sukkot

SYMBOLISM OF THE SUKKAH

THE SUKKAH'S SYMBOLISM of Jewish homelessness is a familiar theme of sermonic literature. However, that was not its original symbolic image. The Bible speaks of the Sukkah as a reminder of God's protection when he provided Sukkot for the Jews who had come out of Egypt (Lev. 23:43). In times of distress, one prayed to the Almighty to be enveloped in a protective Sukkah (Ps. 27:5, 31:20). The inhabitants of a Sukkah are as secure as a lion in his den. Hence the application of the term Sukkah to a lion's den (Ps. 10:9). A king who enjoys divine protection has his seat in a Sukkah. When he loses that protection, his Sukkah collapses (Amos 9:11). As a symbol of protection, the Sukkah is also a symbol of peace—*Sukkat Shalom*.

In talmudic times the Sukkah also assumed the symbolism of joy and beauty. Thus we were told that there are seven joyous elements in the festival of the harvest, one of them is the Sukkah (*Vayikra Rabba* 30). "You are pretty" when you dwell in a Sukkah (*Shir HaShirim Rabba* 4:1). One should decorate a Sukkah and make it beautiful (*Sukkah* 28b). Relaxation is an important ingredient of the mitzvah of Sukkah. If one is ill or if it rains, he is exempt from the mitzvah (*Sukkah* 26a). In time to come the Almighty will build a Sukkah for all the pious people (*Yalkut Job* 927). One of the missions of the Messiah will be to bring the nations of the world the mitzvah of Sukkah (*Shochar Tov*, Ps. 21).

Philo the Alexandrian viewed the Sukkah as a symbol of leisure. With the end of the harvest season, the people no longer had to sleep in the open near the crops. They were freed from their chores and could return to a life of leisure in their booths.

A SYMBOL OF HOMELESSNESS

The post-talmudic period of repression brought a new moralistic twist to the Sukkah symbol. The Sukkah served as an admonition to man not to become overconfident because of affluence. Like his ancestors in the desert, who dwelt in a Sukkah, one's survival is contingent upon the grace of the Almighty (Rashbam, Lev. 23:43). Man must leave his permanent home and move into a temporary abode which is devoid of wealth and security to remind him that he depends upon the Almighty (Menorat HaMaor). The new interpretation of the Sukkah symbol was foreshadowed in one midrashic source: "The Sukkah is built after Yom Kippur. The Almighty sits in judgment on Rosh HaShanah. On Yom Kippur he seals the verdict. If they were sentenced to go into exile, they build a Sukkah wherein they dwell and are thus exiled from their homes to the Sukkah. The Almighty deems it as if they had gone into exile to Babylonia" (Pesikta D'Rav Kahana 28). This was the first intimation that the Sukkah is symbolic of Jewish wandering and homelessness. This interpretation gained popularity as conditions in the diaspora deteriorated.

It is conceivable that the two interpretations are linked to two ancient traditions. Both are mentioned in the Book of Jubilees. According to the first tradition, the Sukkah commemorates the first booth built by Abraham when he greeted the three angels (Bamidbar Rabba 14). It was a joyous occasion. The second tradition describes the Sukkah ceremony as a commemoration of the Sukkah built by Jacob after he fled from Laban (Gen. 33:17). That transpired at the time when he was a homeless wanderer.

THE DATE OF SUKKOT

Rabbi Elijah Gaon offered the following explanation for the date of Sukkot: When Moses broke the Tablets of the Law, he observed that "the people had become exposed" (Exod. 32:25). According to a midrashic comment, "The protecting clouds were removed, and they were not restored until they started the construction of the Tabernacle." Moses requested donations for the building fund on the eleventh of Tishri (Rashi, Exod. 31:18). The contributions were brought in on the twelfth and thirteenth of Tishri (Exod. 36:3—*baboker baboker*). On the following day, Moses asked that further contributions be discontinued (Exod. 36:6). On the next day, the fifteenth of Tishri, he began the construction of the Tabernacle. That was the moment when the "clouds of glory" reappeared. The Sukkah is symbolic of the "clouds of glory" (*Sukkah* 11b; *Yalkut, B'Shalach* 227). The observance of Sukkot was therefore set for the fifteenth of Tishri.

In addition to the Gaon's ingenious explanation, there are other old traditions which attempt to shed light on the date of Sukkot. According to Jubilees (chap. 16), Abraham was the first person to observe Sukkot. There is a rabbinic tradition which similarly links Sukkot to Abraham. As a reward for his hospitality to the angels, whom he had invited into the Sukkah, the Almighty later built Sukkot for his descendants upon their departure from Egypt (*Bamidbar Rabba* 14:8). The angels visited Abraham on the twelfth day of Tishri (*Pirke D'Rabbi Eliezer*, chap. 29). The rabbis set aside the entire period between Yom Kippur and Sukkot as Sukkah-building time (*Vayikra Rabba* 30:7).

The commemoration of Abraham's Sukkah highlights his outstanding trait of hospitality. The Zohar embellished this tradition by the *Ushpizin*, the heavenly guests who nightly visit the Sukkah. Abraham, appropriately, is the first night's guest (Zohar, *Vayikra* 103).

The tradition of Abraham's Sukkah sheds some light on the following enigmatic rabbinic passage: "He who fulfills the mitzvah of Sukkah in this world, the Almighty will give him a share, in time to come, in the Sukkah of Sodom, which he will allot to the pious of all tribes" (*Pesikta D'Rav Kahana* 29). One of Abraham's visiting angels was entrusted with a rescue mission in Sodom. His Sukkah was therefore identified as the Sukkah of Sodom.

The Book of Jubilees considers Jacob the founder of the festival of Sukkot (23:6). This is based on the biblical reference to Jacob's Sukkot (Gen. 33:17). Jacob was born and buried on the fifteenth of Tishri. We thus discover a link between Jacob and the date of Sukkot. It should be noted, however, that according to the ecclesiastical calendar of the Book of Jubilees, all of the pilgrimage festivals begin on the fifteenth of the month.

The most logical explanation for the date of Sukkot may be found in the biblical text which brackets the festival of Sukkot with the exodus: "That your generations may know that I made the children of Israel to dwell in booths, when I brought them out of the land of Egypt . . ." (Lev. 23:43). Passover and Sukkot are accordingly related to the exodus from Egypt, and both are observed on the fifteenth day of the month, the anniversary of the exodus. Passover marks the attainment of the end of bondage and religious freedom (Exod. 5:1). Sukkot marks the attainment of national and territorial independence, the essential ingredients of sovereignty. This implication of Sukkot might have led to the analogy between Sukkot and Chanukah in II Maccabees. Due to its emphasis on economic abundance, the celebration of the festival of Sukkot was postponed to the month of Tishri, when the harvest season is ended.

In concluding the discussion of the date of Sukkot, it is helpful to refer to the views of some of the great biblical exegetes. Nahmanides and Ibn Ezra agree that Sukkot is an exodus festival (Lev. 23:43). They attribute the date to the fact that the building of booths by the exodus generation did not begin until the cool season of Tishri. Baal HaTurim states that the ritual booth would not stand out in the summer, when people normally live in airy booths. The celebration was, therefore, held in the cooler season of Tishri. The Karaite scholar Aaron b. Elijah repeats some of these explanations and adds a few of his own (Nemoy, *Karaite Anthology*, p. 187).

A FESTIVAL OF NATIONAL INDEPENDENCE

The assumption that Sukkot is a festival of national independence may explain why the early Babylonian diaspora apparently suspended the observance of some of the Sukkot rituals, in view of the loss of national independence. This is clearly implied in Nehemiah: "And they found written in the law which the Lord had commanded by Moses, that the children of Israel should dwell in booths in the feast of the seventh month" (8:14). The Sukkah ritual was obviously unknown to many of the repatriates.

The prophet Zechariah urged the speedy restoration of Palestine's religious authority through the rebuilding of the Temple. He was painfully aware that political independence was still beyond their reach. He voiced his aspiration in an enigmatic prophecy: "And it shall come to pass that everyone that is left of all the nations which came against Jerusalem shall even go up from year to year to worship the king, the Lord of Hosts, and to keep the feast of Sukkot. . . . And if the family of Egypt go not up, and come not, there shall be no rain upon them; this shall be the plague wherewith the Lord will smite the nations that come not to keep the feast of Sukkot" (Zech. 14:16, 17, 19). To go to Jerusalem to keep the feast of Sukkot was Zechariah's way of prophesying the recognition of the independence of Israel by the nations of the world. Egypt's refusal to do so would bring upon it divine retribution.

EZRACH and GER

The interpretation of Sukkot as an exodus holiday, marking the attainment of national independence, may also clarify the unique biblical stress of the terms *ezrach* and *ger* in connection with the observance of Passover (Exod. 12:19, 49), the Second Passover (Num. 9:14), Sukkot (Lev. 23:42), and Yom Kippur (Lev. 16:29). *Ezrach* designates a native Jew, and *ger*, a convert to Judaism. A convert is entitled to the privileges of native Jews and is subject to their obligations. Of what significance is the specific mention of the *ger* in conjunction with the observance of the enumerated holidays? The Bible seems to emphasize that the commandments which are based on historical events are mandatory upon a *ger* even though his roots do not descend into the Jewish past. Passover and Sukkot are based on the exodus. Yom Kippur is based, according to tradition, on the transgression of the golden calf.

It should be noted that there are also a number of historically motivated injunctions in which *ezrach* and the *ger* are similarly used. Following the warning: "After the doings of the land of Egypt, wherein ye dwelt, shall ye not do . . ." (Lev. 18:3), the passage concludes: "Ye shall therefore keep my statutes . . . the *ezrach* and the *ger* who lives among you" (Lev. 18:26). The same applies to the laws of drink-offerings, which were decreed after the incident of the twelve scouts (Num. 15:13). This is also true of the dietary laws (Lev. 17:15), which were based on the premise that Jews, descendants of a holy people, must assume additional burdens. (Deut. 14:21).

HOSHANA RABBA

Hoshana Rabba is distinguished from the other days of Sukkot by three features: (1) Hakafot. The congregation marches with lulav and etrog seven times around the bimah. (2) A day of judgment. Hoshana Rabba is traditionally considered to be the concluding day of the judgment period which commences with Rosh HaShanah. (3) Aravot. A bundle of willow branches is used in a special defoliation ritual at the morning services.

The reason for the hakafot is obscure, but the practice is very ancient. The custom was well known in the early talmudic period (*Sukkah* 45a). No reason was indicated either for the practice itself or for the number of hakafot on Hoshana Rabba. We may find it rewarding, however, to look for the reason in an analysis of the symbolic interpretations mentioned in rabbinic literature for the ritual of the lulav and etrog.

There are three distinct interpretations indicated for this ritual. According to one interpretation, the lulav was designed to give man an opportunity to express his joy and his gratitude to God. One may draw an analogy to the human practice of expressing joy and love for a child by lifting him up. Similarly, a Jew expressed his happiness and gratitude to the Almighty by lifting up the "four species." The following are some of the illustrative passages: " 'You shall rejoice before the Lord'—it is to the joy of the lulav to which the text has reference" (Jer. *Sukkah*, chap. 3:13). " 'The fulness of joy' [Ps. 16:11] refers to the four species of agricultural products which make up the set of the lulav" (*Vayikra Rabba* 30). " 'Four are comely in going' [Prov. 30:29]—this text refers to the four species of the set of the lulav which every Jew acquires in order to praise the Almighty" (*Vayikra Rabba* 30).

The second interpretation of the lulav points to its symbolism as a sacrificial offering upon the altar. Like the offering of the Omer, which is brought on the second day of Passover, so the etrog and the other species, which ripen in the fall, are brought as an offering on Sukkot. The Omer is waved in all directions to contain the ill winds. The lulav, too, is similarly waved with the same prayerful intent (*Menachot* 62a). He who fulfills the mitzvah of lulav is considered to have brought an offering upon an altar which he has built (*Sukkah* 45a).

The third interpretation is tied in with the tradition that Sukkot is the concluding holiday of the judgment period and Hoshana Rabba is the culminating day. The lulav is the symbol of victory and vindication on the judgment day. There is particular emphasis on the contest between the nations of the world and Israel. "Rabbi Ovin said: 'When two men appear before a judge, we know not who won. When one emerges with palm branches in his hand, we know that the verdict was in his favor. Israel and the nations of the world come before the Almighty on Rosh HaShanah to exchange mutual charges. We do not know who won. However, when Israel comes out with lulav in hand, we know that the verdict was in its favor' " (*Vayikra Rabba* 30).

It is the third interpretation which apparently was alluded to by the author of the following midrashic passage: The Messiah will teach six mitzvot to the nations of the world, among these the Sukkah and lulav (*Shochar Tov*, Ps. 21). The Sukkah is a symbol of national independence. The lulav is a symbol of exoneration from the charges brought by the nations of the world against Israel. The author thus holds out the promise that in the messianic period, the existence of Israel will be secure and society will be free from anti-Semitism.

The significant role of the lulav as a symbol of judgment, and its connection with the hakafot, is pointed out in the following midrash: " 'and I will circle thy altar, O Lord'—the reference is to the lulav, with which Jews march around the altar once daily on Sukkot and seven times on Hoshana Rabba" (*Yalkut Shimoni*). The biblical quotation in this midrash is from the twenty-sixth chapter of Psalms, which begins with the verse: "Judge me, O Lord, for I have walked in mine integrity." There are other references to Sukkot as a period of judgment. Thus there is an ancient tradition that the amount of rain which is to fall during the year is decreed on Sukkot (*Rosh HaShanah* 16a). It was left to the Zohar to officially declare Hoshana Rabba a day of judgment.

The three interpretations of the lulav evolved at different periods and ultimately continued to coexist to give shape and meaning to divergent customs. The Talmud, for instance, does not mention the practice of hakafot in the post-Temple period. This leads to the conclusion that it had been discontinued. An inquiry of Rav Hai Gaon in the eleventh century about this custom also indicates a lapse (*Otzar HaGeonim*). It is evident that the interpretation of the lulav as a ritual offering motivated the march around the altar and the limiting of the marchers to Kohanim only (*Sukkah* 43b). The same interpretation led to the suspension of the hakafot after the destruction of the Temple. The introduction of the other interpretation of the lulav made possible the ultimate reinstatement of hakafot and the inclusion of all Israelites in the ranks of the marchers.

The theme of the international relations of Israel as one of the symbols of the lulav gives insight to the parallel drawn by Rabbi Chiya between the single daily hakafah on Sukkot plus seven hakafot on Hoshanah Rabba and the marches of Joshua around the walls of Jericho (*Yalkut Shimoni*).

The various customs pertaining to the time of the hakafot in the order of the Morning Service also seem to hinge upon the particular interpretation of the lulav which one adopts. In some communities the hakafot are conducted after Musaf (*Tur* 65a). It is in the Musaf part that a plea for the restoration of Zion follows a confession of sins. The hakafot complete the service in the spirit of a judgment day. A different custom calls for the hakafot to follow the reading of the Torah, while the Scroll is still on the *bimah* (Rav Saadia Gaon, quoted by the *Tur*). The Torah lectern is the substitute for the altar, and the hakafah is a symbolic offering. Still another custom places the hakafot after the recitation of the *Hallel*. This conforms to the interpretation of the lulav as an expression of joy and thanksgiving.

The ritual of aravot is very ancient. According to one talmudic source, it is indicated by implication in a biblical text. According to another tradition, the ritual was communicated orally to Moses on Mount Sinai (*Sukkah* 44a). The custom was suspended in the Babylonian diaspora and restored by the prophets (*Sukkah* 44a).

What is the symbolic significance of the aravot? One may point to the coincidence of the ritual of aravot on the twenty-first day of Tishri and the traditional birthday of Joseph, which falls on that day. According to a midrashic interpretation, the willow branch symbolizes the life of Joseph. The willow withers sooner than the myrtle and lulav, like Joseph, who died in the lifetime of his brothers (*Vayikra Rabba* 30). The ritual of aravot might have been set on Hoshana Rabba, the twenty-first day of Tishri, as a memorial to Joseph. The destruction of the willow branches may convey a prayer for long life. Another explanation for the stripping of the willow branches may lie in the midrashic allegation that the aravot symbolically represent the common people, who are devoid of scholarship and good deeds (*Vayikra Rabba* 30). They may become useful, however, when integrated within the community. The willows are therefore included in the traditional set of the "four species." As an independent unit they may become harmful and must be stripped of power.

SIMCHAT TORAH

The Haftarah selection on the last day of Sukkot originally began with verse 22, chap. 8 of I Kings (*Megillah* 31a). The subject of that passage is the dedicatory prayer delivered by King Solomon on the seventh day of Sukkot. The earliest post-talmudic sources reveal the substitution of a different Haftarah. The new selection, beginning with Joshua 1:1, opens with the sentence: "And it came to pass after the death of Moses . . ." It is generally assumed that the post-talmudic custom of celebrating the completion of the reading of the Torah on Simchat Torah led to the change of Haftarot. The conclusion of the reading of the Pentateuch is an appropriate occasion to recall the death of Moses and the assumption of leadership by his successor. From a chronological point of view, it would seem that the reading of that Haftarah would be even more appropriate in the week preceding Adar 7, Moses' traditional yahrzeit. However, the end of Moses' career is also traditionally linked to Shmini Atzeret and Simchat Torah. According to *Midrash Ptirat Moshe Rabbenu*, Moses was informed on Shmini Atzeret of his impending death. According to *Tanchumah* (*Chukat* 24), Moses waged his last war on the twenty-third of Tishri.

5
Chanukah

INTRODUCTION

CHANUKAH IS A well-documented festival. Most of the historical source material relating to this holiday was written within 250 years of its inception. In spite of the antiquity of Chanukah, it still awaits exhaustive analysis and interpretation. This essay falls short of that goal. Our limited objective is to trace the few stages of transformation through which Chanukah passed before it was finally cast into its permanent mold by the talmudic rabbis at the end of the first century. Specifically, we would like to know: What event does Chanukah commemorate? When was the name Chanukah adopted? Why was it celebrated for eight days? Was the manner of celebrating the festival defined at the outset?

INITIAL OPPOSITION

It is axiomatic that every new institution meets with some resistance before it is universally accepted. The addition of Yom HaAtzmaut to our modern calendar gives us valuable insight into the evolutionary course of such innovations. Is Yom HaAtzmaut a secular holiday? Does it have any religious significance? If so, will there be a clearly defined ritual of observance? Our questions may not be answered until a century or two have elapsed. Diversified forms of celebrations are born out of the confusion and dissension which inevitably attend the birth of a new historic "day."

Purim met with strong rabbinic opposition in its early stages. The Talmud records the well-grounded compunctions of the sages (*Megillah* 7a, Jer. *Megillah*, chap. 1). There must have been powerful elements opposed to Chanukah too. The holiday was closely identified with the Hasmonean dynasty. Assimilated, anti-Hasmonean Jews had no reason to react sympathetically to Chanukah nor would they be inclined to believe the story of the miracle of the oil. Jews under Seleucid hegemony must have felt impelled to denounce the innovation in the same manner that some Jews behind the iron curtain denounce Israel. Jews of Alexandria must have had some misgivings about Chanukah due to its nationalistic implications. The early anti-Hellenic course of the Hasmonean rebellion did not harmonize with the Hellenic predilections of the Alexandrian Jewish community. The letter addressed to the Jews of Alexandria, which prefixes II Maccabees, pleads for the observance of Chanukah. It is a clear indication that the addressees of the letter were slow in accepting the Hasmonean edict. Philo the Alexandrian, who lived in the first half of the first century, does not mention Chanukah in his dissertations on the Jewish holidays. It is conceivable that even the Pharisees in Judea experienced a temporary coolness to Chanukah when the Hasmonean dynasty joined the Sadduceans under Alexander Jannai (103–76 B.C.E.). The brief reign of the beloved Queen Salome Alexandra (76–67 B.C.E.) might have restored Chanukah to its original prominence as a national and religious festival. The loss of independence with the invasion of Pompey in 63 B.C.E. could not but affect the status of the new holiday by toning down its nationalistic overtones and stressing its religious significance. The destruction of the Temple and the loss of the last vestiges of Jewish sovereignty (70 C.E.) must have accelerated the trend which converted Chanukah into a purely religious holiday.

The various ancient Chanukah documents, which are fortunately available to us, reflect the changing moods of time and place. The number of discrepancies between the different sources are very welcome to the historian because they tell a story of growth and development and trace the course of evolution. The following are the main Jewish historical sources covered by this study, listed in the order of their chronological priority: I Maccabees, II Maccabees, Josephus, *Megillat Antiochus*, *Megillat Taanit*, and the Talmud.

I MACCABEES

I Maccabees is assumed by many historians to have been written in the period between 100 and 70 B.C.E. In view of the Pharisaic sympathies of the author of I Maccabees, one must be inclined to accept the earlier date. Alexander Jannai succeeded to the throne in 103 B.C.E. and instituted a wave of persecution against the Pharisees, dimming temporarily the luster of the Hasmonean name. It is hardly conceivable that any Pharisee would have written a book glorifying the Hasmoneans during his reign. This work is the basic source for the story of Chanukah. Josephus followed it very closely, and the Talmud, too, mentions some of the incidents related in this book. It gives an authentic account of the history of that period. Its reliability is not impugned by the fact that *Megillat Antiochus*, an early rabbinic work to which scholars have paid scant attention, contradicts it in many important details.

It is to I Maccabees that we turn first for a description of the events immediately preceding the inception of Chanukah. Judah Maccabee is reported to have urged his followers: "Let us go up to cleanse and dedicate the Sanctuary." Whereupon they pulled down the altar of burnt-offerings because it had been profaned. They put away the stones on the mountain of the Temple and built a new altar. (This incident is also related in the Talmud, *Yoma* 16a; *Megillat Taanit* chap. 9). They made new vessels (Maimonides and Baal HaMaor disagree on the need for new vessels in the event of profanation—see *Avoda Zara* 52b; Maimonides' statement is obviously based on a historical fact rather than on halachic requirements) and brought into the Temple the menorah, the altar of burnt-offerings and of incense, and the table. (They made a new menorah according to the Talmud, *Rosh HaShanah* 24b, *Menachot* 28b.) They burned incense on the altar, kindled the candles to provide light in the Temple, and set the loaves upon the table. The Korban Tamid (daily communal burnt-offering) was offered early in the morning on the twenty-fifth day of Kislev. (The offering of the Tamid was very significant because it signaled the resumption of the daily service at the Temple. The cessation of the Tamid prior to the destruction of the Temple by the Romans brought about the institution of the national fast day of Shiva-Asar b'Tammuz, *Taanit* 26b; *Psikta d'Rav Kahana* also stresses the importance of the Hasmonean resumption of the Tamid.) The altar was then dedicated with songs of praise and instrumental music. They brought offerings of deliverance and praise, and celebrated the dedication of the altar for eight days. Judah and his brothers and the whole congregation of Israel then ordained that the eight days of the dedication of the altar should annually be kept in their season with mirth and gladness, beginning with the twenty-fifth day of Kislev (I Macc. 4).

An analysis of I Maccabees provides an answer to some of our questions, though not to all of them. Chanukah commemorates the restoration of the offering of the Tamid and the general resumption of Temple functions. The name Chanukah was not yet identified with the festival at the time the book was written, but the basis for the name (which means "dedication") was laid in the edict in which Judah asked that "the days of the dedication of the altar should be kept in their season from year to year." No explanation is offered for the length of the festival. Judah's dedication ceremonies lasted for eight days though the biblical dedicatory festivals lasted only seven days.

Prof. S. Zeitlin, in *The Rise and Fall of the Judaean State* (vol. 1, p. 106), drew a distinction between the consecration of a new building, which is limited to seven days, and the reconsecration of an old building, which lasts for eight days, as in the case of King Hezekiah (II Chron. 29:17). However, II Chronicles deals with a cleansing period of eight days rather than a celebration.

No specific ritual for celebrating the festival of Chanukah was prescribed. The Hasmonean edict called for an annual celebration "with mirth and gladness" (cf. Ezra 6:16). This vague term was clearly understood by ancient Jews. The Bible used similar language in connection with the holidays. Thus the injunction

Ve-samachto b'chagecha—"thou shalt rejoice in thy feast" was interpreted to include the bringing of offerings (Deut. 26:11, Jer. *Chagigah* 1) and the provision of good food and fine clothes (*Pesachim* 109a). (The feasting aspect of Chanukah was eliminated after the destruction of the Temple.) The offering of sacrifices as one phase of the celebration of Chanukah must have been optional rather than obligatory. To construe it otherwise would lead to the introduction of a fourth Pilgrimage Festival for the entire household of Israel. That was surely not anticipated. In fact, Nikanor Day, another Hasmonean festival (*Megillat Taanit*, chap. 12), which originated a few years after Chanukah, was also to be observed as "a day of great gladness" (I Macc. 7), and there were no ritual offerings involved in the celebration at all.

II MACCABEES

II Maccabees, the second-oldest Chanukah chronicle, is alleged by its author, an Alexandrian Jew, to be a condensed version of a five-volume work by Jason of Cyrene. Historians do not agree on the date of II Maccabees. One places it as early as 125 B.C.E., another considers the author to be a contemporary of Josephus and suggests 73 C.E. as the date of this work.

We are able to approximate the date from a few chance expressions as well as from the general tenor and objective of the author. In his prefatory remarks he speaks of the "Temple renowned all over the world" (chap. 2). This expression gives the impression that the Temple was still in existence at the time of the writing of the book. In the last chapter, in the author's epilogue to Judah's conclusive victory over Nikanor, he states: "And from that time forth the Hebrews had the city in their power." This places the date in a period when the Jews were still masters of Jerusalem—that is, prior to the year 63 B.C.E., when Pompey conquered the holy city and a Roman garrison was permanently stationed there. We may narrow the possible period in which the book was written even further if we realize that the main objective of II Maccabees was the glorification of the Temple in Jerusalem. Egyptian Jews had their own temple, which was built by Onias IV after the religious persecutions of Antiochus triggered a wave of refugees from Palestine into Egypt. The Alexandrian Jews had accepted the Temple because it offered them an opportunity of bringing sacrificial offerings at home without the need for making the hazardous trip to Jerusalem. The Hasmoneans, who had restored the Jerusalem Temple to its primacy, must have looked askance at the rivalry of Onias' temple. The Pharisees, too, could not but regard it as a serious violation of Mosaic law. They were apparently unable, however, to exert a strong influence on the Alexandrian Jewish community with its predominantly Hellenic culture. The reign of the anti-Pharisaic Alexander Jannai (103–76 B.C.E.) must have affected the cultural and religious structure of Alexandria's Jewry through the influx of a strong Pharisaic element, which fled to Alexandria from Jannai's persecutions. Among the leading Pharisees who sought refuge in Alexandria were Rabbis Joshua b. Prachyah, Judah b. Tabbai, and Simon b. Shatach. They undoubtedly left a profound mark upon the Jewish community. The death of Alexander Jannai and the return of the Pharisees to power in the year 76 B.C.E. was an opportune moment to start a drive to enlist the loyalty of Egyptian Jewry to the shrine of Jerusalem. II Maccabees appears to have been a powerful instrument in that campaign. It was most likely written in the period between 76 and 63 B.C.E. in an effort to get the Alexandrian Jews to celebrate Chanukah and as a result reaffirm their allegiance to the Temple in Jerusalem.

It is a sound assumption that II Maccabees was written about forty years after I Maccabees. We may also take it for granted that the author of the second book was not familiar with the first book. While the older book glorifies the Hasmoneans, the later work glorifies the Temple. They also disagree on some minor historical details which would have been reconciled had the author been acquainted with the earlier book. I Maccabees lists the five Hasmonean brothers in the following order: Jochanan, Simon, Judah, Eliezer, and Jonathan. II Maccabees, on the other hand, lists the four brothers of Judah in the following order: Simon, Jochanan, Jonathan, and Eliezer. (Josephus, in the *Wars of the Jews,* and *Megillat Antiochus* list Judah as the eldest.) I

Maccabees reports that the purification of the Temple took place on the defeat of Lysias, one year after the defeat of Nikanor, and three years after the profanation of the Temple. II Maccabees reports that the purification took place on the defeat of Nikanor, two years after the defilement of the Temple.

In a study of the early history of Chanukah, it is extremely helpful to know that II Maccabees is not a mere reflection of I Maccabees, but that the two books are independent works, drawing upon independent sources and oral traditions available to the authors at the time of writing.

Did Chanukah undergo any evolutionary change in the period which elapsed between the publication of the two books? Both authors agree in substance in their reports on the origin of Chanukah. II Maccabees describes the cleansing of the Temple, the building of a new altar, the resumption of the sacrificial ritual, the setting forth of incense, the lighting of the menorah, and the placing of the showbread. When the process of purification was completed, Judah prayed for God's continued protection and he observed eight days with "gladness." He also ordained that every Jew should annually keep these days. This account of Chanukah presents an independent tradition which parallels and corroborates the earlier tradition. However, II Maccabees introduces two new elements—the story of the ancient miracle of the celestial fire, which is indirectly linked to Chanukah, and an analogy between Chanukah and Sukkot.

THE MIRACLE OF THE FIRE

The story of the ancient miracle of the fire is given great prominence in the letter allegedly written by Judah Maccabee to the Jews of Egypt. This letter prefixes the Second Book of Maccabees. The Egyptian Jews were exhorted in the letter to observe Chanukah "as the feast of Tabernacles and the fire which was given to us when Nehemiah offered sacrifices after he had built the Temple and the altar." A long explanatory paragraph follows in which the story of the miracle is related. Nehemiah is said to have sent some priests to locate the celestial fire of the First Temple. The fire had been hidden in a cave at the command of the prophet Jeremiah. The hiding place was to remain secret until such time as God would redeem his people and restore them to the Holy Land. Nehemiah was sure that the time of redemption had come, and he dispatched some priests to find the cave. The priests located the cave and found in it thick water but no fire. Nehemiah sprinkled the water on the wood and the offering. When the sun came out a great fire was kindled. Every one present marveled at this great miracle. The fire had originally come down from heaven in the days of Moses, whereupon he offered the sacrifice of the dedication of the Tabernacle. King Solomon, too, was granted celestial fire, whereupon he celebrated the dedication of the Temple for eight days. (Solomon's feast of dedication lasted only seven days, II Chron. 7:9.) Nehemiah, too, dedicated the altar after the heavenly fire consumed the offering. (The Talmud states that there was no celestial fire in the Second Temple, *Yoma* 21b.) The author makes no claim that the Hasmoneans were also granted celestial fire. Indeed such a claim would glorify the Hasmoneans beyond the implied objective of the work. He merely states in chapter 10: "And having cleansed the Temple, they made another altar and striking stones, they took fire out of them and offered a sacrifice." (*Josippon,* a 10th-century work, mentions the issuance of fire from the stones in the altar in answer to Judah's prayers.)

Why was the story of the miracle of the fire given such prominence? I believe that it was the prime objective of the author to prove the sanctity of the Second Temple and its superiority over Onias' temple in Egypt. The celestial fire, a reminder of providential intervention, was granted to the Second Temple as a sign of heavenly approval. The Hasmoneans, too, obtained pure fire by striking stones and did not make use of the flame which the pagans had defiled. The author also sought to impress his readers with the traditional link between the inauguration of a sacrificial fire and the observance of a festival or dedication.

The emphasis on the story of the miracle of the fire presents some points of interest to the reader. It indicates the beginning of the trend to minimize the personal glory of the Hasmoneans and the shift of focus to the event in the Temple. If we are correct in assuming that the book was written shortly after the death of Alexander Jannai, the enemy of the Pharisees, then we may also assume that it reflects the new mood of the times. Chanukah was to become a monument to God but not to the Hasmoneans.

The story of the miracle of the fire is evidence of another important historical milestone—the appearance of the first recorded account of miracles linked with Chanukah. There is no doubt that stories of Chanukah miracles must have been widely circulated by the time II Maccabees was written, about a century after the inception of Chanukah. In addition to the miracle of the fire, the author also speaks of "the manifest signs that came from heaven unto those that behaved themselves manfully to their honor for Judaism, so that being but a few they overcame the whole country" (chap. 2). The author reflects, thus, a current tradition of miracles. It is possible that even if he had heard reports about a miracle of oil he preferred to use the more ancient story of the miracle of the flame, which would be more readily believed by the Egyptian Jews. Incidentally, the term "miracle" is not mentioned in II Maccabees nor is it used even in the later rabbinic work, *Megillat Antiochus* (1st cent.). The phrase "Chanukah miracle" was first popularized by the Talmud.

CHANUKAH AND SUKKOT

The analogy between Chanukah and Sukkot is mentioned in both letters which prefix II Maccabees and in the book itself. There seems to be a dual purpose in this analogy. First the author brings out the similarity in circumstances between the Jews wandering in the desert and Judah's wandering in the mountains like a beast of prey. To highlight the affinity between Chanukah and Sukkot, the author describes Judah's celebration with branches, fair boughs and palms, and the singing of psalms of thanksgiving (chap. 10). The comparison is ostensibly drawn in an effort to explain the length of Chanukah. Thus he concludes: "And they kept eight days with gladness as in the feast of Tabernacles" (ibid.).

The true motive for the analogy between Chanukah and

Sukkot might be explained by a reference to the symbolic significance of Sukkot. The ancients interpreted the booth as a symbol of freedom. Philo states that with the conclusion of the harvest season, the Jewish farmers no longer had to sleep in the open on their farms. They were now freed from their exacting chores and obligations and could retire to their booths. Hence the interpretation of the booth as a symbol of freedom. The palm branch, too, was an ancient symbol of independence. When Simon minted the first Hasmonean coins, he engraved a palm branch as a symbol of newly won independence. The palm, as a symbol of victory, is reflected in later rabbinic works (*Vayikra Rabba* 30). An understanding of the significance of the palm makes the objective of the author apparent. As an Alexandrian Jew, his message was directed to the Jews in the diaspora, citizens of many nationalities. To add force to his exhortations, he states that the original Hasmonean edict of Chanukah was addressed to "the whole nation of Jews" (chap. 10). He then sought to reassure his fellow Jews in the diaspora that they could celebrate with pride the restoration of Judea by using ancient biblical religious symbols and thus avoid the opposition of the nations amongst whom they reside.

The reiterated comparison between the two festivals might have prompted some people to label Chanukah by the name of Sukkot. In the second letter prefixed to II Maccabees, the Jews of Egypt were urged: "And now see that ye keep the feast of Tabernacles in the month of Kislev."

II Maccabees is the only ancient source which stresses the similarity between Chanukah and Sukkot. Its traces can be found, however, in the Talmud. Thus one rabbi explained the opinion of Bet-Shammai that one should light eight candles on the first day of Chanukah and then decrease by one on each successive day by comparing this arrangement to the decreasing number of ritual offerings brought daily on the festival of Tabernacles (*Shabbat* 21b). It seems that Bet-Shammai wanted to retain the independence symbolism of Chanukah under the very noses of the Romans. In Jerusalem *Sukkah* (chap. 3), Rav compares the ritual benediction over the lulav to the benediction over the Chanukah candles. While his reasoning rests on the strictly halachic principle of *a fortiore,* there might have been also a psychological basis to his argument. The same might be true of Rabbi Joshua b. Levi's statement (*Shabbat* 22a) about the utilization of sukkah decorations and the utilization of Chanukah lights. The link between the two festivals is reaffirmed in a late midrash (*Midrash L'Chanukah*) in a comment on a verse in Ecclesiastes (11:2), " 'give a portion to seven and also to eight'—he who has a share [in preserving] the seven candles which always burn in the Temple and the eight days of the festival [Sukkot], no creature will be able to stand up to him." In another passage it is stated: "The Almighty said [to the pagans], you wanted to eliminate the seven candles [menorah] and the eight days of the festival [Sukkot]". The affinity between Sukkot and Chanukah is also mentioned by the author of *Rokeach (Hilchot Chanukah)* and Baal HaTurim (Lev. 24:2).

A recapitulation of II Maccabees provides the following answers to our original questions: Chanukah commemorates the dedication of the altar, the victory of the Hasmoneans, and the manifestation of miracles at the time of the deliverance. The festival had as yet no definite name when it reached its first century of existence. The author was obviously baffled by the length of the festival and offered erroneous reasons in an effort to explain it. There was no prescribed ritual for observing the festival, except for the general statement that it was to be kept with "gladness." The book broadened the base of Chanukah, but it had little influence on early rabbinic writings, particularly since it was written in Greek. The two letters which prefix II Maccabees were written originally in Hebrew. They were possibly circulated independently and were known to some people. The prayer of *Al Hanisim,* which was first formulated in *Masechet Sofrim* (8th cent.), bears a strong resemblance to a passage in Judah's letter: "And the manifest signs which came from heaven [*Al Hanisim*] . . . so that being but a few they overcame the whole country . . . [*rabim b'yad meatim*] . . . and chased barbarian multitudes . . . [*vezedim*] . . . and upheld the Law . . . [*oske Toraratecha*) . . . which were going down [*leha-aviram me-chuke retzonecha*] . . . the Lord being gracious unto them [*b'rachamecha harabim*]." It is very possible that the phraseology of this letter inspired the author of the prayer. One may also attribute another bit of lasting influence to the book. The heroic and beloved tale of a mother and her martyred seven sons, which appeared first in II Maccabees, found its way, with some minor variations, into the Talmud (*Gittin* 57b) and *Josippon.*

JOSEPHUS

Our third source, the *Antiquities of the Jews,* was published 258 years after Judah's victory. Josephus adds little that is new to the story of Chanukah because he adheres closely to the account in I Maccabees, merely elaborating, on occasion, in his customary expansive style. There are a number of variations which are undoubtedly the result of an oversight rather than a difference of opinion. The most significant discrepancy between the two authors is in the time of the lighting of the menorah. I Maccabees definitely implies that the menorah was lit on the evening of Kislev 24 and that the burnt offering was brought on the new altar early in the morning of Kislev 25 (I Macc. 4). Josephus, however, states that they lighted the lamps and dedicated the altar on Kislev 25 (*Antiquities* 12.7). The time of the lighting of the menorah was obviously immaterial to Josephus in view of his definition of the holiday as a "festival of the restoration of the sacrifices in the Temple." He therefore regards the twenty-fifth of Kislev to be properly the first day of Chanukah. However, the talmudic view of Chanukah as a festival commemorating the miracle of the oil must be in accord with I Maccabees that the menorah was kindled on the evening of the twenty-fourth. If the lighting had taken place on the evening of the twenty-fifth, Chanukah would begin a day later. It is, of course, possible that the lighting took place on the morning of the twenty-fifth, except for the implication of I Maccabees that the menorah was kindled in the evening.

The following is an illustration of Josephus' elaboration upon the original source material. I Maccabees reports that Judah observed the dedication of the altar for eight days and offered burnt offerings with "gladness." Josephus states that Judah celebrated the festival "and omitted no sort of pleasures thereupon, but he feasted them upon very rich and splendid sacrifices."

FESTIVAL OF LIGHTS

Did Chanukah evolve any new aspects by the time it had reached its 250th anniversary? In this respect Josephus is very enlightening. Chanukah had acquired a distinct name in certain localities. It is not the fact that it was finally given a name that is important. It is the implication of the name that has far-reaching significance. I refer to Josephus' statement (*Antiquities* 12:7) "and from that time to this we celebrate this festival and call it 'Lights.' " It is curious that Josephus is the only Jewish source which mentions the name "Lights."

Shortly after the publication of the *Antiquities*, the festival was given its traditional name—Chanukah—by the talmudic rabbis. Josephus labors hard to link the name "Lights" with freedom of worship. Regardless of its philosophic connotation, the name indicates beyond any doubt that for a long time prior to Josephus' generation Jews had celebrated the festival by kindling lights. At some period between the time of the writing of II Maccabees (ca. 70 B.C.E.) and the beginning of the first century, the practice of candle-lighting on Chanukah had become widespread.

It is hard to pinpoint the time when the practice of candle-lighting was first introduced. We may reasonably assume that the new custom was not the result of a rabbinic edict. The leading rabbis of that period were Rabbi Simon b. Shatach, Shmayah and Avtalion, Hillel and Shammai. The Talmud does not attribute to any one of them a takanah of such great importance. We must therefore accept the view that candle-lighting was a spontaneous custom which grew and spread until it received rabbinic sanction and became a mitzvah.

Customs do not spring out of thin air. We are fortunately familiar with a Temple festival, Simchat Bet HaShoavah, which became very popular and was celebrated with great pomp soon after the death of King Alexander Jannai. At the same time, as a result of the strong anti-Hasmonean sentiments caused by Jannai's tyranny, Chanukah evolved into a commemoration of a Temple event rather than a Hasmonean victory. I believe that part of the ceremonial of Simchat bet HaShoavah was spontaneously copied on Chanukah or it was simultaneously introduced into both festivals.

Simchat Bet HaShoavah was a ritual of libation of the altar with water drawn from the spring of Siloam. The ritual was repeated for seven days beginning with the second day of Sukkot after the morning burnt-offering (*Yoma* 26b). This practice was very ancient, and the Talmud attributes its source to an oral tradition from Moses (*Taanit* 3a). There was apparently little publicity attached to this custom until it became a controversial issue between the Sadducees and the Pharisees. When Alexander Jannai, who was both king and high priest and a follower of the Sadduceans, publicly refused to pour the water on the altar, the congregation became so enraged that it pelted him with etrogim (*Sukkah* 48b, *Antiquities* 13. 13). In the aftermath of this incident, he is said to have massacred more than six thousand of his fellow Jews. When the Pharisees regained power after Jannai's death, the Pharisaic ritual was reinstated. The occasion was given great publicity, and it was celebrated with boundless joy. Huge golden candelabra were lit, and people danced with burning torches in their hands. The flames were so bright that all of Jerusalem was lit up (*Sukkah* 51a). The kindling of the lights was primarily designed to enhance the festivity, yet it soon assumed the status of a mitzvah. Thus the Talmud (*Shabbat* 21a) discusses the question whether the restrictions applicable to Sabbath lights also embrace the Simchat Bet HaShoavah lights as well as the Chanukah lights.

Simchat Bet HaShoavah and Chanukah had much in common. I previously stressed the tradition which linked the festivals of Sukkot and Chanukah. In this case there was an even greater similarity. Simchat Bet HaShoavah was a ceremony performed at the altar after the sacrifice of the Tamid. Chanukah commemorated the dedication of the altar and resumption of the Tamid. It might be of interest to note another similarity. The

Talmud bases the festivities of Simchat Bet HaShoavah on the verse in Isaiah (12:3): "And you shall draw water with joy" (*Sukkah* 48b). The post-talmudic Midrash *Maaseh Chanukah* quotes the same verse and describes the fulfillment of Isaiah's prophecy when the Almighty created springs of water in every home after the Syrians had proscribed ritual immersion. This very likely reflected an ancient tradition which linked the two celebrations. The use of candlelight and torches to enhance a festivity was a recent innovation. It was only natural to introduce this innovation in the home celebration of Chanukah. This most likely took place shortly after the death of Jannai (76 B.C.E.). Originally no special significance was attached to the number of candles. Each family generally used one light (*Shabbat* 21b). Rabbinic sanction of this custom gave it greater meaning as a commemoration of the "miracle of the oil." With the deterioration of the Jewish political situation, particularly after the destruction of the Temple, the need for spreading the inspiring story of the miracle became urgent. It was then that the schools of Bet Shammai and Bet Hillel proposed the addition of more lights. In concluding the discussion of the custom of kindling lights, it is noteworthy that the Talmud and the midrashim do not attribute to the Hasmoneans the mitzvah of Chanukah lights. (*Megillat Antiochus* is the sole exception. Ritva [*Megillah* 14a] states that the rabbis instituted candle-lighting on Chanukah.) The *beraita* merely alleges that on "the following year they set aside and declared it a holiday for thanksgiving and praise" (*Shabbat* 21b). The same is true of the nonrabbinic sources.

Josephus published his *Antiquities* in the year 93. Eighteen years earlier, in the year 75, he had published his first work, the *Wars of the Jews*. It was primarily a history of the war against Rome, but it is prefaced by a few chapters which give a sketchy account of the Hasmonean wars and of Chanukah. This early version includes many historical inaccuracies. It is invaluable, however, to our study of the development of Chanukah. When Josephus wrote his first book, he was not yet aware of the content of I Maccabees, which was apparently not available in Judea. Josephus' early account mirrors the information about

Chanukah current in Judea at the time of the destruction of the Temple. It is significant that the story in the *Wars* is in agreement on some major details with *Megillat Antiochus,* the earliest rabbinic work on Chanukah, which, in my opinion, was published about the same time as the *Wars.* The two agree, for instance, that the cleansing of the Temple followed the killing of Bacchides (*Megillat Antiochus* calls him Begris). I Maccabees, which gives an authentic history of the Hasmoneans, brings Bacchides into the war against Judah at a considerable time after the dedication of the Temple. Furthermore the general killed Judah and returned to Syria in triumph. On the other hand, the *Wars* and *Megillat Antiochus* also disagree in many details about the role of Judah. This illustrates the various contradictory reports about Chanukah circulating in Judea at the time of the destruction of the Temple, prior to the rediscovery of I Maccabees. As to the events which transpired immediately before and during the dedication of the Temple, Josephus early account is consistent with the later version of the *Antiquities* and is substantiated by I Maccabees. He sums it up briefly as follows: "He . . . cleansed the whole place and walled it round about and made new vessels. . . . He also built another altar and began to offer the sacrifices" (*Wars* 1. 1). The story of the dedication of the altar by Judah was thus well known to the Jews of Judea throughout the 235 years which elapsed from the Maccabean victory until the destruction of the Temple. It is thus understandable why the name Chanukah persistently clung to the festival in spite of the shift of emphasis by the rabbis from the Hasmoneans to the miracle of the oil.

MEGILLAT ANTIOCHUS

Megillat Antiochus, originally written in Aramaic, is the earliest rabbinic work on Chanukah. It is a very important document because the story of the miracle of oil appears in it for the first time. The accounts of this miracle in the Talmud (*Shabbat* 2lb, *Megillat Taanit,* chap. 9) are based on this scroll. Scholars have pointed to the purity of its Aramaic style as evidence of its antiquity. According to one opinion, it antedates the Books of

Maccabees. This is obviously wrong in view of the mention made in the seventy-second sentence of the scroll of the destruction of the Temple (there are seventy-four sentences in the scroll). One may be tempted to suggest that the last three sentences were appended at some later period since they constitute merely a postscript to the main story of Chanukah. However, there is evidence to the contrary. The Scroll of Antiochus closely follows the style of the Scroll of Esther. The opening and concluding phrases of the Chanukah scroll are modeled after its famous predecessor. Thus the Book of Esther begins: "And it was in the days of Ahasuerus . . ." The ninth chapter of the Book of Esther, which finishes the story of Purim, concludes with the information that Esther decreed the writing of the book. Since the Hasmoneans had not decreed the writing of the story of Chanukah, the author could not use the last sentence of the Book of Esther as the model for his own concluding sentence. He therefore selected the preceding sentence as the model for his own conclusion. In that sentence we were told that the edict of Purim "was decreed for themselves and their seed" (kiymu al Nafsham v'al zaram). Megillat Antiochus ends similarly by stating that "they decreed it for themselves and their children's children for ever" (kiymu aleihem v'al b'nai bnaihem ad olma). It is obvious that the last sentence of Megillat Antiochus was an integral part of the scroll as it was originally written. We must therefore definitely conclude that the scroll was written after the destruction of the Temple.

Some scholars are of the opinion that Megillat Antiochus was written in the seventh century. There are a number of indications, however, that it must have been written shortly after the destruction of the Temple. In the first place, the name Chanukah is not mentioned in the scroll. The earliest appearance of this name in the Talmud is in the legal controversy between Bet Hillel and Bet Shammai (Shabbat 21b). Since these schools ended their existence in the days of Rabban Gamliel II, we conclude that the name Chanukah was already known at the very latest by the end of the first century.

The scroll, therefore, must have been written in the period

between 70 and 100 C.E. There is ample evidence to corroborate this conclusion. The author of the scroll tells us that the Hasmoneans set aside a period of a "day of joy like the days of joy of the holidays written in the Torah." The Talmud eliminated the "joy and festivity" and attributed to the Hasmonean edict the designation of "days of thanksgiving and praise." The scroll unquestionably antedated this development and was written at a time when Chanukah was still theoretically a festival of joy. Furthermore, the scroll employs a legal formula which was popularized by *Megillat Taanit* shortly after the destruction of the Temple and was widely used at that period: "These eight days . . . no eulogy for the dead is to be delivered during this period and no fast is to be decreed." We are further aided in the dating of the scroll by the fact that the term "miracle," so very popular in the Talmud, does not yet appear in it. Our last bit of evidence is based on the implication in the scroll that if an individual had already made it a custom to fast on Chanukah, he may continue doing so. No seventh-century sage could have written that opinion in view of the definite talmudic prohibition, to which no exceptions were made (*Rosh HaShanah* 18b). We are thus led to the conclusion that *Megillat Antiochus* was written in the short interval between the destruction of the Temple and the final adoption by the talmudic rabbis of the traditional form of Chanukah, by the end of the first century.

The Scroll of Antiochus presents two enigmas which must be solved because they hold the key to the turning point in the evolution of Chanukah. The first amazing feature is the apparent downgrading of Judah Maccabee. He is said to have been killed early in the encounter with Bacchides, whereupon Mattathias assumed the military leadership and finally proceeded to cleanse the Temple after he had scored many victories. (Mattathias is lauded by I Maccabees as the initiator of the rebellion but is not credited with an active part in it. II Maccabees ignores him completely.) In the place of Judah, his brother Jochanan emerges as the real hero of the Hasmonean wars. The heroic tale of Judah's life was well known to the Jews at the time of the destruction of the Temple as is evidenced by Josephus' *Wars*. Why did the author of the scroll play it down?

Another striking feature is the omission of the story of the dedication of the altar in the Scroll of Antiochus. The author, like Josephus in the *Wars*, reports the cleansing of the Temple and the rebuilding of the broken gates. Unlike Josephus, he does not mention the dedication of the new altar and vessels and the resumption of the sacrificial ritual. Instead, he proceeds immediately with the story of the jar of oil. Thus the historical basis of Chanukah, as described in Maccabees and Josephus, seems to have been eliminated by him. What motivated this change?

The Scroll of Antiochus is the first rabbinic interpretation of Chanukah. It reflects the views of the early Chasidim and the subsequent generation of rabbis during the rebellion against Rome. Wars are to be sanctioned only if they are waged in defense of faith and life. The attainment of political ends, even the defense of independence, does not warrant bloodshed, particularly where the fighting against heavy odds could only lead to fame but not to victory. There is good reason to assume that Judah Maccabee lost the backing of the Chasidim prior to his last battle against Bacchides. According to I Maccabees (chap. 11), Judah had only three thousand men in his army when he faced Bacchides. Of this small army only eight hundred were left to engage in battle; the rest deserted him out of fear of the formidable enemy. The fact that Judah had so small an army to begin with, and the unprecedented desertions, speak of disaffection rather than cowardice. The story of his last battle is related in I Maccabees immediately after the account of his alliance with Rome. Raphall (*Post-Biblical History of the Jews*, vol. 1, chap. 6) pointed to a passage in the post-talmudic *Midrash Chanukah* which reflects a rather violent opposition to foreign entanglements. To the Chasidim it was a betrayal of trust and confidence in God. The midrash describes the overpowering array of Bacchides' armies. It then tells of Jewish fears and hopes. "At that time the Jews looked toward the eastern mountains in the hope that the pagan Parthians would come to their assistance. [The Parthians were opposed to the Syrians.] Then Mattathias, the high priest, became angry and said to the Hasmoneans: 'It is written, 'Cursed be the man who places his dependence on flesh, while from the Lord his heart departs;

but blessed is the man who trusts in the Lord' (Jer. 17:5)." In addition to the objections of a strong segment of religious Jews to the foreign alliance which Judah, Jonathan, and Simon continued to promote, there was objection to the fusion of the positions of high priesthood and royalty which the outspoken Eleazar voiced later to Hyrcanus. There was also a disturbing awareness of the fact that the Hasmoneans had defied the ancient tradition that royalty would be invested upon a scion of the house of David. At the time of the destruction of the Temple, the Jews had good reason to rue the first treaty of alliance which Judah had concluded with Rome. The Romans, no doubt, would have come to Judea regardless of any treaties. The author of the Scroll of Antiochus and the Pharisaic leadership, however, must have reacted very unfavorably to Judah's overtures, which had directed Rome's attention to Judea.

In the eyes of the Chasidim, only Mattathias and his sons Jochanan and Eleazar emerged with heroic stature and their reputations unstained. Mattathias sparked the rebellion. His only objective was freedom of religion. That met with the whole-hearted support of the Chasidim. Jochanan and Eleazar were the only two Hasmonean sons who did not attain political leadership and power. They were not involved in the promotion of foreign entanglements. Both sons, like their father, pursued purely religious ends. Jochanan is said to have served as high priest. In light of the Pharisaic attitude toward the Hasmoneans, which had hardened by the time of the destruction of the Temple, the Chanukah account of *Megillat Antiochus* can be readily understood.

The author of *Megillat Antiochus* must have ignored the story of the dedication of the altar for several reasons. The dedication of the altar was linked historically to Judah Maccabee. The practical elimination of Judah's part in the rebellion left the story of the dedication untold. There was a more cogent reason, however, for the author's silence. With the destruction of the Temple, the dedicatory aspects of the festival lost their significance. The shift of emphasis to the story of the jar of oil was the beginning of a new orientation in which the altar and ritual sacrifices were to play no part.

The impact of *Megillat Antiochus* on the Talmud was profound. I believe it was due to the influence of the scroll that the Talmud never singled out the name of Judah in the story of Chanukah. Only Mattathias is mentioned by name (*Megillah* 11a, *Shmot Rabba* 15).

SIMON THE JUST

The text in *Megillah*, just referred to, needs some elucidation. It reads as follows: " 'I did not despise them'—in the days of the Greeks, when I set up for them Simon the Just, and the Hasmonean and his sons, and Mattathias the high priest." The name Hasmonean in the above quotation is synonymous with Mattathias, and yet it is listed here alongside Mattathias as if he were another, additional person. Prof. S. Hoenig (*The Great Sanhedrin*, chap. 4) offers a most ingenious suggestion to amend the text as follows: "I set up for them Simon the Just, Hasmonean (as a prince), the son of Mattathias, a high priest." He accordingly assumes that the entire passage refers to one person only, namely, Simon, the son of Mattathias, who is also known as Simon the Just. This interpretation places Simon in the exalted position of being the sole recipient of talmudic credit for the events "in the days of the Greeks."

In spite of the attractiveness of S. Hoenig's suggestion, one may hesitate to accept it for a number of reasons. In the aforementioned passage in *Megillah*, the Talmud designates the persons who had become divine instruments in heaven's intercession for the Jewish people. One would expect the Talmud to designate the name of a person who was prominent at the most crucial period of the Greek oppression—at the outset of the rebellion, when the survival of Torah was at stake—rather than a person who became prominent at a later period. It is hardly conceivable that Simon, even if he was the first Hasmonean to restore Jewish independence, should be given precedence over Mattathias or Judah, who restored the Temple service. Furthermore, in selecting the various leading individuals whom God had sent in times of trouble, the same talmudic passage is careful to give credit to more than one person. Thus,

Daniel, Hananiah, Mishael, and Azariah were the divine
instruments in the time of the Chaldeans. Mordecai and Esther
were assigned a divine mission in the days of Haman. There is
no reason why Simon should be given exclusive credit for the
victory over the Greeks. Our final objection rests on the fact that
whenever Simon the Just is mentioned in the Talmud, regardless of the identity of the particular Simon the Just, the name of
his father is never appended to his.

The text in *Megillah* is definitely garbled, and I would
therefore suggest the following corrected version: "Simon the
Just and Mattathias the high priest, the Hasmonean and his
sons." This construction corresponds to the opening sentence of
the prayer *Al Hanisim:* "In the days of Mattathias the son of
Yochanan the high priest, Hasmonean and his sons . . ." The
passage in *Megillah,* therefore, gives credit to Simon the Just,
who warded off the wrath of Alexander the Great at the opening
of Judea's Greek epoch, and to Mattathias and his children, who
fought off Antiochus at the outset of the rebellion. The author of
Seder HaDorot (Yochanan Kohen Gadol) quotes the same
passage (*Megillah* 11a). His version parallels my suggested
correction—viz., "Simon the Just and Mattathias the son of
Yochanan the high priest, Hasmonean and his children." The
only distinction between his version and the one in our Talmud
is the name of Mattathias' father, Yochanan, which does not
appear in our text.

If we accept the corrected version of our text, we must explain
the reference to Mattathias as the high priest. The early
nonrabbinic sources state that he was a priest. There is no
mention of his being a high priest. There seems to have existed a
rabbinic tradition that Mattathias was a high priest. The text of
our version in *Megillah* calls Mattathias a high priest. There are
versions which contain a similar reference in *Megillat Taanit*
(chap. 6). The *Midrash Masseh Chanukah* has a few references to
"Mattathias the high priest."

Maimonides (Preface to *Seder Zeraim,* chap. 6) states that
Yochanan the high priest, who is mentioned in the Talmud
(*Maaser Sheni* 5:15), was the son of Mattathias the Hasmonean
(not his father). It follows, therefore, that the reference in the
prayer of *Al Hanisim* to "Mattathias the son of Yochanan the high

priest" speaks of Mattathias the high priest, the son of Yochanan. The M'iri, in his preface to *Avot*, disagrees with Maimonides. In his opinion Yochanan the high priest who is mentioned in the Talmud was the father of Mattathias and not his son. The reference in the prayer of *Al Hanisim* is to Mattathias the son of Yochanan the high priest. It seems that Maimonides based his opinion on *Megillat Antiochus*, which refers to Yochanan the son of Mattathias as the high priest. There is evidence elsewhere that Maimonides derived some of his information from the scroll. His statement (*Hilchot Megillah* 3:2) that "the sages of that generation set aside an eight-day period, beginning with the twenty-fifth day of Kislev, as a day of joy and praise" is based on the scroll, which speaks of Chanukah as days of "joy," a phrase later eliminated in the Talmud. The *Shulchan Aruch* (*Orach Chaim, Hilchot Chanukah* 670:2) correctly states the rabbinic view that "they did not set them aside for feast and joy."

THE KINDLING OF LIGHTS

Before I conclude the discussion of the scroll, I would like to point out that it is the only source which attributes to the Hasmoneans themselves the order to kindle lights as part of their original edict of Chanukah. The Talmud, which presents a more balanced picture of Chanukah, apparently did not accept this view. (See Ritva, *Megillah* 14a, *Veamrinan*. He speaks of a rabbinic ordinance of Chanukah lights.) This does not diminish, of course, the overall influence of *Megillat Antiochus* on the development of Chanukah and on the talmudic and midrashic comments on this festival.

The story of the miracle of the oil, the focal point of Chanukah, as related in *Shabbat* (21b) and *Megillat Taanit* (chap. 9), was based, as I previously mentioned, on the Scroll of Antiochus. The *beraita* in *Shabbat* reads as follows: "On the twenty-fifth day of Kislev, the eight days of Chanukah [begin]. One should not eulogize the dead or fast then . . ." Rabbi Elijah Gaon deletes the reference to fasting. He probably made this correction because there is no reference to fasting in the text of *Megillat Taanit*. However, a comparison of the two texts reveals many

other variations. The *Shabbat* version reads as follows: "When
the royal house of the Hasmoneans [*malchut bet Chashmonai*]
became strong . . . they found only one jar of oil with the seal of
the high priest on it. . . . the following year they designated and
set them aside as holidays with praise and thanksgiving." The
Megillat Taanit version reads: "When the house of the Hasmoneans [*Bet Chashmonai*] became strong . . . they found only one
jar of oil with the seal of the high priest on it which was not
defiled. . . . the following year they designated an eight-day
holiday." The scholiast, who quoted from the *beraita* in *Shabbat*,
had before him a slightly different version than the one which
we have today. An examination of the two versions reveals an
ancient effort to conform to *Megillat Antiochus*. It also indicates
the changes which were introduced by the Talmud in order to
give Chanukah its final traditional form. The scroll mentions
that there is to be no eulogy or fasting on Chanukah. This
conforms to our version in *Shabbat*. It also speaks of the "house
of the Hasmoneans" who entered the Temple. This records
correctly the fact that the Hasmoneans were not yet a royal
house when they cleansed the Temple. It conforms to the
scholiast's version in *Megillat Taanit*. It is possible that our
version of the *beraita* is a later one when the expression *malchut bet
Chasmonai* became standard in the Talmud (*Rosh HaShanah* 24b,
Megillah 6a). The scroll also speaks of the jar of oil "which they
knew to be undefiled." This, too, corroborates the version of the
scholiast. Both the *beraita* in *Shabbat* and the scholiast use the
expression "a miracle happened to it." The scroll, however,
states: "then God in heaven, who rested his name there, gave it
his blessing, and it burned for eight days." The talmudic
introduction of the word "miracle" was placed there by design.
It was used to accentuate the new significance of the festival.
The scroll states that it designated "these eight days, days of joy
like the joyous holidays which are written in the Torah." This
conforms more closely to the scholiast's version. Our version is
the later one. It qualifies the holiday with the post-exilic view
that they are to be days of prayer rather than festivity.

In spite of the profound influence of the Scroll of Antiochus, it
was never officially sanctioned by the talmudic authorities nor

was there a special effort made to preserve it. Its many historical inaccuracies might have weighed heavily against it. There was also a basic reason for the official reserve with which it was treated. The Scroll of Antiochus was written in the style of the Book of Esther and was probably intended for public reading at services on Chanukah. The rabbis looked askance at the publication of any written books outside the canon, particularly if they simulated biblical style, In reference to Chanukah there is a specific statement in the Talmud (*Yoma* 29a) that the story of Chanukah was not to be written but rather handed down orally.

TALMUDIC SOURCES

The destruction of the Temple and the catastrophic defeat at the hands of the Romans brought about far-reaching changes in Jewish life. The Temple, which had been the symbol of national and religious unity, was gone. Geographic dispersal made the need for new symbols of religious and cultural cohesiveness more urgent. The rabbinic academies, the synagogue, and the home itself were converted into new symbols. Under such circumstances Chanukah could be made to play a vital role. With the destruction of Onias' temple in Egypt in the year 73, and the removal of its spurious claim to religious leadership, the door was widely opened to the spread of Chanukah throughout the diaspora. In this hour of national anguish it was imperative to preach a message of hope. The memory of "miracles" cushioned the harshness of defeat and blunted the sharp edge of Rome's total triumph. Confidence in ultimate salvation and restoration of independence was carefully nurtured through religious observance of past miracles. The people were told that there was no reason for despair because miracles could occur again. *Pirsumo niso,* the publicizing of miracles, became a chief preoccupation of the rabbis. The reading of the Scroll of Esther was made obligatory because it publicized an ancient miracle (*Megillah* 3b). Women were included in this injunction because they, too, were saved by the miracle (*Megillah* 4a). The four *kosot* of wine of the Seder night were given great prominence because of their symbolic reference to redemption. Here, too, women were enjoined to participate in the mitzvah because they had been included in the original miracle (*Pesachim* 108b).

Chanukah offered an excellent opportunity for spreading the word of God's miracles. It had the advantage of commemorating a comparatively recent miracle. The dedication of the altar was one phase of the festival which had lost its significance. The military victory of the Hasmoneans could not be safely proclaimed without arousing the hostile reaction of the enemy. (The story of the victories was restored in the prayer of *Al Hanisim*, which was composed in the eighth century.) The publicizing of the miracle of oil was timely and helpful. The lighting of candles at home brought the story of the miracle to each family. Instead of the single light, multiple lights were introduced to give the miracle greater publicity. There, too, the mitzvah was made obligatory even for women because they had been included in the miracle (*Shabbat* 23a). A special prayer of thanks for the performance of miracles was composed. Unlike Purim, festivities were deemed improper because the miracle related to a Temple function which unfortunately was no longer in existence.

RABBAN GAMLIEL II

The duty of reinterpreting Chanukah must have fallen to Rabban Gamliel II, who headed the Sanhedrin during the crucial years 80–118. He instituted many new provisions to help adjust Jewish life to the new conditions. Under his leadership many new important prayers, including major parts of the Haggadah, were written. Old prayers which had been forgotten, some dating from the time of the Hasmoneans, were restored (*Megillah* 17b). It was during his lifetime that the name Chanukah was finally adopted, for the sake of historical continuity and accuracy.

The retention of the name Chanukah ("dedication") for a festival commemorating a miracle of oil led to much confusion in later generations. This is the significance of the talmudic question, *Mai Chanukah?*—"What do we commemorate on

Chanukah?" The scholiast reflects this confusion in his lengthy and labored efforts to explain Chanukah. The inconsistency of the name with the theme of the festival gave rise to new interpretations of the word Chanukah by such great scholars as Abudarham, Ran, Kalbo, Tur, etc. The historical dedication of the altar had been totally glossed over since the days of the Scroll of Antiochus, and no one looked to our remote history for the key to the name.

The author of *Josippon*, who lived in the tenth century, speaks of this "dedication of the altar" on the twenty-fifth day of Kislev. This passage apparently escaped the attention of the great medieval rabbis. The Maharsha was the first of the great talmudic scholars to rediscover the ancient link in his commentary on Shabbat. (See Zevin, *Moadim Be-Halacha*, Chanukah. He quotes Rabbi Isaac of Kenna, the author of *Or Zarua*, who lived in the fourteenth century. He, too, had already recognized the link between Chanukah and the dedication of the altar.)

RABBINIC CHANUKAH

By the end of the first century, the basic outlines of the talmudic Chanukah had been delineated. It seems to have made little headway during the remainder of the tannaic period, which terminated roughly by the end of the second century. No new rituals and regulations were evolved, and the festival apparently remained confined mainly to Palestine. The fact that Rabbi Judah HaNasi never included the *beraita* which discusses the origin of Chanukah in his edition of the Mishnah is highly revealing. (Chanukah is mentioned in Mishnah *Bikkurim* 1:6).

What caused the interruption in the development of Chanukah? One may venture to suggest a psychological reason. The second century was dominated by Jewish activists. The spark of rebellion and direct action was not yet extinct. Many Jews had refused to consider the defeat in the year 70 as final. They declined to accept the early post-Hasmonean message of Chanukah that their future restoration could henceforth be brought about only through miraculous and divine intervention. The rebellion of Bar Kochba was to sweep the nation with its courage and daring. When that failed there was still hope of a peaceful arrangement with the Romans for autonomy and a semblance of independence.

The Talmud refers to an incident which reflects the disregard of Chanukah. The people of Lydda had declared a fast during Chanukah. There was a widespread feeling that the festivals of *Megillat Taanit*, including Chanukah, were no longer in force. The strong protests of Rabbi Eliezer and Rabbi Joshua reimposed the restrictions of Chanukah upon the people (*Rosh HaShanah* 18b). Rabbi Judah HaNasi, who had attained a state of peaceful coexistence with the Romans, sought to do away with some of the exilic fasts and to minimize the importance of Purim (*Megillah* 5b). He failed, however, to win over his colleagues, and his views were overwhelmingly rejected. This showdown was undoubtedly the turning point which renewed the active interest of the rabbis in Chanukah. The deterioration of the political situation aided the views of the majority. With the opening of the amoraic period, the development of Chanukah resumed its rapid pace. Within a few pages of tractate *Shabbat* (21–24), we find no less than thirty Amoraim engaged in the discussion of Chanukah rituals. These include both Palestinian and Babylonian Amoraim of the first through the fifth generation (ca. 200–370). The opening of the Babylonian academies assured the widespread introduction of Chanukah to Babylonian Jewry and thence throughout the diaspora. The main efforts of the rabbis during these two centuries was directed toward the publicizing of the miracle of the oil. The emphasis on the kindling of the lights and the rituals pertaining to it led the editors of the Gemara to include the Chanukah discussions in tractate *Shabbat* in context of the laws of the Sabbath candles. From a historical point of view, this subject should have been incorporated in tractate *Megillah*, which expounds the laws of another major post-exilic festival. Both Maimonides and the *Shulchan Aruch* group the laws of Chanukah and Purim in the same chapter.

VERNACULAR TERM

Before we bring the discussion of rabbinic Chanukah to an end, it may be of interest to note that in addition to its religious connotation, Chanukah also acquired, at one time, a secular significance, synonymous with a "winter festival" or the winter season. The three Pilgrimage Festivals were always identified with seasons of the year. Passover was a spring festival; Shavuot, a summer festival, and Sukkot, a fall festival. There was a long hiatus, however, during the winter months. The introduction of Chanukah filled the gap. It was soon popularly identified as the opening of the winter season. The rabbis, too, adopted that concept on occasion. Thus they expressed the fact that heads of leek (*kaplatot*) were available in Palestine in the summer and the fall by saying that they were available from "Shavuot to Chanukah" (Jer. *Dmai*, chap. 2).

The use of the vernacular concept of Chanukah as a subdivision of the calendar helps clarify some talmudic passages which might otherwise appear obscure. In discussing the deadline for the delivery of the tithes which had fallen due over the triennial cycle (Deut. 14:28), the Talmud considers the suggestion that Chanukah become a terminal point (Jer. *Maaser Sheni*, chap. 5). It may sound rather puzzling that the rabbis named a postbiblical festival as the possible deadline of a biblical period. Yet here, too, the use of Chanukah is merely synonymous with winter. The rabbis had suggested that the time of delivery was extended to the winter of the fourth year. In the end they conclude that the period of grace is extended until Passover, or the spring of the fourth year.

The same interpretation is to be given to the statement in the Mishnah (*Bikkurim* 1:6) that one may offer his *bikkurim* during the period between Sukkot and Chanukah, but without the confessional prayer which is part of the ritual. Here, too, Chanukah seems to be out of place in a consideration of biblical periods. However, the usage of the term Chanukah as a designation of a season puts the term in the proper perspective. *Bikkurim* are to be offered beginning with Shavuot. It was therefore a summer offering. It may be offered properly throughout the summer—from Shavuot until Sukkot. It is accepted also in the fall, but the terminology of the prayer is no longer applicable to the season. It is therefore offered without a prayer between Sukkot and Chanukah. A post-Chanukah or winter plant is considered a product of the succeeding year. Its *bikkurim* fall due on the following Shavuot.

SUMMATION

1. Chanukah originally commemorated the dedication of the altar and the resumption of the daily sacrificial rites.
2. The festival was initially known as the Days of Dedication.
3. In the first century of its existence, the festival was celebrated with voluntary sacrificial offerings and feasting.
4. The practice of kindling lights was spontaneously adopted shortly after 76 B.C.E. The observance of Chanukah was mainly confined to Judea.
5. The name Chanukah was adopted about the end of the first century C.E. The emphasis of the celebration was the miracle of oil.
6. The festival spread throughout the diaspora with the opening of the Babylonian academies in the third century.

6

Purim

RABBINIC IDENTIFICATION OF AHASUERUS

THE IDENTITY OF the Persian king in the Book of Esther has never been definitely ascertained. It is generally assumed that Ahasuerus was not a proper name but a royal title borne by a number of Persian and Median sovereigns. Daniel mentions "Darius the Mede," who received the kingdom of the Chaldeans (6:1). He was described as the son of "Ahasuerus, descendant of the Medes" (9:1). Cyrus conquered Media in 550 B.C.E. and Persia in 551 B.C.E. Upon the fall of Babylonia in 538 B.C.E. he appointed Darius the Mede, who was of royal Median descent, vassal king of the province of Chaldea.

Ahasuerus, the father of Darius the Mede, is not to be confused with the Ahasuerus of Purim fame. It is to avoid such confusion that the opening sentence of the Book of Esther attempts to identify the king in question: "And it came to pass in the days of Ahasuerus, he is the Ahasuerus who reigned from India even unto Ethiopia over 127 provinces." We are thus informed that the Persian Ahasuerus is distinct from the Median Ahasuerus.

The name Ahasuerus is mentioned again in the Book of Ezra (4:6). Ezra listed four Persian kings: Koresh, Daryavesh, Achashverosh, and Artachshasta. At this point it might be helpful to record the chronology of the Persian kings of that period: Cyrus, 558–529 B.C.E.; Cambyses, 529–522 B.C.E.; Pseudo-Smerdis, 7 months; Darius Hystaspes, 521–485 B.C.E.;

Xerxes, 485–465 B.C.E.; and Artaxerxes Longimanus, 465–424
B.C.E. We may now attempt to identify the four kings listed by
Ezra as follows: Koresh is Cyrus, Daryavesh is Darius Hystaspes, Achashverosh is Xerxes, and Artachshasta is Artaxerxes.
If we are to assume that the Ahasuerus listed by Ezra is the
Ahasuerus of the Book of Esther, and there is a talmudic
tradition to that effect (*Megillah* 11a), we must arrive at the
conclusion that the story of Mordecai and Esther took place in
the reign of Xerxes, 485–465 B.C.E. This conclusion, however, is
open to challenge. Since the name Ahasuerus was a royal title
rather than a proper name, it is conceivable that any of the
Persian kings listed in the Book of Ezra could have been the
Ahasuerus of the Book of Esther. Indeed one rabbi identified
Ahasuerus with Artaxerxes (*Esther Rabba*, chap. 1). There is
another rabbinic tradition that Cyrus and Darius were the only
proper names of Persian royalty. All the other Persian names
mentioned in the Scriptures are merely titles (*Seder Olam Rabba*
30). This tradition renders the identification of Ahasuerus even
more difficult.

The Book of Esther does not provide us with substantial clues
to help resolve the king's ambiguous identity. We are told that
the king ruled over an empire stretching "from Hodu unto
Kush." Kush is traditionally translated as Ethiopia. If this
translation is correct, we must eliminate Cyrus as one of the
kings who might be equated with Ahasuerus. Ethiopia was first
conquered by Cyrus' son, Cambyses. Furthermore, the assumption that the province of Hodu is Indus would eliminate
Cambyses, too. Indus was first annexed by Cambyses' successor, Darius. However, we cannot be sure of the geographic
location of Hodu and Kush. The term *Kushi* was applied to all
dark-skinned people. The Midianite Zipporah was called a
Kushite (Num. 12:1). Indeed one rabbi expressed an opinion
that Kush was a province adjoining Hodu and not on the
opposite end of the empire (*Megillah* 11a). The name Indus,
technically the northwestern province of India, was also loosely
applied to other territories. We need not, therefore, exclude
Cyrus and Cambyses from consideration.

THE DATE OF MORDECAI

The scriptural introduction to Mordecai, which could help us in ascertaining the approximate date of Purim, is also somewhat ambiguous. "There was a certain Jew in Shushan the castle, whose name was Mordecai, the son of Jair, the son of Shimei, the son of Kish, a Benjamite; who had been carried away from Jerusalem with the captives that had been carried away with Jeconiah, king of Judah, whom Nebuchadnezzar the king of Babylonia, had carried away" (Esther 2:5–6). We know that Jeconiah was taken into captivity in the year 597 B.C.E. We cannot tell from the text, however, whether it was Mordecai or his ancestor, Kish, who had been exiled with the king. If it was Mordecai who was deported in 597 B.C.E., then we must confine the events of Purim to the comparatively short period from the conquest of Babylonia by Cyrus in 538 B.C.E. to the death of Mordecai. Assuming that Mordecai was a young man of twenty at the time of his deportation, he would have been an old man of seventy-nine at the time of the fall of Babylonia. Even if he were blessed with longevity, one cannot normally attribute active leadership to him beyond the age of ninety. We would therefore reach the conclusion that the story of Purim took place within the period of 538–528 B.C.E.

For the sake of comparison we have the record of another biblical figure, Daniel, who was also deported at the time of the captivity of Jeconiah (Dan. 1:6). We assume that he, too, was a very young man at the time of his deportation. He lived in Babylonia until the fall of that empire. The latest date mentioned by him in the Book of Daniel is 536 B.C.E. (10:1). He was about eighty years of age at that time. We may assume that he died shortly thereafter. (The Daniel who joined Ezra in the second aliyah [Ezra 8:2], and who was also a collaborator of Nehemiah [Neh. 10:7], is not to be confused with the author of the Book of Daniel, who would have reached by then his 170th year.) Mordecai and Daniel were contemporaries and belonged to the same generation. We have no reason to assume that Mordecai survived Daniel by a considerable number of years.

A passage in the Midrash (*Shir Hashirim Rabba* 3:6) states that Daniel received his political promotion in the reign of Darius. There is also a talmudic statement (*Megillah* 15a) that Mordecai, Daniel, Haggai, Zechariah, and Malachi prophesied in the second year of Darius (519 B.C.E.). These passages seem to indicate a rabbinic tradition that Daniel and Mordecai were still alive in the year 519 B.C.E., at which time they would have been close to one hundred years. This would be contrary to a normal expectancy of life. There is no mention anywhere in the Talmud, not even in the aggadic literature, that either one of these two men had lived an exceptionally long life. We must therefore assume that the tradition that Mordecai and Daniel had lived in the early years of King Darius' reign referred to Darius the Mede, the contemporary of King Cyrus. In dating his visions, Daniel referred on some occasions to the reign of Darius the Mede (9:1). Since Haggai and Zechariah prophesied in the early years of the Persian Darius (521 B.C.E.), the two traditions were erroneously merged into a single tradition, listing the name of the men who had prophesied in the reign of Darius.

The conclusion that Mordecai died in the reign of King Cyrus and that the latter is to be identified with Ahasuerus is predicated upon the construction of the biblical text (Esther 2:5–6) that it was Mordecai who had been exiled in 597 B.C.E. On the other hand, if the text refers to Kish as the man who had been exiled in 597 B.C.E., it would be conceivable that Mordecai lived a century or 150 years later. This is a reasonable assumption, inasmuch as the genealogical list of Mordecai's forebears does not include every link in the chain of his ancestry. This alternate interpretation of the text allows us to accept the theories which place Mordecai at various periods in the reign of Darius, Xerxes, and even Artaxerxes.

RABBINIC VIEWS

A considerable number of talmudic rabbis seem to have favored the view that it was Mordecai who had been deported in 597 B.C.E. The major reason for this tradition was undoubtedly the fact that a man named Mordecai is listed among the individuals who had accompanied Zerubbabel on his journey to Palestine in 538 B.C.E. (Ezra 2:2, Neh. 7:7). He was commonly identified with the Mordecai of the Book of Esther (*Menachot* 65a). The rabbis also interpreted the name Bilshan, listed after Mordecai in the Books of Ezra and Nehemiah, not as the proper name of another individual but as a noun, meaning "linguist." Thus the text called him "Mordecai the linguist." This gave rise to the tradition that Mordecai had been a member of the Sanhedrin prior to his deportation. It was generally assumed that a linguistic qualification was a prerequisite to an appointment to the Sanhedrin (*Megillah* 13b).

There might have been other reasons leading to the conclusion that Mordecai lived at the time of the early captivity of 597 B.C.E. The text in Esther states that Mordecai (or Kish) was a Benjamite (2:6). One might wonder what significance this information adds to the life of Mordecai. It is true that the tribal composition of the kingdom of Judea, consisting of the large tribe of Judah and the small tribe of Benjamin, was preserved by the Babylonian captivity. The tribal distinction was retained in captivity as an expression of confidence in the ultimate return to Zion and resettlement in ancestral lands. This distinction was still maintained in Palestine after Zerubbabel returned to Jerusalem in 538 B.C.E. (Ezra 4:1), at the time when Ezra arrived there in 457 B.C.E. (Ezra 10:9), and when Nehemiah joined him in 444 B.C.E. (Neh. 11:4). There was no reason, however, for continuing the tribal designation in Babylonia after the first aliyah of Zerubbabel. Those who remained in Babylonia did so by choice, moved by a decision to remain outside Palestine. To these Jews the tribal label was no longer important. As a result of the gradual obliteration of the tribal designation, the name "Jew" emerged early in the diaspora (Esther 2:5, Neh. 1:2). The adjective *Yehudi* in the text of Esther no longer had a parochial, tribal, connotation but rather a broad national identification. (The term *Yehudim* in Jeremiah 52:28, 30, still retained a tribal identity.) Mordecai, a member of the tribe of Benjamin, was also known as a Judean man, or Jew. In earlier references to the Jews of the captivity, the accepted label was "the children of Israel" (Dan. 1:3, Ezra 2:5, 3:1). "Israel" was a comprehensive term, embracing even the remnants of the ten tribes. Their ultimate absorption by the Babylonian captivity brought about the gradual adoption of the name Judeans or Jews.

The newly coined name Jew originated in Babylonia, among the Aramaic-speaking Jews, and then drifted slowly southward into Palestine. In the Book of Ezra we find the name only in the Aramaic passages of the text (6:7, 14). The Hebrew passages still use the old names: "The people of Judea" (4:4), "The children of the captivity" (6:19), and "Israel" (7:28). The Book of Nehemiah, on the other hand, makes liberal use of the name Jew (1:2, 2:16, 4:6, etc.), indicating a widespread acceptance of the term.

The authorship of the Book of Esther was attributed by the Talmud to the Men of the Great Synagogue (*Baba Batra* 15a), which was traditionally founded by Ezra and Nehemiah. At the time of the writing of Esther, the word Jew had already been well publicized and widely used. Indeed, the age-old conflicting connotations of "Jew"—religious (adopted by the medieval church), racial (preached by Hitler), and national (emphasized by modern Zionism)—had already made their appearance in ancient times. The text of Esther (2:5–6) seems to give the name a national connotation by calling Mordecai a Jew because he had come from Jerusalem, where he had been a Judean national. The rabbis in a later age suggested that he was called a Jew because he had defended monotheism (*Esther Rabba*, v. 5). Zeresh, Haman's wife, anticipated the Nazi racial theories by speaking of Mordecai who is "of the seed of the Jews" (6:13), thus giving the name a racial overtone.

With the widespread adoption of the name Jew, the tribal identification of Mordecai by the Men of the Great Assembly might have appeared somewhat redundant to later rabbis. They might have concluded, therefore, that the tribal label is to be attached to Kish, an ancient ancestor of Mordecai, who was the father of King Saul. The significance of the tribal reference thus becomes apparent—it lends importance to Mordecai, who was of royal lineage.

The conclusion that Kish was not a close ancestor of Mordecai appears to have been further reinforced by the listing of three of his forebears. It was common practice to add to the name of an

individual the name of his father in order to facilitate identification (Isa. 1:1, Jer. 1:1, etc.). The listing of additional antecedents
would normally be limited to instances where the author seeks
to trace descent from an illustrious ancestor (Josh. 17:3, Judg.
20:28). In the chronology of Kish (Sam. 9:1), five preceding
ancestors are listed. The first in the chain is apparently an
anonymous person, merely identified as a Benjamite. One may
wonder why his genealogy was traced to an anonymous person.
It is possible that the concluding phrase, "a mighty warrior"
(gibor chayil), refers to the Benjamite and not to Kish. I venture to
suggest that the Benjamite who was the "mighty warrior" may
be identified with Jephthah, who had acquired great fame
during the years of his leadership. Jephthah was one of two
judges described as "a mightly warrior" (Judg. 11:1). The
Ammonites had crossed the Jordan in order to wage war against
the tribes of Judah, Benjamin, and Ephraim (Judg. 10:9). The text
does not indicate the tribe of which Jephthah was a member. It is
very likely that he was a Benjamite. The traditional period of
time between the judgeship of Jephthah and the reign of Saul is
101 years. This may be the period covered by the chronological
list of Saul's ancestors. One can understand the author's desire
to trace Saul's ancestry to a judge as famous as Jephthah. Yet he
chose to cloak the judge's name with anonymity because of the
questionable legitimacy of his birth (Judg. 11:1), the shady
reputation of his youth (Judg. 11:3) and his tragic, reckless vow
(Judg. 11:31). In the text of the Book of Esther, however, one fails
to discover any reason for the listing of his three ancestors. If
they were Mordecai's immediate forefathers, they were apparently little-known individuals, and their names would add no
luster to the status of Mordecai. The rabbis might have therefore
preferred the tradition which identified Kish with the father of
King Saul. By the same process of reasoning they identified
Mordecai's ancestor Shimei with the famous Shimei who had
been the adversary of King David. Jair, on the other hand, might
very well have been the name of Mordecai's father.

   The foregoing consideration might have influenced some of
the talmudic rabbis in their interpretation of the text of Esther
that it was Mordecai who had been exiled in 597 B.C.E. This, in

turn, would confine the time of Purim to approximately the decade after the fall of Babylonia, in the reign of King Cyrus. The fact that Cyrus granted permission to rebuild the Temple, but apparently rescinded the permission soon after the Temple foundation was laid (Ezra 4:5, 24; Kaufman, *Historia shel Bayit Sheni*, vol. 1, chap. 14), indicated a change in the political climate. This might have provided a psychological background favorable to the rise of Haman.

SURVEY OF RABBINIC PASSAGES

A survey of rabbinic passages on this subject reveals a substantial number in accord with the preceding conclusion. Such is the opinion of *Esther Rabba* (on Esther 2:3); Rabbi Nehemiah said it "was the third year since the suspension of the construction of the Temple. At the end of the three years of suspension of Temple work, he made a feast for the officers and vassals." The original foundation of the second Temple was laid in 537 B.C.E. The work was stopped in the same year, and it was not resumed until 522 B.C.E. Upon the resumption of work, the Persian governor, Tattenai, made another attempt to interrupt the construction (Ezra 5:3), but he failed when Darius confirmed the right of the Jews to proceed with the work (Ezra 6:7). The midrashic reference to the suspension of the construction of the Temple could only point to the year 537 B.C.E. The famous feast of Ahasuerus is alleged to have been given three years later, i.e., 534 B.C.E. Cyrus was still king of Persia in that year.

In another passage in *Esther Rabba* (chap. 7), Rabbi Levi states that it was Haman who had advised Ahasuerus to suspend the construction of the Temple. This allegation leads to the same conclusion that the date of Purim is to be fixed in the reign of Cyrus.

Rav identified Hathach (Esther 4:5) with Daniel (*Megillah* 15a, *Esther Rabba*, chap. 8). Daniel is presumed to have died within the first decade after the fall of Babylonia. We must therefore conclude that Rav, too, fixed the date of Purim in the reign of Cyrus.

Rava stated that Ahasuerus' feast was given seventy years

after the captivity of Jeconiah in the year 597 B.C.E. (*Megillah* 11b). The date of the feast was therefore, according to Rava, the year 527 B.C.E. Cambyses was the king of Persia at that time.

Rav Nachman apparently disagreed with the view that Mordecai was a contemporary of Cyrus. He identified Mordecai with the prophet Malachi (*Megillah* 15b). The active period of Malachi extended approximately from 475 to 420 B.C.E. Accordingly, Ahasuerus might be identified with Xerxes I (485–465 B.C.E.), Artaxerxes (465–424 B.C.E.), or Darius II (424–404 B.C.E.).

Midrash Aba Gorian identifies Darius as the father of Ahasuerus. Accordingly, the latter must be equated with Xerxes I.

Rabbi Levi identified Ahasuerus with Artachshasta (*Esther Rabba* I). Presumably Artachshasta is Artaxerxes. However, the inference of Rabbi Levi's statement in *Esther Rabba*, chap. 7 (see above), points to a much earlier date of Purim, coinciding with the reign of Cyrus. This inconsistency might possibly be explained by the statement of Josephus (*Antiquities* 4. 6) that Ahasuerus was Artaxerxes Longimanus, who was also named Cyrus. The tradition that Artaxerxes was also named Cyrus might have led to a confusion between the first and second Cyruses. According to the *Seder Olam* (chap. 30), it was Darius who was also known to be Artachshasta and as Cyrus the second.

The Jerusalem Talmud (*Megillah* 1:5) quotes a letter addressed by Mordecai and Esther "To our rabbis" (*L'rabbotenu*). The salutation indicates that the letter was alleged to have been written at the earliest after the founding of the Great Synagogue, when the title "rabbi" came into use. Here again we must conclude that this letter, which was presumably written soon after the proclamation of Purim, was sent not before the reign of Artaxerxes.

A summation of the talmudic passages bearing on the subject of the date of Purim reveals the absence of a uniformly accepted traditional date. A collation of the various views leaves us with the conclusion that the traditional time of Purim is to be confined to the period of 534–420 B.C.E. The years 534 and 527 B.C.E. are the only specific dates indicated in the rabbinic literature.

The absence of precise knowledge of the time of Purim applies also to the manner and pace of development of the festival. Purim, like Chanukah, met with considerable resistance in the early period of its history. This resistance is clearly indicated in the Book of Esther, which states that Mordecai's original decree, proclaiming the festival of Purim, had to be followed up by a second decree, backed by the authority of Queen Esther (9:29). The Amora Rabbi Samuel b. Judah read a historical sequence into these two decrees. The first set up Purim in Shushan; the second, in the rest of the world (*Megillah* 7a). This view undoubtedly reflects the gradual spread of Purim from Shushan to the remote provinces of the empire.

THE FEAST OF AHASUERUS IN HOMILETICS

Rabbi Solomon Alkabez (16th cent.), author of the hymn *Lcha Dodi*, asserted in his commentary on the Book of Esther that the feast of Ahasuerus was concluded on the eighth of Nisan. There is no historical basis for this assertion, and we quote it merely as a folk tradition. This alleged date opens the door for the establishment of other traditional dates, not fixed in the Bible or in the early rabbinic works. It also provides a new homiletic framework for some of the events in the Book of Esther.

The banquet of Ahasuerus, which allegedly was concluded on the eighth of Nisan, had commenced 180 days earlier, on the eighth of Tishri. This sheds some light on the rabbinic statement that Ahasuerus ordered the feast because he had become convinced that Solomon's Temple would never be rebuilt and that the precious vessels of the Temple would remain in his custody (*Megillah* 11b). According to Rabbi Nehemiah, the feast began three years after the suspension of the construction of the Second Temple (*Esther Rabba* 2:3). The eighth of Tishri was the anniversary of Solomon's feast of dedication of the Temple. The feast of Ahasuerus was inferentially set for the same day to signify the fact that he had become heir to Solomon's throne and glory.

When the national banquet was concluded, Ahasuerus tendered to the people of Shushan a local banquet, lasting for seven days, from the ninth to the fifteenth of Nisan, the first day of Passover. The chief instigator of this banquet, according to a rabbinic allegation, was Haman, who schemed to trap the Jews into sin (*Drash L'Purim*).

THE TIMING OF HAMAN'S DECREE

Haman's decree of extermination was published on the thirteenth of Nisan (Esther 3:12). The timing lent credibility to the belief that the decree was a retributive measure for the transgression of the Jews, who the year before had joined in the Shushan festivities in that very same week.

Queen Esther instituted the three-day fast on the thirteenth of Nisan. The fast was to end on the fifteenth of Nisan, the anniversary of the last day of the Shushan banquet. Thus the fast was to be an atonement for the Jewish transgression in the week of the festivities.

The appearance of Esther before the king was set for a time which she must have considered propitious for two reasons. Due to the fast she was confident of the Almighty's forgiveness. She also had reason to anticipate the king's sympathetic reception because she was to appear on the anniversary of the death of Vashti, who was executed on the last day of the banquet (Esther 1:10). The king had regretted his hasty judgment in the case of Vashti, and he was unlikely to condemn Esther to death on the anniversary of her predecessor's execution.

Ahasuerus accepted Esther's invitation to be her guest at a dinner to be tendered by her for him and Haman. The old Jewish transgression was now to be erased through a reversal of situations. In place of the Shushan feast, where the Jews ate defiled food as the guests of Ahasuerus and Haman, the latter were now to be the guests of Esther at a feast which she was to prepare in accordance with Jewish dietary requirements.

Esther's banquet was to be given on the same day on which her invitation was extended. This was done for the sake of protocol to indicate the urgency of her voluntary appearance. She could not wait another day in the hope of receiving a summons from the king because the banquet had to be given on the very day of her appearance before the king. Unfortunately, the fifteenth of Nisan was the last day of her fast period. She was free to act as a hostess, but she could not participate in the festivities. This is indicated in the text: "So the king and Haman came to the banquet which Esther had prepared" (Esther 5:5). However, due to her fast she could not partake of her own meal. Her abstention might have chilled some of the congeniality which she had attempted to create. She therefore requested that the king and Haman come again on the next day, the sixteenth of Nisan. This time Esther was able to join in the festivity. This, too, is indicated in the text: "So the king and Haman came to drink with Esther, the queen" (Esther 7:1).

Retribution followed swiftly. Haman was hanged on the sixteenth of Nisan, one day after the termination of the fast. With the disclosure of Esther's racial origin, the king appointed Mordecai in the place of Haman and decreed the cancellation of the anti-Jewish laws.

This calendar of events, gleaned from rabbinic homiletic sources, brings to light another curious coincidence. The king's national banquet, to which the distress of the Jews was attributed by the rabbis, was begun on the anniversary of King Solomon's dedication of the Temple. The reversal of Ahasuerus' policies and the proclaimed salvation of the Jewish people came on the anniversary of King Hezekiah's rededication of Solomon's Temple (II Chron. 29:17).

OPPOSITION TO PURIM

The Babylonian Talmud mentions a social objection offered by opponents of the introduction of the new festival of Purim (*Megillah* 7a). There was a legitimate fear that the celebration of Purim might provoke Gentile resentment. The Jerusalem Talmud also mentions a religious objection (*Megillah* 1). The religious objection was based on Deuteronomy 13:1, which prohibits the introduction of new religious laws. The latter objection did not turn out to be a serious bar to the acceptance of Purim in view of the early decision by the Men of the Great Synagogue, who had reconciled the establishment of Purim with Mosaic law (*Megillah* 7a). The social objection, however, must have seriously hampered the progress of Purim, particularly in remote Jewish communities of the diaspora, exposed to the wrath of non-Jewish majorities.

It is important to take note of another variation in the Purim versions of the Jerusalem and Babylonian talmudic texts. The Jerusalem Talmud quotes an early tradition about a letter addressed by Mordecai and Esther to the rabbis inquiring of the latter whether they would agree to accept the designation of Purim as a festival to be annually observed by all Jews. According to this version, the proclamation of Mordecai and Esther remained the sole source of authority for the observance of Purim. In view of the fact that the authority of Mordecai was political rather than religious or juridical, it stands to reason that the opponents of Purim had the right to deny the validity of his proclamation. The Jerusalem version reflects a rationalization used in the period of strong resistance. The Babylonian Talmud, however, quotes a letter in which Mordecai and Esther are said to have requested the rabbis to proclaim Purim an annual festival (*Megillah* 7a). Their affirmative reply gave Purim a religious basis which could no longer be questioned by any opponent. This version represents the second stage in the development of the festival.

There is another version in the Babylonian Talmud which may help shed some light on the early history of Purim. In this version Mordecai and Esther wrote to the rabbis: "Put down our story in writing for the generations to come" (*Megillah* 7a). This raises a question of authorship. Who wrote *Megillat Esther?* Many scholars assume that this letter merely requested rabbinic canonization of a book which had already been written (see *Divre Chiba*, Ritvah, *Megillah* 7a). The Talmud (*Baba Batra* 15a) states that the Book of Esther was written by the Men of the Great Synagogue. This possibly means that the book in our possession was edited in its final form by the Men of the Great Synagogue, based on the original *Igeret* distributed by Mordecai and Esther. We may assume that according to this tradition the Book of Esther must have been in existence by the year 400

B.C.E., or shortly thereafter. This leads us to the question, did this book gain immediate and widespread recognition?

DATE OF INTRODUCTION OF *MIKRA MEGILLAH*

The answer to this question is related to another question. When did the reading of the *Megillah* become part of the Purim ritual? On the one hand there is a definite statement in the Talmud that the prophets instituted the practice of *mikra Megillah* (*Megillah* 14a). There is also another talmudic statement which attributes to the Men of the Great Synagogue the designation of the days when the *Megillah* is to be read (*Megillah* 2a). Rashi, commenting on this passage, states that the designation of the days was made in the lifetime of Mordecai and Esther. Even if one is inclined to question the basis of Rashi's assertion, there is no doubt that the talmudic tradition reflects an assumption that the practice of reading the *Megillah* was instituted at a very early date. This is corroborated by the statement that the Kohanim used to interrupt their Temple functions so that they could go to hear the reading of the *Megillah* (*Megillah* 3a). On the other hand, there is considerable evidence that the Book of Esther was not available to most people, and therefore very few people had the opportunity to read it on Purim. This is particularly true of the first few centuries after Purim, before the widespread establishment of local synagogues and before the practice of public reading in the synagogue had been instituted.

The Dead Sea Scrolls, which date, according to most historians, from the first century B.C.E., include fragments from all the biblical books except the Book of Esther. This would indicate that the Book of Esther had not yet been canonized at that time and consequently had not yet gained a wide circulation. One could hardly expect widespread reading of the *Megillah* when the book itself was not available to most people. In the fourth century, by which time the practice of *mikra Megillah* had been firmly established, we are told that the demand for the scrolls was so great that the scribes supplied them at the low rate of one *zuz* each (*Baba Batra*, 155b). The relation between the reading of the *Megillah* and its availability is obvious.

THE SEPTUAGINT

It seems likely that in the early period after the establishment of Purim, wherever the festival was observed, the people relied on oral accounts of the content of the book and also on the Septuagint, upon which all Greek-speaking Jews depended.

There is substantial evidence of the great use which the Jews made of the Septuagint. The latter calls the festival Fruria ("days of protection") and not Purim, as it is called in the Hebrew text. It also omits the verse which describes Haman's casting of lots (*hipil pur*), to which the name Purim is attributed in the Book of Esther. The earliest postbiblical Jewish source to mention Purim is II Maccabees (ca. 75 B.C.E.). In describing Nikanor Day, the author reminds the reader that it falls on "the day before Mordecai Day" (chap. 15). The author of II Maccabees was an Egyptian or Syrian Greek-speaking Jew. He obviously had never heard of the name Purim. It is equally clear that he derived his knowledge from the Septuagint and was unfamiliar with the original Hebrew text.

It is also apparent that even Josephus, who was surely conversant with Hebrew, used the Septuagint as his source of information and was not familiar with the Hebrew Book of Esther. The account in the *Antiquities* (2.6) does not mention the name of Purim and, like the Septuagint, omits the story of Haman's casting of the lots. If the ritual of *Megillah*-reading had been in vogue in his day, the Hebrew Book of Esther could not have escaped his attention.

The *Antiquities* was published in the year 93. By that time the festival of Purim had already become a universally accepted holiday. Thus Josephus writes: " . . . whence it is that even now all the Jews that are in the habitable earth keep these days festival." Josephus mentions only one Purim custom: "and send portions to one another." No mention is made of the custom of *mikra Megillah*.

There is further evidence that the practice of *Megillah*-reading was first started some years after the destruction of the Temple. Thus we find three Tannaim of the second century engaged in a dispute as to which portion of the *Megillah* must be read on Purim, in order to fulfill the requirements of the ritual (*Megillah* 19a). It is inconceivable that this question would not have been resolved sooner if the custom had already been in existence many centuries before their time. Another example is the controversy of Rabban Simon b. Gamliel and Rabbi Eliezer b. Yosi (2nd cent.) whether the *Megillah* is to be read a second time in Adar II if it had been read already in Adar I (*Megillah* 6b). The intercalation of a month was a very frequent occurrence. It is inconceivable again that such a basic question was not resolved sooner in the five hundred years that had elapsed since the beginning of Purim. The answer lies in the fact that the custom of reading the Hebrew *Megillah* was of a much more recent origin and these questions had to be resolved by the Tannaim of the second century.

To adopt such a view, however, and to deny the fact that a *mikra Megillah* was practiced in the earlier centuries is wholly inadmissible, in face of the positive talmudic statements to that effect. We must therefore look for an answer to a reinterpretation of the mode of the ancient *mikra Megillah* as it was undoubtedly practiced from the very beginning of Purim.

THE PROPHETS' DECREE

The Talmud ascribes the reason for the prophets' decree of *mikra Megillah* to a comparison to the *Shira* recited by the Jews after the crossing of the Red Sea (*Megillah* 14a). The exodus from Egypt and the emancipation from slavery had been commemorated from time immemorial by a special recitation of the Passover story. It was justly felt that the festival of Purim, commemorating the redemption of the Jews from death and extinction, should be observed in similar fashion. The use of Passover as a precedent for Purim is important to bear in mind, in order to understand the early development of the Purim ritual.

The recitation of the Passover story was for a long time an

extemporaneous home ceremonial, without any definite, pre-scribed form. The heads of households elaborated or abridged the recital in accordance with the mood of the narrator and the occasion. The Haggadah did not take shape until sometime after the destruction of the Temple. When the final ediction of the Haggadah was completed, it did not become a canonical work but, like a prayer book, was used as an aid in the home service.

Most likely a similar pattern of observance evolved after the establishment of Purim. The early *mikra Megillah* was not necessarily a reading of the *Megillah* itself but a recitation of the events recorded in the *Megillah*. As a home ceremony it was informal, extemporaneous, and embroidered with individual imagination and interpretation. It is highly improbable that the *Megillah* was recited in the synagogues prior to the canonization of the Book of Esther. The Jerusalem Talmud implies that the custom of reciting the *Megillah* in the synagogue was first introduced in the second century, in the time of Rabbi Judah HaNasi (Jer. *Megillah* 2). In the Tosefta, however, there is a different version which omits the reference to the synagogue (*Megillah*, chap. 2). In any event it is clear the *mikra Megillah*, which, according to the tradition, was instituted by the prophets, must have preceded the time of the widespread establishment of synagogues. In that early period it was, of necessity, a private home ceremonial. However, some parts of the Hebrew *Megillah* were read in public in Jerusalem in the first century C.E. (*Megillah* 3a). Due to the informal character of the early *mikra Megillah*, as a family rather than community function, the custom must have spread slowly in the initial stages of its development. It is also apparent that very few individuals made use of the Hebrew *Megillah*. The price of the *Megillah* must have been prohibitive for the average man, even if it were not written on parchment. The original small demand for *Megillot* must have discouraged mass production. In addition to the price factor, the language barrier must have contributed to the low circulation of the Book of Esther. Aramaic and later Greek displaced Hebrew as the mother tongue of a growing number of people. The Jews of Egypt and Syria, for whose benefit the Septuagint was pub-lished, undoubtedly used the Greek version of the *Megillah* for their personal information and the Purim ritual. The rise of large Greek-speaking Jewish communities led to the popularization of this Greek version. The spread of Christianity in the first century greatly increased the demand for and supply of the Septuagint. Widespread use of the Greek Esther is reflected in the view of Rabban Simon b. Gamliel (2nd cent.), who sanctioned the reading of the *Megillah* in the Greek language (*Megillah* 18a). Rabbi Meir, a contemporary of Rabban Simon b. Gamliel, went to Asia Minor to intercalate a second Adar. This trip was probably undertaken during the period of the Hadrianic persecutions, when the practice of Judaism was banned. It is said that Rabbi Meir was unable to obtain a *Megillah* there for Purim (*Megillah* 18b). It may seem puzzling that a sizable Jewish community in Asia Minor did not possess a single *Megillah*. This is even more surprising in view of the fact that the ritual of public reading of the *Megillah* in the synagogue was well established by that time. The Tosefta on *Megillah* (chap. 2) fortunately adds one detail which clears up this point. The Tosefta states that "he could not find there a *Megillah* which was written in Hebrew." Obviously most Greek-speaking Jewish communities in Asia and Africa used the Septuagint for the Purim service. (Rabbi Isaac b. Sheshet [d. 1409] prohibited the reading of the *Megillah* in Spanish for the benefit of women who did not understand Hebrew.)

CANONIZATION OF THE BOOK OF ESTHER

The canonization of the Book of Esther was a decisive turning point in the history of the ritual of public reading of the *Megillah*. Circumstantial evidence points to the patriarchate of Rabban Gamliel II (80–118) as the momentous period when many of our postexilic customs took final shape. The shattering experience of the destruction of the Temple had depressed the morale of the people to a new low. It was imperative to focus scholarship and faith as the mainstays of Jewish existence and survival. It was also urgent to reemphasize the ancient miracles as a means of reviving Jewish hopes. *Pirsuma nisa* (publicizing of the miracle) became the rationale for many decrees ordained by Rabban Gamliel and his court. He added an important part of the Passover Haggadah to bring it up to date with conditions resulting from the destruction of the Temple. The Chanukah miracle was given new prominence by fixing the ritual of the Chanukah lights. The Purim miracle was to be publicized, too, through the reading of the Book of Esther. The schools of Hillel and Shamai held different opinions on the degree of sanctity of the Hagiographa (Megillah 7a). Rabbi Akiva and some of his colleagues, however, declared that "the Book of Esther was stated by divine inspiration" (Megillah 7a). This statement undoubtedly led to the canonization of the book. Since Rabbi Akiva was a much younger man than Rabban Gamliel, we may assume that the canonization took place in the second century, in the concluding years of Rabban Gamliel's patriarchate. Rabbi Yochanan b. Nuri, another younger contemporary of Rabban Gamliel, is the earliest sage mentioned in the Talmud to have read the Megillah on Purim (Jer. Megillah 1). Rabban Simon b. Gamliel II, who succeeded his father to the patriarchate, continued to elaborate upon the postexilic ordinances of his father's court. He discussed the ritual of mikra Megillah in an intercalary year, a moot question which had to be resolved in view of the widespread adoption of public reading of the Megillah (Megillah 6b).

The continued development of the Purim ritual was temporarily halted when Rabbi Judah HaNasi succeeded to the patriarchate of his father. Moved by a desire to reestablish friendly relations with Rome, he sought to deemphasize the commemorative days which helped perpetuate the memory of Roman cruelty and the festive days which marked Jewish victories over foreign oppressors. He minimized the importance of Chanukah by omitting a discussion of the origin of Chanukah and its ritual from the Mishnah. He also publicly engaged in weekday activities on Purim (Megillah 5a), thus relegating the festival to the privacy of the synagogue and the home. For the same reason he considered the revocation of the fasts of the seventeenth of Tammuz and the ninth of Av.

The evolution of the Purim ritual was accelerated under the dynamic leadership of Rabbi Joshua b. Levi (3rd cent.), head of the Lydda academy. As a patron of the nationalist Jewish youth, he used Jewish historical festivals as a means of promoting lingering nationalistic sentiments and bolstering resistance to the Romans. He upheld the ancient tradition that women, like men, should drink four cups of wine on the Seder night because they were also witness to the miracle of Passover (*Pesachim* 108a). He gave the same reason for the obligation imposed upon women to listen to the reading of the *Megillah* (*Megillah* 4a). He similarly offered the same explanation for the law requiring women to light Chanukah candles (*Shabbat* 23a). He thus tried to make every Jewish person aware of the great historical miracles which had saved the Jewish people at the most crucial junctures of its fabled existence. In order to give maximum publicity to the Purim story, he issued an order that the reading of the *Megillah* on Purim eve, heretofore a voluntary custom, was now a mandatory obligation (*Megillah* 4a). With the promulgation of this ordinance, the salient features of the Purim ritual may be said to have been fully established by the end of the first half of the third century.

SUMMATION

1. The events of Purim, according to talmudic sources, took place in the period between 534 and 420 B.C.E. The years 534 B.C.E. and 527 B.C.E. are two specific dates indicated in the rabbinic literature.
2. There was little observance of the festival prior to the publication of the Septuagint in the third century B.C.E.
3. Most Jewish communities were not familiar with the Hebrew text of the Scroll of Esther prior to the second century C.E. The festival was variously known at that time as the Day of Mordecai or Fruria ("days of protection"). It was observed by informal home recitations of the story of Esther and the exchange of gifts. There was a public reading of the *Megillah* or parts of it in Jerusalem in the first century C.E.

4. The Hebrew text gained wide circulation after the canonization of the Book of Esther in the second century C.E.
5. Public reading of the *Megillah* on the morning of Purim was introduced by the end of the second century C.E.
6. The rituals of Purim, as we know them today, were established in the third century C.E.

7

Passover

I.
CHAG HAPESACH

THE SACRIFICIAL RITE of the paschal lamb and its consumption were the main features of the ancient Passover pageantry which ushered in the holiday. As a ritual it was unique in many respects. The lamb was slaughtered in the afternoon of the fourteenth of Nisan, prior to the commencement of the festival (Lev. 23:5). This was an exception to the general rule that all festival offerings are to be sacrificed on the day of the festival. Furthermore, the lambs were slaughtered by Israelites, and the priests poured the blood on the base of the altar. All other offerings were generally slaughtered by the priests. There was yet another exception. No offering could normally be brought after the evening whole-offering (Karban Tamid). This rigid rule did not apply to the paschal lamb (*Pesachim* 58a).

It should be pointed out that the paschal lamb and its accompanying Karban Chagigah (festival offering) are the only offerings commemorated by a symbolic dish, even after the destruction of the Temple. The exceptional nature of the Passover celebration is illustrated further by the biblical tradition which set the principal observance of the Passover rites on the evening of the fourteenth of Nisan, not on the first day of the festival (Exod. 12:18). This included the eating of the paschal lamb, matzah, and maror (Exod. 12:8). Even after the destruction of the Temple the biblical obligation to eat matzah remains in effect only on the evening of the fourteenth of Nisan (*Pesachim* 120a).

The explanation for the uniqueness of the Passover celebration may be found in its commemorative aspects. The Bible repeatedly emphasized this facet of Passover: "And this day shall be unto you for a memorial . . ." (Exod. 12:14); "And Moses said unto the people: remember this day in which ye came out from Egypt, out of the house of bondage . . ." (Exod. 13:3); "Thou shalt well remember what the Lord thy God did unto Pharaoh . . ." (Deut. 7:18); "that thou mayest remember the day when thou comest out of the land of Egypt all the days of thy life" (Deut. 16:3).

A careful reading of the above and other passages clearly indicates the general function of the Passover pageant to serve as a permanent reminder of the crucial period in the early formative years of the Jewish people. The celebration was designed to keep fresh the memory of the momentous struggle against slavery and the revelation of God through Moses. It was also to reassure the people that the Almighty would smite all future tyrants as he had done to Pharaoh. The memory of the people was to be annually refreshed not only through the recitation of an account of that great day, as recorded in the Bible, but primarily through an actual reinactment of the events of that day. It is in the reinactment of those events that we find the key to the colorful rituals of the Passover pageant.

Philo the Alexandrian (1st cent.), in his treatise entitled *On the Ten Festivals* (trans. of C. D. Younge), alluded to the annual reinactment of the exodus: "And this festival is instituted in remembrance of, and as giving thanks for, their great migration which they made from Egypt . . . . and what was then done the law enjoined to be repeated once every year as a memorial of the gratitude due for their deliverance." Philo was right in his reference to the reinactment of "what was then done." However, he failed to mention the educational and morale-building objectives of the holiday, which are clearly indicated in the Bible.

What were the memorable events of the historical fourteenth of Nisan? The first important event was the slaughtering of the paschal lamb on the afternoon of that day. The significance of the paschal lamb may perhaps be best understood by a reference to the initial request of Moses that Pharoah permit the Jews to go on a three days' journey into the desert to bring an offering to God (Exod. 5:3). This constituted a petition for freedom of religion, which had been denied to them. The need for the journey was attributed to the opposition of the Egyptian population, which would have regarded the slaughtering of lambs as an abomination (Exod. 8:22). The triumphant conclusion of the drawn-out contest between Moses and Pharaoh was demonstrated by the order to proceed with the slaughtering of the lamb. This move was symbolic of an open and defiant practice of freedom of religion. The symbolic significance of the paschal lamb as a confirmation of the Abrahamitic covenant with God was most likely the reason for the biblical prohibition of aliens joining in this feast (Exod. 12:43).

A study of the history of the patriarchal period sheds further light on the great importance attached to the paschal lamb ritual. It is enlightening to read the account of the first covenant concluded between God and Abraham. In return for Abraham's declaration of faith (Gen. 15:6), he was promised that Palestine would be given to his descendants (Gen. 15:18). The fulfillment of this promise was to come at the end of an interlude of four centuries of wandering, persecution, and slavery. Thus the faith of his offspring would be put to further test. At the end of that period the persecutors would be "judged," and the Jews would go out with substantial wealth to begin their new life as an independent people (Gen. 15:14).

This covenant, which was to form the basis for the future relationship between Israel and God, could not become binding and immutable until the provisions contained therein were fully met. Abraham was subsequently reassured again that "I will confirm my covenant between me and thee and thy seed after thee" (Gen. 17:7). Such repeated confirmation was advisable in view of the contingent nature of the original covenant. Abraham and his children were ordered to engrave upon their flesh the seal of the covenant by circumcising all their males (Gen. 17:10). The rite of circumcision and the shedding of their blood were to symbolize the conclusion of a covenant in accordance with Semitic custom (see Gen. 15:10).

When the time for the redemption from Egyptian slavery approached, the Almighty requested the Jews to borrow silver and gold from their Egyptian neighbors. The Talmud notes the tone of urgency in the request that Jews accept such gifts. The urgency is explained by the necessity for the fulfillment of the original promise of future wealth, inasmuch as the preceding forecast of persecution and slavery had come true (*Berachot* 9b). The implication is also clear that without the fulfillment of the promise of material reparations, the Jews would not have been bound by Abraham's covenant.

The offering of the paschal lamb by the emancipated Jewish slaves, as a religious mode of worship of God, became a decisive symbolic act which marked the conclusive establishment of the ancient covenant between God and his people. The Jews reaffirmed their faith as the Almighty was in the process of fulfilling the providential commitments. The Bible refers several times to the covenant concluded between God and the Jews who had come out of Egypt: "But I will for their sakes remember the covenant of their ancestors, whom I brought forth from the land of Egypt in the sight of the nations, that I might be their God; I am the Lord" (Lev. 26:45); "Then men shall say: 'Because they forsook the covenant of the Lord, the God of their fathers, which he made with them when he brought them forth out of the land of Egypt' " (Deut. 29:24). This covenant was also mentioned by Jeremiah (31:31). The anniversary of the exodus is also the traditional anniversary of the Abrahamitic covenant (*Seder Olam*, chap. 5).

THE RITE OF CIRCUMCISION

The affinity between the rite of circumcision and the paschal lamb, prominently pointed out in the midrashic literature, is easily understood in light of their common symbolism of Jewish adherence to the covenant. No uncircumcised Jew was permitted to partake of the paschal lamb (Exod. 12:48). This affinity is further evidenced by the punishment prescribed for the failure to observe the rite of circumcision and the paschal lamb—extirpation (*karet—Keritot* 2a). These are the only two positive commandments in the Bible the neglect of which is punishable by *karet*. In view of the symbolic significance of these two rites, it is understandable that the failure to carry them out is an act of self-exclusion from the covenant and the household of Israel, with extirpation as the consequence. Both rites were suspended after the exodus from Egypt and were not resumed until after the Jews crossed into Palestine. We must note the sole exception when the suspension was lifted and the paschal lamb was offered—on the first anniversary of the exodus (Num. 9:2). No explanation is given for this exceptional event. We may assume, however, that the need for the second paschal lamb was due to the golden calf incident, which constituted the first major breach of the covenant. The divine forgiveness of this serious violation, which was sealed with a new covenant (Exod. 34:10) had to be confirmed by a second declaration of faith on the part of the Jewish people. This was done again through the offering of the paschal lamb. Thereafter the suspension of both rites continued until the end of the sojourn in the desert. There were practical reasons for this suspension due to desert conditions. It is also possible that the suspension was due to the fact that one of the providential promises made to Abraham, the giving of Palestine to his children, had not yet been fulfilled. It is noteworthy that the crossing of the Jordan was timed for the Passover season and that the first two official rites ordered by Joshua were the rites of circumcision and the paschal lamb (Josh. 5:3, 10). Thereafter the covenant was complete and irrevocable. The annual paschal lamb, brought on the fourteenth of Nisan, was to be a visible reminder to the Jews of their historic declaration of faith and their obligation under the covenant concluded on that day.

The fact that the annual paschal lamb was a reinactment of the original paschal lamb of the fourteenth of Nisan helps to clarify the technical character of this offering. The original paschal lamb (*pesach*) was not an "offering" (*karban*) in the technical sense of the word. There were as yet no consecrated priests to perform the normal rites of an offering, nor was there any altar upon which to perform such rites. The laymen were told to slaughter the animal as they would normally do in preparation for a feast. However, it was made clear that this feast was not to be a purely social occasion but a religious celebration, "a paschal lamb unto the Lord" (Exod. 12:11). This phrase is repeated almost every time the *pesach* offering is mentioned in the Bible, indicating the need for stressing the religious aspect of the Passover feast.

The Bible never labeled the paschal lamb a *karban*. In reply to a child's request for a definition of the lamb, the Bible orders us to tell him it is a *zevach*, a slaughtered animal (Exod. 12:27). This is in contrast to the designation of *karban* given to "a burnt offering" (Lev. 1:3), to a meal-offering (Lev. 2:1), and to a "peace-offering" (Lev. 3:1). Similarly, the process of preparing the paschal lamb is described as *ve-shachatu ha-pesach* ("kill the paschal lamb," Exod. 12:22), *ve-Asa hapesach* ("and he will make the paschal lamb," Exod. 12:48), and *vezavachta hapesach* ("you shall slaughter the paschal lamb," Deut. 16:2). The technical verb *vehikravta* ("you shall offer," related to the noun *karban*), frequently used in connection with other offerings, is never hyphenated with the *pesach*. The only exception to this rule was the biblical term *karban haShem*, "the Lord's offering," mentioned in Numbers 9:7, 13. That term was used in connection with the second *pesach*, offered on the fourteenth of Iyar by those who were unable to offer the first *pesach* on the fourteenth of Nisan. That practice was promulgated after the priests had been consecrated and an altar had been built and the technical designation of *karban* had come into being. However, the phrase *karban pesach* was not used even in connection with the second *pesach*. The earliest mention of the term *karban pesach* is found in *Targum Yonatan b. Uziel* (Lev. 9:12). It was never duplicated in the Talmud. Only in the post-Geonic literature do we find extensive usage of the designation *karban* attached to *pesach* (see Rashi, Exod. 12:11; Maimonides, *Hilchot Karban Pesach* 1; *Chinuch, Bo* 5).

The term *zevach* ("a slaughtering," the biblical designation of the *pesach*) was applied broadly to any feast where a slaughtered animal was the central feature of the festivities. It had no religious significance. In that sense it was used in Genesis 31:54, Deuteronomy 12:21, and I Samuel 20:29. The term *zevach* was also applied, however, to peace and thanks offerings where a major portion of the meat was consumed by the owners (Lev. 19:5, 22:29). The paschal lamb had the same degree of sanctity as a peace-offering (*Zevachim* 12b).

The sacrifice of the paschal lamb on the afternoon of the fourteenth of Nisan was followed by a special ritual which was never duplicated again. The Jews were ordered to "take a bunch of hyssop, and dip it in the blood that is in the basin, and strike the lintel and the two side-posts with the blood that is in the basin" (Exod. 12:22). The smearing of the blood on the doorposts, unlike the slaughtering of an animal, was not a regular mode of worship, and therefore was not in itself a religious function. The blood was placed at the entrance of the home to indicate to all that the occupant had participated in the religious ritual of the paschal lamb and had thereby rejected paganism and declared his faith in God. This public demonstration was the reason why the Lord "passed over the houses of the children of Israel in Egypt when he smote the Egyptians" (Exod. 12:27). This act of divine grace, linked to the Jewish profession of faith, was perpetuated by the name given to the lamb, *pesach*, and it was the primary event to be commemorated on that day by the Jewish people.

The smearing of blood on the doorposts did not become a permanent part of the Passover pageantry. There might have been a practical reason for this omission. With the erection of the Temple, all paschal lambs were slaughtered and consumed in Jerusalem. Most of the people were far from home, and it would have been impossible to smear the blood on the doorposts of their homes. One may also speculate that the attachment of a mezuzah to the doorposts served the same religious purpose as the smearing of the blood in Egypt—a declaration of faith (see *Mechilta*, Exod. 12:23). The link of the mezuzah to the exodus is implied in Deuteronomy. Following the famous passage of the *Shema*, which is concluded with the verse: "And thou shalt write them upon the doorposts of thy house" (Deut. 6:9), the text continued: "And it shall be when the Lord thy God shall bring thee into the land . . . then beware lest thou forget the Lord who brought thee forth out of the land of Egypt. . . . When thy son asketh thee in time to come . . . then thou shalt say unto thy son:

'We were Pharaoh's bondmen . . . and the Lord brought us out of Egypt with a mighty hand' '' (Deut. 6:10, 12, 20, 21). The mezuzah, which replaced the smearing of the blood as a permanent symbol of our declaration of faith, sheds new light upon the sequence of the verses in the above passage.

In spite of the fact that the smearing of the blood was never reinacted, this event was nevertheless subsequently perpetuated through a symbolic rite at the Seder table, as we will point out later.

THE PASSOVER PAGEANTRY

With the conclusion of the preliminary rituals, the Festival of the Paschal Lamb was ushered in on the evening of the fourteenth of Nisan. On that night the Jews were ordered to eat the paschal lamb. There were a number of restrictive rules attached to this feast. "And they shall eat the flesh in that night, roast with fire; with unleavened bread and bitter herbs they shall eat it" (Exod. 12:8). They were not to eat it rare or boiled in water (Exod. 12:9). They were not to leave the meat over past the conclusion of the night (Exod. 12:10). They were not to break any of the bones of the lamb (Exod. 12:46). No alien sojourner, hired servant, or uncircumcised person may eat the meat of the paschal lamb (Exod. 12:43–45). The feast was to be held in one house, and no part of the meat was to be taken outside the house (Exod. 12:46).

A variety of explanations are offered for the aforementioned rules. Some scholars regard the injunction to have the lamb fully roasted as a demonstrative departure from ancient pagan spring-festival rites, when meat was eaten raw or half-boiled. This does not explain the reason for the prohibition of boiled meat. The *Chinuch* (no. 7) suggested that the emancipation of the Jewish slaves converted them into a "priestly kingdom." The *pesach* was therefore served as a royal feast, and it was to be eaten in the manner of royalty. Consequently the meat was to be well roasted, a process preferred by royalty because the taste of the meat is brought out to best advantage. Similarly no bones were to be broken because royalty discards the bones whole, but the poor break the bones so that they can pick them bare of their meat. This homiletic interpretation is not consistent with the provision for the eating of the lamb with matzah and bitter herbs, in commemoration of affliction and bitterness. One could hardly commemorate royalty and poverty at the same time. We are inclined to agree with the opinion that the reason for the roasting is the fact that it is the fastest process of preparing meat. In view of the urgent need for haste, in the event of a sudden order of expulsion, it was necessary to have the meat prepared in as little time as possible. The meat was to be well roasted so the blood would be completely drained. Since the blood smeared on the doorposts became the symbol of religious allegiance, it would have been improper to consume any part of the blood of the paschal lamb. Haste was also apparently the reason for the injunction against the breaking of the lamb's bones. This would prevent the people from tarrying too long over their meal in the manner of those who spend leisurely hours over succulent bones. The feast was to be confined to the night so that they would be ready to begin their march in the morning. Non-Jews and uncircumcised Jews were precluded from participating in the feast because of the religious significance of the occasion as an affirmation of the covenant. The paschal lamb was to be eaten in one house, and no part of the meat was to be taken out because each household slaughtered its own lamb and the head of the household was the religious functionary for the occasion. Each group of celebrants was to remain together as a unit during the festivities so that the feast should not degenerate into a social event, with different people dropping in on one another.

All these rules and conditions affecting the original paschal lamb were incorporated into the Passover pageantry which was to be annually reenacted by posterity. Since the first lamb was not a *karban*, all subsequent lambs similarly were not designated *karban* but merely *zevach*, or simply *pesach*. Hence the law which prohibited the bringing of a *karban* after the daily whole-offering of the evening did not apply to the paschal lamb.

The Passover pageant does not include two events of the historic fourteenth of Nisan. One is the smearing of the blood on the doorposts, which we have already discussed. The other is the order for a state of readiness for instantaneous departure. Thus the Jews were told to eat the lamb "with your loins girded, your shoes on your feet, and your staff in your hands, and ye shall eat it in haste—it is the Lord's Passover" (Exod. 12:11). One may well understand why this dramatic effect was left out of the pageant. The purpose of these props was to impress the people with the need for preparedness for a sudden exodus from the land. Such a ceremonial would be unsuited in Palestine, which was their ultimate destination and which they had hoped never to leave.

One may sympathize with some of the Jewish communities in the diaspora which demonstrated an urge to reinact the dramatic biblical pre-departure pageant. Abraham Ibn Ezra (12th cent.) mentioned a contemporary community guilty of such a practice, and he harshly berated it for such heresy (Exodus 12:10). A dramatization of the exodus from Egypt was also part of the Passover celebration of the Moroccan Jews, who put packs on their shoulders and ran through the streets shouting: "This is how our forefathers came out of Egypt." Similar pageants were acted out by Jews of remote communities in different parts of the world.

The paschal feast, the highlight of the biblical Passover celebration, was not originally designed to be a gay occasion in the popular concept of the word. One may rather say that it was a solemn moment of religious awareness and introspection. The symbolism of the paschal lamb, matzah, and bitter herbs spoke of an unhappy past and warned the people of the consequences of a breach of the covenant. The Passover message was a call to piety and human dignity.

Philo aptly described the character of the Passover feast as it appeared in his day: "and those who share the feast come together, not as they do at other entertainments to gratify their bellies with wine and meat, but to fulfill their hereditary customs with prayers and songs of praise." The distinctive rituals of the first night did not call for an expression of joy or a happy celebration, inasmuch as they marked the pre-exodus period. Indeed, the customary biblical exclamation ve-samachto ("and thou shalt rejoice"), mentioned in connection with Shavuot and Sukkot, was omitted on the occasion of Passover.

Did the historical exodus also give rise to a happy celebration of freedom without undue emphasis on the oppression of Egyptian slavery? Indeed, the joyous phase of the exodus came to the fore on Shavuot, which the rabbis considered to be the concluding period of Passover (*Pesikta* 30:163; *Shir HaShirim Rabba* 7). The prayer associated with the *bikkurim* rite on Shavuot read in part: ". . . and the Lord brought us forth out of Egypt . . . and has given us this land, a land flowing with milk and honey . . ." Then follows the injunction: "And thou shalt rejoice in all the good which the Lord thy God hath given unto thee . . ." (Deut. 26:5–11). To a lesser degree, Sukkot, too, marked the joys of the post-exodus era.

II.
CHAG HaMATZOT

The feast of the paschal lamb (Chag HaPesach) coincided with the beginning of the festival of matzot (Chag HaMatzot). The principal feature of this holiday is stated in the Bible: "Seven days shall ye eat unleavened bread" (Exod. 12:15). This commandment is repeated in the same chapter: "In the first month, on the fourteenth day of the month, in the evening, ye shall eat unleavened bread until the twenty-first day of the month at evening" (Exod. 12:18). In addition to these two verses, there is a prior injunction to eat matzot with the paschal lamb: "And they shall eat the meat in that night roast with fire, and unleavened bread, with bitter herbs they shall eat it" (Exod. 12:8). There are thus two distinct sources and two distinct reasons for the eating of the matzot on the first evening of Passover.

MATZOT: SYMBOL OF REDEMPTION

The matzah in the paschal lamb ritual was symbolic of *lechem oni*, "bread of affliction." The lamb, matzot, and bitter herbs depicted the story of Jewish martyrdom in Egypt—they were impoverished and their lives were embittered, but when they cried out to God and declared their faith in him, they were released from bondage. On the other hand, the matzot that were to be eaten for seven days on the festival of matzot were no longer symbolic of *lechem oni* since the Jews had departed from Egypt with ample compensation in silver and gold. These matzot commemorated the speed and abruptness with which the Jews had to leave Egypt, testifying to the decisive intervention of the Almighty, which compelled Pharaoh to suddenly release the Jews in spite of his relentless opposition. The matzot were thus symbolic of redemption.

Chag HaPesach lasted only for part of a day. What was the reason for the seven days of Chag HaMatzot? Abraham Ibn Ezra attributed the length of the Passover festival to the fact that Jews had to eat matzot for seven days until they crossed the Red Sea, inasmuch as Pharaoh did not allow them to pause long enough to bake bread (Exod. 12:15). The implication of a talmudic passage (*Kiddushin* 38a), however, points a rabbinic view that matzot were eaten for thirty days. *Targum Yonatan b. Uziel* (Exod. 16:2) stated that the dough taken out of Egypt lasted for thirty days. It is possible to reconcile both views by assuming that for the first seven days they ate matzot while during the balance of the thirty days they ate bread. Josephus (*Antiquities* 2. 15) mentions the tradition that the food taken out from Egypt lasted for thirty days. He definitely erred, however, when he said that the matzah which we eat on the feast of the unleavened bread is to commemorate the want and privation of the Jews in the desert. He undoubtedly confused the symbolism of this matzah with the matzah which was eaten with the paschal lamb. Philo, a contemporary of Hillel and Rabban Gamliel the Elder, correctly stated that the matzah was symbolic of Jewish redemption. We are amazed that this statement escaped Josephus' attention. At any rate, it is clear that by the time the *Antiquities* was published (ca. 90 C.E.), the definitive interpretation of Rabban Gamliel II had not yet been made or was unknown to Josephus.

The pre-exodus and post-exodus symbols of the matzah were

both included in the same verse in Deuteronomy (16:3). Following the command: "and thou shalt sacrifice the Passover offering unto the Lord thy God," the text continues: "Thou shalt not eat leavened bread with it; seven days shalt thou eat unleavened bread therewith [the matzah which is to be eaten on the first night together with the paschal lamb, and the matzah which is to be eaten on the seven days], even the bread of affliction [the symbol of the matzah on the first night]; for in haste didst thou come forth out of the land of Egypt; that thou mayest remember the day when thou comest forth out of the land of Egypt all the days of thy life [the symbol of the matzah on the seven days]." (See Nahmanides' comment on this verse). Posterity was thus bid to commemorate both aspects of the matzah symbolism.

The injunction to eat matzah was obligatory only on the first night, at the paschal feast (*Pesachim* 120a). There is no obligation, however, to eat matzah during the seven days of the festival of matzot. The text merely requires that one abstain during that period from eating leavened bread. Theoretically, therefore, it was only the "bread of affliction" symbolism which had to be commemorated. The commemoration of the symbolism of redemption was optional.

The main distinction between the Chag HaPesach and Chag HaMatzot lies in the historical area which each seeks to reflect. The Chag HaPesach reinacts the events of the fourteenth of Nisan (the pre-exodus period), and the Chag HaMatzot marks the actual departure from Egypt, which was concluded with the crossing of the Red Sea (the exodus period). Both are component parts of the same festival, the festival of Passover. Our ancient non-talmudic scholars were apparently confused when they spoke of two distinct holidays. Thus Philo listed the festival of Passover as the fourth holiday on his list of ten Jewish holidays. The festival of matzot is number 5 on his list. Josephus, too, speaks of a festival of Passover and the feast of unleavened bread (*Antiquities* 2. 14, 15).

The term Chag HaPesach is mentioned only once in the Bible (Exod. 34:25). Its correct translation is "the feast of the paschal lamb" rather than "the festival of Passover." An erroneous translation might have contributed to the confusion of the nonrabbinic scholars.

DEFINITION OF *ETZEM*

The first biblical link between the Chag HaMatzot and the post-exodus era is mentioned in Exodus 12:17. "And ye shall observe the festival of matzot because in this selfsame day [*b'etzem hayom haze*] I brought your hosts out of Egypt." The Hebrew term *etzem* seems to have been introduced here to pinpoint the exact time of the exodus. Yet its true connotation remains obscure. That this descriptive word was not a mere literary flourish is evident from the fact that it was repeated two more times in the same chapter (Exod. 12:41, 51).

The term *etzem* appears in several biblical accounts: The flood (Gen. 7:13), Abraham's circumcision (Gen. 17:26), the Omer (Lev. 23:14, Josh. 5:11), Shavuot (Lev. 23:21), Yom Kippur (Lev. 23:28, 30), the death of Moses (Deut. 32:48), the burial of five enemy kings (Josh. 10:27), the appearance of Ezekiel (Ezek. 2:3), the siege of Jerusalem (Ezek. 24:2), and Ezekiel's vision of the restoration of Jerusalem (Ezek. 40:1).

Nahmanides noted with great amazement that *etzem* was used only in connection with the observance of Yom Kippur and Shavuot but not the Sabbath and other festivals (Lev. 23:28). He concluded that the Torah employed the term *etzem* only when it was necessary to indicate that it was the "substance" of the day itself that produced a legal effect or status, even when the ritual prescribed for that day could not be performed.

This conclusion is in line with the talmudic interpretation of *etzem* used in connection with the prohibition of new crops prior to the offering of the Omer on the sixteenth of Nisan: "And you shall eat neither bread, nor parched corn, nor fresh ears, until this selfsame [*etzem*] day . . ." (Lev. 23:14). After the destruction of the Temple and the discontinuation of the Omer, Rabban Yochanan b. Zaccai decreed that the new crops may be eaten at the end of the sixteenth day of Nisan (*Sukkah* 41b). The amoraic comment based this decree on the term *etzem*, which hinges the lifting of the ban on new crops on the arrival of the day itself, inasmuch as the offering of the Omer was no longer possible. The phrase *b'etzem hayom* is rendered therefore as if it had been written *hayom b'atzmo* ("the day in itself"). This is also the sense of the *etzem* used by Ezekiel (40:1)—"on this day itself," or on this very same day. A similar interpretation of *etzem* is to be given to the phrase *ad etzem hayom haze* (Josh. 10:27; Ezek. 2:3)—"to this day itself," or to this very day. This conveys a sense of endurance or persistence.

Rabban Yochanan b. Zaccai's interpretation of the text relating to the Omer would permit the use of new crops at sunrise of the sixteenth of Nisan. Yet he decreed the continuation of the ban until the expiration of the day for other reasons stated in the Talmud.

Rabbi Yehuda concurred with Rabban Yochanan b. Zaccai's conclusion but disagreed with his interpretation of *etzem*. He based the continuation of the ban on new crops throughout the sixteenth of Nisan not on rabbinic considerations but on the implication of the biblical *etzem*. According to Rashi, the phrase *etzem hayom* denotes the entire day. This interpretation apparently assumes that the word *etzem* is derived from *otzem*, "closes" (Isa. 33:15). *Ad etzem hayom haze* may therefore be translated "until the close of the day."

Both interpretations of *etzem*, however, cannot be applied to the account of the first new crops related in the Book of Joshua (5:11): "And they did eat of the produce of the land on the morrow after the Passover . . . in the selfsame day [*b'etzem hayom haze*]." According to the Talmud (*Rosh HaShanah* 13a), the Jews first offered the Omer and then ate the new crops. Consequently one cannot construe the sentence that they ate the new crops "at the close of the day" or "by virtue of the day itself." It was the offering of the Omer which lifted the ban on the new crops.

The word *etzem* means "bone" or "bone-structure" and hence "body." This construction makes *etzem* a restrictive adjective, confining the time element exclusively within the body of time specified in a sentence. Thus the admonition in Leviticus (20:30) that a person who does any manner of work on Yom Kippur (*b'etzem hayom haze*), "that soul will I destroy," is interpreted by the Talmud (*Yoma* 81a) to apply only to a violation perpetrated on Yom Kippur but not in the extra time (*tosefet*) added to the holiday before nightfall.

This interpretation of *etzem* was also the basis for the statement of Abudarham that the fast of the tenth of Tevet may never be delayed even if it falls on a Friday (*Bet Yoseph, Orach Chaim* 550). He based his conclusion on the *etzem* (Ezek. 24:2) which restricts the observance of the fast to the tenth of Tevet only.

Midrashic literature provides another definition, which points to a derivation from the noun *otzem*, "strength" (Deut. 8:17). *B'etzem hayom* may therefore mean: "when the day is at its strongest," or at midday. Thus *Sifri* (Deut. 32:48) comments on the *etzem* in the story of the Exodus (Exod. 12:41), "said the Almighty, I will lead them out at midday." This definition carries two implications: (1) something is done in broad daylight for the purpose of securing maximum publicity; (2) something is done publicly in open defiance of all challengers.

Sifri (Deut. 32:48) lists three historical events in connection with which the term *etzem* was employed. It interprets all of them as acts of defiance. Noah is said to have been told to enter the ark in broad daylight (Gen. 7:13), in defiance of open threats to prevent his entry. The Jews were said to have been taken out in broad daylight (Exod. 12:41), in defiance of those who had threatened to prevent their exodus. Moses is said to have been ordered to ascend Mount Nebo in broad daylight (Deut. 32:48), in defiance of the Jews who had threatened to stop him.

Rashi (Gen. 17:23) quotes a midrash which interprets the circumcision of Abraham to have also been an act of defiance. *Sifri*, on the other hand, considered the timing of the circumcision, which was performed in "broad daylight," merely as an effort to give wide publicity to this act so that all would know that Abraham had become "a son of the covenant."

The implication that the exodus from Egypt was an act of defiance sheds new light on a scriptural text (Exod. 12:17). The struggle against Pharaoh is a classic illustration of man's rebellion against slavery and despotism. Had Pharaoh conceded the evil of slavery, this stirring chapter of ancient Jewish history would have ended in total victory. There would have been little need for posterity to commemorate the exodus in a world free from the threat of subjugation and oppression. Unfortunately, the ancient heroic struggle did not attain its full humanitarian objective. Pharaoh was compelled to let the Jews go, but the ideological aims of the rebellion were lost on him. The Egyptian had hoped to the end to prevent the exodus. Posterity was therefore admonished to commemorate the story of the exodus as a reminder of the need for eternal vigilance. The biblical verse may therefore be paraphrased as follows: Remember to observe the feast of Passover for all time, so that you may continue to be on guard against those who would enslave you again. The lust for mastery and domination is ever present in man. Indeed, the ten plagues did not produce a change of heart in the Egyptian taskmasters. Even as I took your hosts out of Egypt, I had to defy the mobs who persisted in challenging your right to freedom.

OBJECTIVES OF PASSOVER

The religious and educational objectives of both phases of Passover are given in the Bible as follows:

1. To teach our children that it was the intervention of God which brought about the redemption of the Jews in Egypt (Exod. 10:2, Deut. 7:18).
2. To recount the wondrous miracles which God performed in Egypt as evidence of his intervention (Exod. 10:2, 13:14; Deut. 4:34, 10:21).
3. To recall the miraculous escape of the Jews from the plagues which had smitten the Egyptians as further evidence of God's divine intervention (Exod. 12:13, 14, 23, 24; Deut. 7:22, 23).
4. To remember that God's intervention was the result of the Jewish profession of faith (Exod. 13:8).
5. To acknowledge that God's intervention marked the fulfillment of his promise to the patriarchs upon the conclusion of the covenant (Deut. 4:37, 7:8).

6. To perceive the ultimate objective of the exodus as a preliminary to their attainment of nationhood in their own land and the exercise of freedom of religion (Deut. 11:8).
7. To realize that the account of the exodus must be an everlasting reminder of their duty to observe God's commandments. (Deut. 10:20–21).
8. To realize that the account of the exodus is an everlasting assurance that the Almighty will smite all enemies of the Jews, provided the covenant remains inviolate (Deut. 7:19).
9. To be ever appreciative of one's status and material condition by recalling the poverty of the Hebrew slaves in Egypt (Deut. 6:12).
10. To be ever sympathetic to the destitute and the enslaved by recalling the bitter lot of our ancestors in Egypt (Deut. 5:15, 16:12).
11. To relate the story of the exodus to our children in order to implement the historic objectives of Passover (Exod. 13:8).

The greater part of the foregoing objectives were reflected in the symbolism of the paschal lamb, matzah, and bitter herbs. To serve its educational purpose, however, the Passover ritual required elaboration and elucidation. There was, therefore, the need for an explanatory commentary to go along with the paschal feast to make it meaningful to the young as well as the old. Such expository remarks were called for by the Bible: "And thou shalt tell thy son . . ." (Exod. 13:8). To meet this need, the Passover night service, modest and ritualistic at the outset, was gradually expanded into a stirring religious and educational experience. The creation of the Haggadah ultimately made it possible to give due emphasis to all the Passover objectives and thus fully implement the biblical function of the holiday.

III.
FROM JOSHUA TO RABBAN GAMLIEL II

The significance of the Passover rituals gave this festival a special centrality in the religious life of ancient Jewry. In surveying the history of that phase, we must also take note of the evolutionary process which enriched the Passover pageantry and gave it new form and direction.

The description of the observance of the first Passover in Palestine touches upon the offering of the paschal lamb and the eating of matzot in accordance with Mosaic law. The ritual was undoubtedly simple, but Joshua's eloquence must have stirred the people. He left us a sample of his reference to the exodus: "Thus saith the Lord . . . Your fathers dwelt of old time beyond the river . . . and they worshipped other gods. And I took your father Abraham from beyond the river and led him throughout the land of Canaan and multiplied his seed . . . and Jacob and his children went down into Egypt. And I sent Moses and Aaron and I plagued Egypt . . . and afterwards I brought you out . . . and you crossed the Jordan and came into Jericho . . . and I gave you a land for which ye did not labor, and cities which ye built not, and ye dwell therein. . . . Now therefore fear the Lord and serve him in sincerity and truth; and put away the gods which your fathers served beyond the river and in Egypt . . ." (Josh. 24:2–14). Joshua thus stressed the classic message of Passover— the humble origin of the Jewish people, the covenant with Abraham, God's intervention in Egypt, the fulfillment of his promise, and the reaffirmation of faith.

The powerful religious stimulus of the public Passover celebration could have exercised a profound influence upon the people had it not been for the chaotic conditions which followed shortly after the death of Joshua. The neglect of all Mosaic traditions was compounded by an ignorance of the recent past of the Jewish people. The memory of the exodus faded, and a widespread relapse into idolatry followed. (Judg. 2:10–13). This trend was the result of a lack of leadership and central administration. The Pentateuch, deposited in the custody of the priests, was unavailable to the people. The anarchical conditions prevailing under the tribal set-up of the nation and the constant harassment by hostile neighbors disrupted the contact of the people with the Tabernacle and its priestly leadership. The sporadic emergence of energetic "judges" brought only temporary relief to the generally dismal scene. We may safely assume that for three centuries after the death of Joshua Passover played no role in the national life of the people, becoming the private domain of a traditionally minded minority. Gideon, beset by crisis, evoked the memory of God's wondrous works in Egypt. Yet even he echoed the skepticism of the people (Judg. 6:13).

The appearance of Samuel in the eleventh century B.C.E., at the end of the period of the judges, ushered in a great religious revival. Under his leadership the Jews rejected idolatry and restored old traditions (I Sam. 7:4). There is no doubt that under his influence Passover assumed once again its prime function as a religious festival. The memory of this revival lingered long in the minds of our ancient historians. About four hundred years after Samuel, during the religious revival in the reign of King Josiah (637–607 B.C.E.), reference was made to a ceremonious Passover celebration with the parenthetical remark that "there was not kept such a Passover from the days of the judges that judged Israel, nor in all the days of the kings of Israel, nor of the kings of Judah" (II Kings 23:22). The phrase "from the days of the judges" testifies to the fact that there had been a period in the time of the judges when Passover was celebrated with great pomp and ceremony. Who was the judge of that period? The Book of Chronicles is more specific on this point: "And there was no Passover like to that kept in Israel from the days of Samuel the prophet; neither did any of the kings of Israel keep such a Passover as Josiah kept . . ." (II Chron. 35:18). We may take it for granted that the religious revival which began with Samuel continued through the reign of David and reached its zenith under Solomon, with the construction of the Temple in Jerusalem. This interlude lasted a little over a century.

PASSOVER PAGEANTRY IN THE TEMPLE

The construction of the Temple (ca. 960 B.C.E.) and the provision of spacious grounds to accommodate the multitudes of pilgrims lent new magnificence to the Passover celebration. An early mishnah describes the Temple ritual on the fourteenth of Nisan. While this mishnah dates from the period of the Second Temple, it reflects the procedure in the First Temple. "The paschal lamb was slaughtered in three groups . . . . when the first group entered and the Temple court was filled, the gates of the Temple court were closed. A *tekiah, truah,* and again a *tekiah* were then blown on a shofar. The priests stood in rows, and in their hands were basins of silver and basins of gold. . . . An Israelite slaughtered his offering and the priests caught the blood. The priest passed the basin to his fellow, and he to his fellow, each receiving a full basin and giving back an empty one. The priest nearest to the altar tossed the blood against the base of the altar. While the ritual was performed the Levites sang the *Hallel* . . ." (*Pesachim* 64a).

There are a number of biblical references which indicate that the preceding procedure was also followed in Solomon's Temple. Following the rededication of the Temple by King Hezekiah, the priests are described as tossing the blood of the paschal lamb upon the altar (II Chron. 30:16). The Levites and priests are also described as having "praised the Lord day by day [*Hallel*], singing with loud instruments unto the Lord" (II Chron. 30:21). The same ritual is described again in the public Passover observed in the reign of King Josiah. There is a reference to the priests pouring the blood on the altar (II Chron. 35:11). There is also a reference to the "singers, the sons of Asaph, were in their place, according to the commandment of David" (II Chron. 35:15).

The religious interlude which started with Samuel came to an end with the death of King Solomon and the partition of the nation into the kingdoms of Judea and Israel, in the year 932 B.C.E. Jeroboam, the first king of Israel, reintroduced idolatry. The survival of many God-fearing individuals in that kingdom is attested to by the Bible in numerous places. The majority, however, soon lapsed into the paganism of the non-Jewish neighboring nations. Paganism spread also to the kingdom of Judea in the reign of Rehoboam, the son of Solomon. This reduced further the number of Jews who made the pilgrimage to Jerusalem.

The first brief religious revival in Judea took place after a lapse of more than two centuries, with the accession of King

Hezekiah, in the year 720 B.C.E. Twelve kings had preceded him since the partition of Solomon's kingdom. Of these, seven are described as having done "that which was right in the eyes of the Lord." Yet not one of them was willing or able to erase paganism from the land. The pagan shrines remained unmolested. The Assyrian invasion of the kingdom of Israel in 722 B.C.E. had created the climate for a thorough religious reformation in Judea. Hezekiah set out to restore and renew the ancient covenant. In his address to the assembled priests and Levites he said: "Now it is in my heart to make a covenant with the Lord, the God of Israel . . ." (II Chron. 29:10). The renewal of the covenant was to be formalized by a national celebration of Passover in which the entire people of Judea and the remnants of the kingdom of Israel were to participate. The paschal lamb ritual, the ancient symbol of the conclusion of the covenant, was to be the highlight of the celebration. The people responded to the king's appeal for a mass pilgrimage. Most of the Jews of the former kingdom of Israel, however, had long forgotten the significance of Passover and refused to join. The text succinctly describes their reaction to the king's emissaries: "but they laughed them to scorn and they mocked them" (II Chron. 30:10). Hezekiah's achievements were soon undone by his son and successor, Manasseh, who restored the pagan shrines which had been destroyed.

The next religious revival came in the reign of King Josiah (637 B.C.E.). The accidental discovery of the Torah scrolls in the year 619 B.C.E., in the course of repair work done at the Sanctuary, disclosed the extent to which the old traditions had been neglected and forgotten. The king was shocked into initiating a thorough reformation. The revival was projected once again through a ceremonial renewal of the covenant. The inhabitants of Jerusalem were assembled at the Temple and the king read to them "all the words of the Book of the Covenant." Then he "made a covenant before the Lord to walk after the Lord and to keep his commandments" (II Chron. 34:30–32). The ceremonies were climaxed by an imposing public celebration of Passover, which began with the slaughtering of the paschal lambs, the ancient symbol of the conclusion of the covenant. "And there was no Passover like that kept in Israel from the days of Samuel the prophet" (II Chron. 35:18).

The religious revival spearheaded by King Josiah brought far-reaching and lasting results. The masses turned away from idolatry. Old traditional practices had struck deep roots by the time the king was killed in 607 B.C.E. The four succeeding kings, who reigned for a total of twenty-two years, until the destruction of the kingdom of Judea, did not display much ardor for Josiah's reforms, but they did not reverse the popular religious trend. When King Jehoiachin was sent into captivity in Babylonia in 597 B.C.E., together with ten thousand prominent officials and citizens, there were amongst them influential religious leaders who were greatly respected by the people. These laid the foundation of the Babylonian Jewish community, which was to expand with the influx of the captivity of 586 B.C.E. The dominant trend of this community was toward an intensification of ancient religious practices and traditions.

THE BABYLONIAN INTERLUDE

We have little information on the effect of the destruction of the First Temple on the religious calendar and rituals. We know that a number of fast-days, commemorating the destruction of the Temple, were introduced by the Babylonian community. The discontinuance of ritual offerings initiated the development of the prayer service and temporarily altered the basic routine of festival observance. The dominant personality in the early years of the captivity was the prophet Ezekiel (ca. 592–570 B.C.E.). He attributed the fall of Judea to the persisting idolatry, which continued to cling to some of its people, and to the violation of the Sabbath (and also, by implication, the other festivals). He interpreted the Babylonian interlude as the means for purging the Jewish people of its recalcitrant elements. Only those who reaffirmed their allegiance to God would be allowed to return to Zion to reestablish the nation. A great part of his prophecy was dedicated to a vision in which he described the restored Sanctuary and the offering rituals on the Sabbath and festivals. The restoration of the rituals would indicate the final redemption of the Jewish people (Ezek. 45:17, 21, 25). His preaching created the atmosphere for a popular reaffirmation of faith which was expressed through a strict observance of the Sabbath and holidays. There was no paschal lamb to usher in Passover, but the Festival of Matzot was widely observed. It is unlikely that any new ceremonials were introduced into the Passover celebration with a view toward lifting the morale of the people. The faithful regarded their plight as a divine chastisement, to which they submitted with silent resignation. Their prophets had predicted a quick end to the exile, and the ultimate reconstruction of the Temple was never doubted. Their morale was high; there was no need for ceremonial innovations during this brief interlude.

THE SEDER SERVICE

When the construction of the Second Temple was completed in 515 B.C.E., the entire biblical ritual of the Passover holiday was restored to its former glory. The priests and Levites, who had purified themselves, slaughtered the paschal offerings for all the Jews who had returned from the captivity. The new community "kept the Festival of Matzot seven days with joy, for the Lord had made them joyful . . ." (Ezra 6:22). This was the auspicious opening of a new epoch which brought many innovations to Jewish religious life. It is in this epoch that we will also begin to trace the gradual introduction of an expanded Passover pageantry, the forerunner of our Seder service.

When was the first step taken leading to the creation of the home Seder service? I believe that the first step was taken when the Jews who had slaughtered the paschal offerings joined the Levites in the chanting of *Hallel*. The chanting of psalms was originally confined to the Levites exclusively. The text describing the Passover celebration of King Josiah (619 B.C.E.) mentions "the singers, the sons of Asaph, were in their places" (II Chron. 35:15). The Tosefta reflects this ancient custom when it states: "The Israelites slaughter the lambs and the Levites chant the *Hallel*" (*Pesachim*, chap. 4). A subsequent statement in the Talmud (*Pesachim* 95b), however, clearly indicates that this practice had changed. Thus it states: "Is it possible that the Israelites should slaughter their offerings and wave their palm-branches and not chant the *Hallel?*" This innovation was probably introduced in the early period of the Second Temple. The total number of pilgrims was comparatively small at that time, and they might have joined in the chanting in order to enhance the festive spirit of the occasion. The Talmud quotes a tradition (*Pesachim* 117a) that attributes to the prophets the decree which bid all Jews to recite *Hallel* on the anniversary of a salvation from distress. Most talmudic references to prophets who instituted new decrees generally allude to the terminal prophets who brought the era of prophecy to a conclusion. The prophet Haggai is considered the connecting link between the prophets and the Men of the Great Assembly. Many new laws were attributed to him (see *Nazir* 53a, *Zevachim* 62a). We may reasonably conclude that the new practice of collective chanting was introduced sometime between 515 and 450 B.C.E.

The second significant step in the development of the Seder service was the provision for the *Hallel* to be chanted not only at the slaughtering of the offering but also at the feast when the paschal lamb was eaten (*Pesachim* 95a). The paschal lamb was eaten in private homes throughout the city of Jerusalem. The chanting of *Hallel* in these homes marked the beginning of the Seder service. It is most probable that the head of the household informally related the story of the exodus during or after the meal, in keeping with the biblical injunction. There were no further developments, however, for a few centuries after the introduction of the *Hallel*. There is no reference to any home ceremonial in the ancient sources. The few talmudic statements attributed to the early rabbis discuss the paschal lamb and do not mention any home ceremony. Among these sages are Shmayah and Avtalion (50 B.C.E., *Pesachim* 66a), and Hillel (30 B.C.E., *Pesachim* 115a). On the other hand, the Tannaim of the second half of the first century of the common era frequently refer to various phases of the Seder ceremony. Thus Rabbi Eliezer b. Tzadok discusses charoset (*Pesachim* 114a), and Rabbi Joshua b. Chananiah discusses the sequence of Kiddush and Havdalah on a festival night following the Sabbath (*Pesachim* 103a). We have conclusive evidence that very considerable portions of the Seder service were already adopted prior to the destruction of the Temple (*Pesachim* 116a, first mishnah). It is therefore reasonable to assume that some additions were made in the first century B.C.E. and that a substantial development of the Seder continued in the early part of the first century C.E.

TRIUMPH OF RABBINIC JUDAISM

This process was part of a general trend which led to the triumphant emergence of rabbinic Judaism as the dominant force in Jewish life. The trend was a reaction to the abortive attempt of King Jannai (103–76 B.C.E.) to exterminate the Pharisaic leadership. Jannai's oppressive policies, which cost the lives of many sages, fortunately brought only a temporary setback to Pharisaism. When it was restored to power by Jannai's widowed queen, it came back with increased vigor and a changed orientation. Henceforth it was to concentrate its efforts on religious instruction and refrain from political activities which might provoke the antagonism and opposition of the government. This policy enabled the heads of the rabbinic academy at Jerusalem to function throughout the turbulent century and a half which preceded the destruction of the Temple, without interference by the Hasmonean and Herodian dynasties or the Roman officials. The great spiritual force which had been consumed by the fight with the secular government was now released to enrich the religious customs of the people. It also focused its attention upon the social and economic problems of the masses and made provisions to meet them. The dynamism of Ezra (d. ca. 440 B.C.E.), the father of rabbinic Judaism, had lost its impetus in the succeeding generations. To Ezra were attributed ten basic ordinances, most of which are still part of our religious code. He was eulogized by posterity as the man "who had restored the Torah to Israel after it had been forgotten" (*Sukkah* 20a). He founded the Great Assembly, which carried on his work for a few centuries. Yet with the exception of Simon the Just, no outstanding individual came to the fore during that period to leave his name to history. The vibrant

Babylonian community was capable of producing great leaders. But it seems that the restored Palestinian community was still intellectually too poor to produce its own. The great sage Resh Lakish later recalled the prolonged sterility of the Palestinian Jewish community by declaring that when the Torah was forgotten, Ezra came from Babylonia and restored it; when the Torah was forgotten once again, Hillel came from Babylonia and restored it (*Sukkah* 20a). One must take into consideration the political upheavals of those centuries, which created and destroyed great empires. The Persian Empire was carved up by Alexander the Great, and his great empire broke up into its component parts, each of which became expansionist and aggressive in its turn. Palestine became a hapless pawn in the international game of aggression. The unsettled conditions hampered the peaceful reconstruction of the Jewish community. The Hasmonean rebellion (168 B.C.E.) let loose a regenerative nationalism rather than scholasticism. When the Hasmonean dynasty veered toward the Sadduceans, the Pharisee leadership declared its opposition and almost perished in the ensuing conflict. The death of King Jannai (76 B.C.E.) left Rabbi Simon b. Shatach the dominant rabbinic figure of his generation, and with him began the second great epoch of rabbinic Judaism. Tradition accurately summed up his position when it said of him, as of Ezra: "The [Jewish] world was desolate until Simon b. Shatach came and restored the Torah to its ancient glory" (*Kiddushin* 66a).

The new policy of this epoch, concentration on theology and nonentanglement with the government, was formulated by Rabbi Simon b. Shatach's disciple, Shamai: "Love work, hate lordship, and seek no intimacy with the ruling power." This made possible the resumption of Ezra's work, which had been interrupted for almost four centuries. Rabbinic Judaism was to extend its hold upon the people so that no force could ever again challenge its supremacy.

Among the innovations introduced at that early period were the joyous pageantry of Simchat Bet HaShoavah (*Sukkah* 51a); the kindling of Chanukah lights (see chap. 5); a provision for compulsory attendance at elementary religious schools (Jer.

Ketubot 8); a provision for greater stability of the marital status of women (Jer. *Ketubot* 8), "prozbul," to facilitate the obtaining of loans prior to a Sabbatical year (*Gittin* 36a); a provision for the unhampered right of a seller to redeem a house in a walled city (*Eruchin* 9:4). These were followed up in the early part of the first century by a provision to ease the plight of an "agunah" (*Yevamot* 115a); two provisions to prevent a challenge of the legality of a divorce on baseless grounds (*Gittin* 34a); a provision for the allotment of charity to Gentile indigents and the visitation of ailing Gentiles (*Gittin* 61b); a provision for cotton shrouds for the benefit of the poor (*Moed Katan* 27b). It was during this period of great ferment and intellectual productivity that the Passover Seder, too, began to evolve its rich ceremonialism and complexion.

THE SEDER IN THE FIRST CENTURY B.C.E.

We must now trace the development of the Seder in the first century B.C.E., up until the time of the destruction of the Second Temple. It may reasonably be assumed that the first addition since the introduction of *Hallel* at the Passover feast was the recitation of the Kiddush over a cup of wine. This custom was simultaneously ordained for the Sabbath and all festivals. The sanctification of the Sabbath is, according to talmudic interpretation, a biblical injunction (*Pesachim* 106a). However, the formula of the ancient sanctification merely provided for the recitation of a biblical passage (such as *Vayechulu*) or a simple proclamation that "this is a holy day unto the Lord." Such a statement is mentioned in Nehemiah (8:9), and it is likely that it reflected the ancient Kiddush. The use of wine for the Kiddush ritual is not of biblical origin. That was ordained by the rabbis (Tosafot, *Zachrenu*; *Pesachim* 106a; Maimonides, *Hilchot Shabbat* 29:6).

The author of *Magid Mishnah* suggested that the biblical mitzvah of Kiddush was confined to the Sabbath and the rabbis extended it to the festivals as well (ibid. 29:18). It is debatable whether Passover is to be classified in this regard with the other festivals or with the Sabbath. The basis for the biblical Kiddush rests on the verb *zachor* ("remember"). The same verb is used in the Passover text (Exod. 13:3). Maimonides quotes a *Mechilta*: "He has commanded us to remember [the exodus] in the same manner as when he ordained 'Remember the Sabbath day, to keep it holy' " (*Sefer HaMitzvot* 157). In its broader connotation, this statement includes the mitzvah of Kiddush too. Furthermore, the mishnah which discusses the sequence of the Passover Kiddush mentions conflicting opinions of the schools of Hillel and Shamai (*Pesachim* 114a). The original passage containing this classic dispute is mentioned in *Berachot* (51b), where the point at issue was the Sabbath Kiddush. The inclusion of this passage by the editor of the mishnah in Pesachim, in the context of the Passover Kiddush, seems to indicate that the Kiddush of Sabbath and Passover were considered by him to be of equal standing.

The origin of the Passover Kiddush is, of course, not material to the fixing of the date when the ceremony of the Kiddush cup of wine was first introduced. A number of editions of the tractate *Sota* contain a passage which states that the supply of Kiddush wine (*yayin kiddush*) from Senor came to an end with the destruction of the Solomonic Temple (48b). This would seem to indicate that Kiddush wine was already in use at the time of Solomon's Temple. This talmudic passage, however, contains a typographical error. The correct version reads *yayin karush* (a wine jelly), as is evident from the talmudic passage in *Sukkah* 12a. The erroneous version was mistakenly included by the encyclopedic *Otzar HaAggadah* (*kiddush hayom ve-havdalah*).

The earliest Tanna to whom the Talmud attributes a legal opinion relating to Kiddush wine was Rabbi Joshua b. Chananiah (*Pesachim* 103a). He lived in the second half of the first century. However, it is evident from his statement that the ritual had already been in existence for a considerable period before his time. The Talmud (*Berachot* 48a) relates that King Jannai placed a cup of wine before Rabbi Simon b. Shatach and asked him to recite the after-meal benedictions. The fact that they used wine for the benedictions following the meal indicates that the cup of wine had already assumed a ritualistic significance. In view of the fact that the first century B.C.E. marked the beginning of the second period of rabbinic development, we may assume that Kiddush wine, too, was introduced in that century, simultaneously with or a little prior to the after-meal wine.

The further evolution of the Seder service is described in a series of mishnayot in *Pesachim* (114a, 116a). However, the mishnah included also the features which had been added after the destruction of the Temple. A study of the gradual growth of the Seder will therefore require careful selectivity.

THE SEDER OF THE FIRST CENTURY C.E.

The development of the Seder in the first century was guided by the specific function of the celebration—the reinactment of the historic events of the fourteenth of Nisan. This led to the introduction of *yerakot* (herbs), which were dipped in vinegar or possibly red wine and then eaten. The Talmud at a later period explained this practice as an incentive to children to ask questions (*Pesachim* 114b). This explanation is merely to be taken as a suggestion that this custom be pointed out to children and utilized as a stimulant for questioning. The origin of the custom may be traced to the reenactment of the biblical account of the dipping of the hyssop in the blood of the Passover lamb and the smearing of the blood on the doorposts of the Jewish homes (See *Daat Zkenim Baale Tosafot*, Exod. 12:8). The charoset, a reminder of the mortar (*Pesachim* 116a), also fitted in with the broad objective of the early Seder.

The questions asked by the child, in accordance with biblical injunction, were changed three times in the course of time. The earliest form of these questions was preserved by the Jerusalem Talmud (*Pesachim,* chap. 10). The text contains only three questions. The first question begins with the well-known phrase *Mah nishtanah*, which has survived to our day. In these three questions the child listed three practices which distinguish Passover night from all other nights: "On all other nights we dip only once, on this night twice; on all other nights we eat chametz and matzah, on this night only matzah; on all other nights we eat roast or boiled meat, on this night only roast." (Alfasi retained this version with only a slight variation.) The apparent reason for limiting the child to three questions is the desirability of conforming to the biblical texts, which refer three times to a child's questions (Exod. 12:26, 13:14; Deut. 6:20). Three distinguishing features were therefore selected and put in the mouth of the child. The questions followed the order in which these "differences" appear in the course of the Seder.

The first question related to the practice of eating herbs twice on Passover night. The use of the word "dipping" was merely a euphemism for "eating," since it was the ancient custom to eat herbs after they had been dipped in gravy or vinegar. It was generally regarded as an appetizer to be eaten immediately preceding or during the main meal (see Rashi, second mishnah, *Pesachim* 114a). In the Passover ritual the herbs were dipped twice. They were first dipped at the outset of the Seder, right after the Kiddush, in commemoration of the dipping of the hyssop in blood. The second "dipping" referred to the maror, the bitter herbs, which were eaten with the paschal lamb at the conclusion of the meal. The serving of the first herbs as a separate dish, and not as a course of the meal, was the earliest indication to the child that there was something "different" about Passover night.

The second question related to the eating of matzot exclusively. In view of the fact that the matzot were placed on the table before the paschal lamb was brought in, the question about the matzot was properly given precedence.

The third question related to the paschal lamb. Since the paschal lamb was the last dish to be placed on the table (no dessert was permissible), the question followed in the same order.

The father's response was directed toward an explanation of the significance of these distinctive practices on Passover night. There was as yet, at that time, no traditionally fixed answer as was formulated later in the Haggadah. According to the mishnah, the father's answer was to fit the knowledge and understanding of the child (*Pesachim* 116a). There was a broad formula, however, which required the father to include in his account the early period of paganism, the subsequent period of slavery, and the ultimate redemption. The objective of this formula was to spell out the sequence of sin, suffering, repentance, and redemption. Joshua was the first to adopt this formula in reviewing the lesson of the exodus to the first post-exodus generation (Josh. 24:2–14).

The dramatic tale of the departure from Egypt, the pursuit of Pharaoh and his army, the crossing of the Red Sea—all of this was not included in the story told by the first-century father to his son. That phase of the account, it was felt, was out of place in a pageant reinacting the historic events of the fourteenth of Nisan. Thus we find the school of Shamai clinging to this tradition and excluding the recitation of the 114th chapter of Psalms (*B'tzet Yisrael*) at the Seder service because it commemorated the departure from Egypt (*Pesachim* 116b). Such is also the implication of the statement of Rabbi Eleazar b. Azariah (end of 1st cent. and beginning of 2nd), that the reference to the exodus was omitted from the evening prayer of *Shema* until his contemporary, Ben Zoma, offered a new exegetic interpretation, allowing the recitation of that biblical passage even at night (*Berachot* 12b). The former exclusion of the reference to the exodus unquestionably applied not only to the evening prayer of *Shema* but to the Seder service on Passover night as well (hence the inclusion of that talmudic passage by the authors of the Haggadah).

The mishnah which describes the ancient Seder (*Pesachim* 116a) adds a postscript, requiring the father to recite the biblical passage beginning with *Arami oved avi* ("A wandering Aramean was my father . . ."—Deut. 26:5) until the end of the portion. This passage contains two parts. The first part consists of a preliminary paragraph (vv. 5–8), which was recited after the offering of the *bikkurim* on Shavuot and deals with the historical events leading up to and including the departure from Egypt. The second part deals with the conquest of Palestine and the offering of the *bikkurim* (vv. 9 and 10). The rabbinic instruction to recite the portion to the end was obviously not intended to include the second part, which refers to the *bikkurim*. The authors of the Haggadah incorporated the first part into the Haggadah, interspersed with rabbinic comments. However, it is questionable whether the entire first part was recited in the first-century Seder. The concluding verse reads: "And the Lord brought us forth out of Egypt with a mighty hand and with an outstretched arm, and with great terribleness, and with signs and with wonders." This verse refers primarily to events which took place after the fourteenth of Nisan, beyond the scope of the ancient Seder. We may therefore assume that this verse was not included until after the destruction of the Temple. It is of interest to note, in connection with this discussion, two versions—the Jerusalem version, which generally reflects the earliest practice, and the Babylonian version. In the Jerusalem Talmud (*Pesachim*, chap. 10, retained by Alfasi), the father is told to read the passage "until he finishes the whole portion" (*ad Shehu gomer kol haparasha*). This limits the requirement to the reading of the whole subject of affliction, from Jacob on. The eighth verse would hence be excluded. In the Babylonian version, the father is requested to recite "until he is to finish the whole portion in its entirety" (*kol haparasha kula—Pesachim* 116a). This includes the eighth verse too.

The tradition which kept the post-exodus events out of the Passover night pageantry is reflected also in a Tosefta (*Pesachim*, chap. 6), which describes a Seder of Rabban Gamliel and the elders in Lud. It is said that they spent the whole night discussing the laws and traditions of Passover. This contrasts with the account of the famous Seder celebrated later at Bnai Brak, where the rabbis spent the night relating the wonders of the exodus.

The sequence of the Seder in the first century, prior to the destruction of the Temple, may be summed up as follows: (1) Kiddush; (2) dipping of herbs; (3) the child's three questions; (4) the father's answer; (5) the meal, concluded with the eating of the paschal lamb, matzah, maror, and charoset; (6) the cup of wine following the after-meal Grace; (7) the chanting of *Hallel*. The Talmud states that *Hallel* was chanted after the eating of the paschal lamb (*Pesachim* 86a). The commonly accepted reason for the division of *Hallel* in the Haggadah and the chanting of part of *Hallel* prior to the meal is the importance which it lends to the second cup of wine. It stands to reason, therefore, that prior to the introduction of the four cups, the entire *Hallel* was chanted after the meal.

THE SEDER OUTSIDE OF JERUSALEM

There is one more area that we must explore before the
conclusion of this phase of our study. Was there any home Seder
service conducted in the Temple era by Jews who could not go to
Jerusalem for the Passover holiday? There seems to have been
no traditional grounds to preclude such a Seder, and consequently we may assume that it was, in fact, conducted in some
homes throughout the diaspora. Such a Seder was complete as
outlined above, with the exception of the paschal lamb, which
was missing, and possibly minus the chanting of the *Hallel*,
which was required only with the eating of the paschal lamb. In
place of the paschal lamb many Jews in the diaspora roasted a
kid (*Pesachim* 53a). According to the Talmud (*Pesachim* 120a),
there was a biblical obligation to eat matzah and maror when the
Temple was in existence, even if one could not spend the
holiday in Jerusalem. Furthermore, the *Mechilta* (Exod. 13:8)
states that the biblical injunction to relate the story of the exodus
is to coincide with the time when matzah and maror are on the
table. The presence of the paschal lamb is not required. We have
thus spelled out the duty of conducting a Seder even in the
diaspora. This rabbinic passage was inserted in the Haggadah,
preceding the father's answer, as the basis for the Seder in the
diaspora.

Our conclusion that a Seder service was conducted in private
homes outside Jerusalem even in the Temple era seems to be
corroborated by the Jerusalem version of a mishnah in *Pesachim*
(chap. 3). The mishnah describes a phase of the Seder: "When it
is brought before him [the vegetable], he eats the lettuce before
the breaking of the matzah. They bring before him matzah and
lettuce and charoset [and two dishes—Babylonian version],
although charoset is not a religious obligation. Rabbi Elazar b.
Rabbi Tzadok says: 'It is a religious obligation.' And in the
Temple [Jerusalem] they used to bring before him the body of
the Passover offering."

The Jerusalem version apparently retained the original text,
which describes the ritual in the Temple era. The description
covers the practice both in and out of Jerusalem. The Jerusalem

Gemara (ibid.) quotes a *beraita* which seems to supply a detail which was omitted in the Mishnah: "And in the border-towns [*ubigvulin*] one is required to have two dishes, one in commemoration of the *pesach*, and one in commemoration of the *chagigah.*" There is an inference here that even in the period of the Temple they had already used the two symbolic dishes outside Jerusalem. The term *gvulin* could conceivably be interpreted to refer to Jewish communities after the destruction of the Temple. However, in its general usage the term *gvulin* denotes a geographic delineation and has no reference to a specific chronological era (see Jer. *Rosh HaShanah 4, Baba Batra 56a, Mechilta 13:7, Shekalim 7:2*).

The Babylonian version, which includes in the text of the mishnah the "two dishes," presents a later interpolation, as is evidenced from the sequence and structure of the sentence. The intent of this interpolation was to confine the mishnah to the post-Temple era. The Babylonian Gemara likewise does not quote or mention the term *gvulin*. Thus the impression created by the Jerusalem version that the "two dishes" were used outside of Jerusalem even in the Temple era is entirely eliminated. However, this does not preclude the probability of a universal Seder service in the Temple era, with the exception of the "two dishes," which had not yet been introduced at that time.

For practical purposes we must note that there were not too many homes outside of Jerusalem where a Seder was conducted. Rabbinic Judaism made little headway in Alexandria, where a considerable part of diaspora Jewry lived. They had their own temple in Alexandria, which had alienated Alexandrian Jewry from the rest of the Jews, who looked to Jerusalem for religious guidance. Philo, the great Alexandrian Jewish scholar, does not mention a Seder service in his essay on Passover. As for the Jews who were under rabbinic influence, particularly in Palestine and Babylonia, most of them must have made the pilgrimage to Jerusalem. There was a phenomenal rise in the number of pilgrims in the first century. According to a talmudic story, the number of paschal lambs was counted once at the request of King Agrippa. The total amounted to 1,200,000

(*Pesachim* 64b). Since a minimum of ten people was required per lamb, one arrives at the staggering figure of 12 million Jews. Even if we allow for the usual folklore exaggerations, the figures still reflect a vast throng of pilgrims who had come from many countries. Most historians assume that the king mentioned in the talmudic account is Agrippa I (d. C.E. 44). However, Josephus gives an account of a similar census taken at the behest of the Roman general Cestius (*Wars* 6. 9). He was a contemporary of Agrippa II (28–100). It is likely that the census requested by Agrippa II was made by the order of Cestius. The result of the census, according to Josephus, totaled 2,700,500 Jews. This, too, is an amazing total, attesting to the very large numbers who made the pilgrimage to Jerusalem. We may therefore conclude that the home Seder outside of Jerusalem was not yet a prominent feature of Passover.

IV.
THE SEDER IN THE POST-TEMPLE ERA

The destruction of the Temple in the year 70 crushed the morale of the Jewish people and brought a serious crisis to their religious life. Many must have wondered whether the great misfortune was a signal of God's rejection of his people. A very serious responsibility fell upon the rabbinic leadership to bolster the morale of their followers as well as their faith. The successful results of their statesmanship and wisdom is attested by the persisting Jewish spirit of rebelliousness and frequent uprisings against Rome, which enlivened Jewish history for a long time. Only a people with a high morale will stand up to fight for its rights in spite of the hopelessness of the situation. Though most of the rabbis opposed bloodshed, the proud spirit which brought it forth was the product of rabbinic leadership. They did not preach nationalism and were rather inclined toward a fatalistic acceptance of the conqueror, so long as he did not interfere with freedom of religion. However, by bolstering the morale of the people and emphasizing the optimistic outlook of Judaism, which looks toward an ultimate redemption, they indirectly made it possible for nationalism to survive.

In addition to the problems of morale, the destruction of the Temple produced a host of theological questions which had to be answered promptly to avoid a serious breakdown. A major part of the religious ritualism was based on Temple rites. The primary mode of worship through sacrificial offerings was no longer available. The sacrifice of offerings was also the central feature of the observance of most festivals. The end of the pilgrimages which brought most of the people face to face on three holidays and the end of the sacrificial offerings left the festivals without meaning or significance.

Let us observe how the destruction of the Temple affected the celebration of Passover. The popular Passover night celebration needed considerable readjustment in order to survive. There was no communal slaughter of the paschal lamb at dusk nor any communal chanting of the *Hallel* that accompanied it. The many festive offerings which had produced an abundance of meat for the Seder table were also gone. With the discontinuance of the paschal lamb, the chanting of *Hallel* at home was no longer required. The ritual of maror was also linked to the paschal lamb, and therefore it, too, could be dispensed with. There was even a serious doubt whether the biblical obligation to eat matzah survived the destruction of the Temple. All that definitely remained was the negative injunction to refrain from eating chametz. The advisability of retaining a Passover night ceremony which highlighted the slavery, poverty, and affliction of ancient times without compensating for it with an account of the glories of the subsequent redemptions must have been seriously questioned. The people were tired of afflictions and needed a comforting message to give them hope. The duty to reevaluate the Seder and make it a moral force in the struggle for survival fell upon Rabban Gamliel II, the first head of the academy after the destruction of the Temple.

THE DICTUM OF RABBAN GAMLIEL

The rabbis always realized the importance of retaining ancient ceremonies, wherever possible, for the sake of historical continuity and the orderly development of Judaism. However, they lent new interpretations to ancient customs in order to fit them to new exigencies. The first basic statement of the reevaluation of the Passover ceremonial was given in the famous dictum of Rabban Gamliel: "He who does not stress these three rituals on Passover does not fullfill his obligations: the paschal lamb, matzah, and maror" (*Pesachim* 116a). We must precede the analysis of the new interpretations introduced by this statement with the establishment of the identity of its author. Rabban Gamliel the Elder, who lived prior to the destruction of the Temple, and his grandson, Rabban Gamliel II, the head of the first academy in post-Temple era, are both frequently referred to in the Talmud as Rabban Gamliel. Some scholars are of the opinion that the author of our statement is Rabban Gamliel the Elder. This view is based on the phrase which the authors of the Haggadah interpolated after the words "paschal lamb," which open the next sentence in this statement. In the original talmudic version the sentence read: "The paschal lamb, what is the reason for it?" The editors of the Haggadah changed it to read as follows: "The paschal lamb, which our ancestors used to eat when the Temple was still in existence, what is the reason for it?" This would seem to indicate that the original statement was made at a time when the Temple was still in existence. Such a conclusion is erroneous. The editors of the Haggadah inserted many phrases for the sake of elucidation. Thus they interpolated also the word "this" before "matzah" and "maror" for the sake of greater emphasis. Ancient formulas were preserved throughout the talmudic period. Even the child's question about the roast meat was retained in talmudic times though the paschal lamb was no longer there. The editors of the Haggadah, however, eliminated it for the sake of clarity. The fact that the festival is designated in this statement by the name *pesach* is adequate proof that the author lived in the post-Temple era. Prior to the destruction of the Temple the name *pesach* retained its biblical connotation and was confined to the paschal lamb exclusively. In order to commemorate the importance of the paschal lamb, the rabbis not only introduced a symbolic dish for it but also named the festival for it. It is therefore clear that the Rabban

Gamliel who was the author of the statement is Rabban Gamliel II.

We may now return to the substance of Rabban Gamliel's statement. The commemoration of the paschal lamb (*pesach*) is to be stressed as a lesson pointing to the fact that the Almighty had passed over (*pasach*) the homes of our ancestors in Egypt. Heretofore only one phase of the paschal lamb had been paramount—the adherence of the Jewish people to the covenant and their assumption of obligations under it. Rabban Gamliel, however, called for the emphasis of the other phase—the wondrous intervention of God in Egypt on behalf of his people, There had been many miracles performed by Moses. The Egyptians were not always convinced of the origin of these miracles and attributed some of them to witchcraft. The Jews, too, expressed little faith throughout that period. When they saw, however, that every Jewish home had been spared in the midst of a plague which had killed the Egyptian firstborn, they were convinced of God's intervention in their behalf. The rabbis conveyed the same thought by the statement that God revealed himself (*gilui shchina*) when he took his nation out from the very midst of another nation (*Sifri*, Deut. 26:8). This is also the significance of the biblical verse: "And I will set apart on that day the land of Goshen in which my people live, that no swarms of flies shall be there; to the end that you shall know that I am the Lord . . ." (Exod. 8:18). The memory of God's past intervention brought new hope to the people that he would intervene again in the future, in keeping with the divine promise recorded in Deuteronomy (7:19). A new and lasting rabbinic policy was thus formulated. The pageantry of the Seder was no longer to be confined to a reinactment of the events of Nisan 14, with the solemnity of an occasion of a religious reaffirmation. The plague of the firstborn took place after the historic feast of the paschal lamb. Henceforth the doors were opened wide for the recitation on the Seder night of all the great wonders and miracles which occurred prior and subsequent to the departure from Egypt. This included also the momentous miracles which, according to tradition, took place during the crossing of the Red Sea. It was thus to become an experience of joyous exultation and hopeful-ness.

The symbolism of the matzah on the Seder night was also reinterpreted, in keeping with the new rabbinic policy. The destruction of the Temple raised a legal problem with regard to the mitzvah of eating matzah. At issue was the question: Was the commandment to eat matzah on Passover night merely incidental to and part of the mitzvah of eating the paschal lamb, or was it a separate and distinct mitzvah? As an incidental mitzvah it could not survive the discontinuance of the paschal lamb. As an independent mitzvah it could survive even without the paschal lamb. The next question was: If it survived as a biblical mitzvah, was it by virtue of the prior verse which reads: "And they shall eat the flesh in that night, roast with fire, and unleavened bread; with bitter herbs they shall eat it" (Exod. 12:8), or by virtue of a later verse which reads: "in the evening ye shall eat unleavened bread" (Exod. 12:18)? If the former verse remained in force with regard to matzah, even after the destruction of the Temple, then the old symbolism of "bread of affliction" must remain unchanged. If the latter verse, which discusses the eating of matzah throughout the seven days, is to become the basis for the mitzvah of matzah, then only the symbol of "redemption" is to be commemorated.

A reflection of the consideration of these issues is found in a talmudic passage of a much later period. Rava restated the view that matzah remained a biblical commandment even in the post-Temple era. His opponent questioned his view, quoting the prior verse which links matzah to the paschal lamb. To this Rava retorted that matzah "is restored", to its status as a mitzvah by virtue of the later verse (*Pesachim* 120a). This ambiguous an-swer leaves us wondering whether the original matzah of the prior verse, with its symbolism of "bread of affliction" is "restored," inasmuch as the later verse indicates that the mitzvah of matzah is to survive the discontinuance of the paschal lamb; or does the "restoration" mean that a new mitzvah of matzah came into effect upon the destruction of the Temple, based on the later verse, with the exclusive symbolism of "redemption"? The *beraita*, quoted in the same talmudic passage, is more specific on this point. It corroborates the views of Rava. However, unlike Rava, it does not say that the later verse "restored" the mitzvah of matzah. In concluding its statement it says: "It is this verse upon which the obligation [of matzah] rests." The implication of the *beraita* is clear that the original mitzvah of matzah was not a separate and distinct mitzvah, but merely incidental to the eating of the paschal lamb, and consequently could not survive but for the restatement of an independent mitzvah of matzah in the later verse.

Alfasi quotes this *beraita* in his text, including the concluding phrase: "It is this verse upon which the obligation rests." Maimonides, too, quotes the later verse as the basis for the obligation to eat matzah (*Hilchot chametz umatzah* 6:1). Rashi, however, quotes the aforementioned *beraita* but omits the concluding phrase. Nahmanides, the outstanding biblical exegete, in his comments on the prior verse offers two interpretations. At first he gives the classic talmudic construction that the matzah mentioned in it was merely incidental to the eating of the paschal lamb. In his second interpretation, however, he gives the following construction to the verse: "And they shall eat the flesh in that night, roast with fire, and [they shall eat] matzot; with bitter herbs they shall eat it [the flesh]." According to this construction one finds two independent commandments in the verse: (1) to eat the lamb, (2) to eat matzah. The second commandment could remain in force even if the first one was to be discontinued. This interpretation is not necessarily in conflict with the talmudic passage quoted above. It merely means that even though the independent mitzvah of matzah, contained in the prior verse, survived the destruction of the Temple, its symbolism of "bread of affliction" was linked to the paschal lamb and bitter herbs. In the post-Temple era its symbolism is that of the later verse, "redemption." This construction might even help explain the anomoly of the obligatory character of the mitzvah of matzah on the first night but not during the balance of the festival.

Nahmanides' second interpretation is fully supported by the phraseology of the text dealing with the second *pesach*: *Al matzot umerorim yochluhu* (Num. 9:11), "with matzot and bitter herbs they shall eat it." This contrasts with the phraseology of the text of the first *pesach: Veachlu et habasar . . . umatzot al merorim yochluhu* (Exod. 12:8), "and they shall eat the flesh . . . and matzot, with bitter herbs they shall eat it." The second paschal lamb was offered on the fourteenth of Iyar by those who had been unable to offer the paschal lamb in Nisan, due to absence or impurity. There is no mitzvah to eat matzah in Iyar, and chametz is not prohibited. The ritual of the second *pesach*, however, calls for the eating of the offering with matzah and bitter herbs. The latter are only incidental to the offering, and therefore the preposition *al* ("with") precedes both of them. On the other hand, in the first *pesach* there is an independent mitzvah of matzah and the maror is incidental to the offering, and therefore the preposition *al* precedes only the *merorim*.

It is of interest to observe that the cantillation notes of the two verses similarly support Nahmanides' second interpretation. In the first *pesach matzot is accented with a zakef-katan*, indicating the end of a phrase, while *merorim* is thus placed in a separate phrase. On the other hand, in the second *pesach matzot umerorim* is accented by a *mercha tipcha*, which combines them into a single phrase.

The analysis of the legal aspects of the mitzvah of matzah after the destruction of the Temple provides the background for Rabban Gamliel's dictum which associated the symbolism of matzah with the *geulah* ("redemption") rather than with affliction. This was another element which was to contribute a note of gaiety and hopefulness instead of solemnity.

In spite of Rabban Gamliel's reinterpretation, the old symbolism of the matzah was not entirely forgotten. The custom of dividing one matzah (*yachatz*) was attributed by Rav Papa (*Berachot* 39b) to a commemoration of the "bread of affliction." The Jews in Egypt could not afford a whole matzah. It was not until the Geonic period that the old symbolism was prominently reintroduced through the introductory passage of *Halachma anya* ("This is the bread of affliction"). Thus the Geonim did for Passover what they did for Chanukah—they restored the ancient significance of the ritual.

Rabban Gamliel did not change the symbolic meaning of

maror. The rabbis could have dispensed with maror after the destruction of the Temple. But they retained it by rabbinic provision because its presence helped the overall objective of the post-Temple Seder. Courage and perseverance was the message of the new Seder. Regardless of how desperate and hopeless the situation of the Jews in Egypt had appeared, God's intervention brought an end to their suffering.

EVOLUTION OF THE HAGGADAH

The recitation of Rabban Gamliel's new interpretation was made obligatory for all Jewry, thus assuring widespread compliance. The answer of the father was deprived of much of its former spontaneity. A detailed and formalized answer was prescribed for all. The content of the pre-meal portion of the Haggadah was well established by the first third of the second century. Its final form and sequence, however, were still undetermined. Thus we find Rav and Shmuel (3rd cent., *Pesachim* 116a) debating the question whether the father should commence with *mitchila ovde kochavim* or *Avadim hayinu*. The thanksgiving aspects of the holiday, which had originally found expression on Shavuot, were incorporated into the Passover ritual, while Shavuot was given new prominence as the anniversary of the Giving of the Law. The passage of *B'chol dor v'dor* . . . ("in every generation") was included to give every Jew a personal part in the drama of the exodus and to add to his exultation and joy. "Therefore we are under obligation to praise . . . him who had wrought all these miracles." This led to the expression of thanks to God, "who brought us forth from slavery to freedom from sorrow to joy, from mourning to holidays, from darkness to great light, and from servitude to redemption." The recitation of the *Hallel* was retained by rabbinic provision because it fitted in with the spirit of the new Seder.

Rabbi Akiva (d. 135), who lived through the tragic period of the Hadrianic persecutions and was to die a martyr's death, apparently felt that the effusive thanksgiving for "freedom," "great light," and "redemption" might sound unrealistic to a generation plunged into darkness. He therefore added a concluding prayer for a brighter future: "O eternal, our God the God of our fathers, mayest thou grant us to live to observe other holidays and festivals in peace. May we rejoice in the building of thy city and exult in thy service . . . then we will give thanks unto thee with a new song for our deliverance and redemption . . ." (*Pesachim* 116b). This prayer has found a responsive chord in every generation since the days of Rabbi Akiva. It was the same impulse which had led Rabbi Akiva to compose the prayer that prompted the addition to the Haggadah in the fourteenth century of the quotation from the Psalms (79:6) *Shfoch chamatcha* . . . ("Pour out thy wrath").

The occasional allusions to the sad plight of the Jewish people in the diaspora did not change the general tone of the new Seder, which held out the promise of a new redemption. To promote this theme the rabbis proclaimed that "he who elaborates upon the account (*hamarbe l'saper*) of the exodus from Egypt is to be commended" (Haggadah). The desired elaboration is to deal with the newly introduced phase of the Seder—the Almighty's wonders and miracles prior and subsequent to the exodus. This is the phase which would contribute most to the strengthening of morale. Since much of it was new to the Seder ritual, the rabbis emphasized their request by adding special praise to those who conformed with this request. To give greater weight to the change in the ritual, five of the outstanding sages of that generation met at Bnai Brak to celebrate the Seder (Haggadah). Due to the universal respect which Rabbi Akiva commanded, it was held in his home. The meeting of the five famous and beloved men must have attracted widespread attention. The entire night was taken up with the accounts and interpretations of the wonders of Egypt (*hayu msaprim biyetziat mitzrayim*). The nature of their discussions that night can be surmised from other sources, also quoted in the Haggadah. Rabbi Eliezer, one of the participants in the Bnai Brak Seder, stated that there were forty plagues in Egypt and two hundred plagues at the Red Sea. Rabbi Akiva, the host of the Seder, stated that there were fifty and two hundred and fifty plagues respectively (*Mechilta*, Exod. 14:31).

The statement in the Haggadah that it is incumbent upon us to relate the story of the departure from Egypt *(mitzvah alenu l'saper)* is not to be taken as a reference to the biblical injunction to "tell thy son" *(vehigadta l'vincha)*. The verb *l'saper* means to "relate" and has a different connotation than *vehigadta,* which means "you shall tell," explain," or "instruct." The prime objective of the biblical Seder was instruction, and therefore the verb *vehigadta* was used to convey the specific function of the Seder. The verb *l'saper* mentioned in the Haggadah is apparently based on two biblical texts. After the plague of pestilence, Moses informed Pharaoh that not only his cattle but his people, too, could have been wiped out by the plague. The people were spared, however, for good reason: "To show you my power and that my name may be proclaimed [*ul'maan saper shmi*] in the whole land" (Exod. 9:16). Where the theme of the discourse is the greatness of God, the one who relates it is a *mesaper.* A similar expression is used by the psalmist. *Hashamayim mesaprim kvod el* (Ps. 19:2), "the heavens proclaim the majesty of God." The second biblical text is even more specific in its character: ". . . for I have hardened his heart . . . that I might show my wonders in his midst. And that you may tell [*ul'maan tesaper*] in the ears of thy son, and of thy son's son what I have wrought upon Egypt, and my wonders which I have done among them, that you may know that I am the Lord" (Exod. 10:1–2). The proclamation of God's wonders in Egypt was thus made a commendable act (not a mitzvah). But it was not tied to Passover night or to any of its rituals. (This view is apparently contradicted by Maimonides, *Hilchot chametz umatzah* 7:1—"It is a positive commandment of the Torah to relate the miracles and wonders which were performed for our ancestors in Egypt on the night of the fifteenth of Nisan, as it is said: 'Remember this day in which you came out from Egypt.' ") This act was performed on Shavuot, when the *bikkurim* were offered to the priest. It was performed on Sukkot, when the sukkah was interpreted as a symbol of the wondrous shelter provided by God to the Jews in the desert. It was performed on the seven days of Passover, when the symbolism of the matzah was explained. It was performed whenever the portions of the Torah describing God's miracles were read in public. It was performed when the passage from Nehemiah (9:6–11) and the *Shira* are recited as part of the daily prayers. When the rabbis incorporated the proclamation of God's wonders in the Seder service, they used the biblical expression and said "it is a mitzvah to proclaim [*l'saper*] the [wonders] of the departure from Egypt." The rabbinic inclusion of this phase in the Seder was not intended to restrict it to the evening of the fourteenth of Nisan. At the Seder in Bnai Brak, they elaborated upon the ancient miracle all night. On the other hand, the original biblical mitzvah to recount the experiences of the slavery and the affirmation of the covenant was confined to the Seder service (*Mechilta*, Exod. 13:8). Hence it would have normally been limited to the time when the paschal lamb was eaten with the matzah and maror. According to Rabbi Eleazar b. Azariah (one of the participants in the Bnai Brak Seder), the limit is midnight (*Berachot* 9a). This biblical mitzvah is based on the commandment *vehigadta l'vincha* (Exod. 13:8; Maimonides, Sefer HaMitzvot 157). The material which was compiled to meet the requirements of the *vehigadta* "and you shall tell") was therefore called "Haggadah." The earliest rabbi to mention the name Haggadah was Rav Huna (ca. 216–96 C.E., *Pesachim* 115b). As the head of the prominent and large academy of Sura, he was in a position to give extensive publicity to this name. However, it is doubtful whether it was Rav Huna who had coined the name. Rav Huna's student, Rav Acha ber Yaakov also used the name Haggadah (*Pesachim* 116b). On the other hand, Mereimar, a contemporary of the latter, used the Aramaic version, "Agadta" (ibid.). It therefore seems likely that the Hebrew name was not of Babylonian origin but was transmitted to Rav Huna by Rav, who had received his education from the Tannaim in Palestine.

Rabban Gamliel's reinterpretation of the Seder led to the practice of *heseibah*, the tradition to recline at the Seder table (*Pesachim* 99b). According to the Talmud, this posture reflects the free status of an individual because slaves ate their meal in a standing position (Jer. *Pesachim* 10). The observance of this practice was emphasized particularly during the eating of the matzah, which had become the symbol of redemption. There is no need for reclining, however, when one is eating maror (*Pesachim* 108a). The earliest sage who is described as having reclined at the Seder table is Rabban Gamliel (Tosefta, *Pesachim,* chap. 10).

The pattern of the new Seder also resulted in the addition of a fourth question and a change in their sequence. The original version had three questions, listed in the following order: (1) double dipping, (2) matzah, (3) roast. Rabban Gamliel's dictum called for the interpretation of the paschal lamb, matzah, and maror. The questions were therefore addressed to these three rituals. Since the paschal lamb was no longer available, (except for a symbolic dish), preference was given to a new version: (1) matzah, (2) maror (a new question), (3) roast, (4) double dipping. The last question had originally been first because it was the first "difference" which the child had noticed on the Seder night. It was also historically significant because it had reinacted an important event of Nisan 14. Under the new policy of Rabban Gamliel, the reinactment phase was played down while the theme of freedom and God's intervention was played up. Since the Jews had never been enjoined to reinact the smearing of the blood on the doorposts, this question lost its significance. It was retained only for the sake of the preservation of old traditions and also because the double dipping helped focus the child's attention on the uniqueness of the occasion. The question was therefore placed last (*Pesachim* 116a), and it was entirely ignored in the formalized answer provided for the father.

In the Geonic period the form of the questions was changed again. The reference to the roasted meat was omitted for lack of a paschal lamb. A reference to the custom of reclining was substituted in order to preserve the traditional number of questions in vogue during the talmudic period. The latest version follows the following order: (1) matzah, (2) maror, (3) double dipping, (4) reclining. The question relating to the most recent custom was placed last.

THE FOUR CUPS OF WINE

The obligation to drink four cups of wine was another rabbinic provision which was introduced, most likely, within several decades after the destruction of the Temple. Some modern scholars assume that this custom had already been practiced in the Temple era. There seems to be no evidence to support such an assumption. The Talmud states that the custom is of rabbinic origin (*Pesachim* 109b). There is no hint in the statement, however, as to the date of origin. The fact that the Jerusalem Talmud (*Pesachim* 10:1) offers four different explanations for this practice is indicative that there was no single traditional or historical reason which could have motivated the rabbinic provision. Furthermore, the explanations in the Jerusalem Talmud seek to shed light upon the number of cups of wine rather than the reason for the wine itself. We must therefore seek the explanation in the overall objectives of Rabban Gamliel's new Seder—to make the occasion an experience of great joy and happiness. The words of Rabbi Judah b. Beteira seem to offer a clue: "In the time of the Temple one experienced joy by the eating of meat . . . but now that the Temple is no longer in existence, there is only joy through wine" (*Pesachim* 109a). Rabbi Judah b. Beteira did not specifically refer to the Seder, but his words show the motive for the introduction of wine at the Seder—an increase of joy. Maimonides, in his discussion of the various modes of rejoicing on all festivals, stated: "More binding than all these was the drinking of wine, which is best for rejoicing" (*Sefer Hamitzvot* 54). Two single cups of wine were placed at every festive table even prior to the destruction of the Temple, the Kiddush cup and the cup after the recitation of Grace. The number was doubled for the Seder, and every individual was made to drink a full cup. The drinking of the cups was spaced properly to produce joy but to prevent intoxication. To each cup was assigned a special place in the Seder ritual: the first two cups when the story of slavery is recited, and the last two cups when the glory of freedom is related (*Pesachim* 108a). The original function of the wine of Kiddush and Grace was retained even after the number of cups was increased to four (the first and third respectively). The rabbinic interpretation of the four cups mentioned in the Jerusalem Talmud and midrashic literature added to the religious significance of this ritual by making the cups an outstanding symbol of freedom and redemption (*Pesachim* 109a).

There are other clues which seem to support the conclusion that the four cups were introduced after the destruction of the Temple. Thus the Talmud states that the paschal lamb was eaten in Jerusalem on the ground level, which was consecrated. Due to the crowded conditions, many people used to go up to the roofs of the buildings to chant the *Hallel* (*Pesachim* 86a). There is no mention made of the fourth cup of wine, which would normally be drunk subsequent to the completion of the *Hallel*. One also may wonder why the child's original three questions did not contain a question regarding the four cups, which are a more noticeable "difference" than the double dipping. Apparently there were no four cups at that time. Furthermore, an analysis of the names of the rabbis who discussed the basic aspects of the four cups, such as the quality and quantity of the wine, presents another useful hint in determining the approximate date of origin of the custom. The earliest rabbi mentioned by name as having drunk four cups of wine is Rabbi Judah b. Illai (Jer. *Pesachim* 10). He was a student of Rabbi Akiva and active in the middle of the second century. It is said that he drank the full quantity of wine in spite of the fact that the wine could cause him severe physical pain. One gets the impression that the custom was still young and that the rabbi subjected himself to this pain in order to impress the people with the importance of the ritual. The bulk of the sages who contributed to the clarification of the basic rules of the four cups were members of the first generation of Babylonian and Palestinian Amoraim—Rabbi Chiya, Rabbi Hoshea, Rabbi Yochanan, Rabbi Joshua b. Levi, Rav, and Samuel. The span of activities of these men bridged the second and third centuries. Had the four cups been in existence in the Temple era, it would have surely had some of its important aspects discussed by prior generations of rabbis.

Research fails to produce any opinion by our great talmudic

commentators which places the four-cups ritual within the Temple era. The one notable exception is Raabad, the celebrated twelfth-century scholar. His view is expressed in a comment on Rabbi Zerachiah Girondi (Rif, *Pesachim*, chap. 10) regarding the maximum number of cups which may be drunk on the Seder night. The Mishnah prohibits the drinking of wine between the third and fourth cups (*Pesachim* 117b). The Jerusalem Talmud attributes this prohibition to the need of preventing drunkenness (Jer. *Pesachim* 10). In view of the traditional repugnance against intoxication, one may construe the statement of the Jerusalem Talmud as the real objective of the prohibition. In another statement in the Jerusalem Talmud, it is said that one must drink four cups of wine but not get drunk on them (Jer. *Pesachim* 10). Diluted wine was therefore preferred to the marketable, potent, and concentrated drink. The concern of the rabbis with the result of the four cups can be easily understood in light of ancient popular folk-sayings describing the effects of four cups of wine. According to one of these sayings: "He who drinks one cup of wine, containing a *reviis*, loses one fourth of his mind . . . he who drinks four cups loses his whole mind" (*Bamidbar Rabba* 10). Another saying declared: "One who drinks one cup of wine possesses modesty and humility . . . he who drinks four cups is like unto a pig who wallows in mud" (*Yalkut* 58:61). Still another saying described the frightful effect of four cups on women, who may lose, as a result of the wine, all sexual inhibitions (*Ketubot* 65a). The four cups on the Seder night were therefore not drunk successively but at intervals, to prevent the saturation which produces intoxication. The Talmud also states that wine which is drunk with the meal, in addition to the four cups, does not contribute to intoxication because it is diluted by the food (Jer. *Pesachim* 10).

The majority of our great medieval sages and commentators elaborated upon the reason stated in the Jerusalem Talmud. They felt, apparently, that it was not drunkenness in itself that the Talmud was so much concerned with as the fear that drunkenness would prevent the completion of the Seder service. Most of them cite the concern that the chanting of the *Hallel* might be omitted by a drunken person. Thus the offensive state of drunkenness would be compounded by a religious violation. Since the *Hallel* is chanted between the third and fourth cups, the prohibition against additional wine was specifically confined to the interval between the third and fourth cups of wine. The Raabad is the only one of the great scholars who broadened his comments to include both the Temple era and the post-Temple era. In the time of the Temple the prohibition against additional wine was aimed to prevent the paschal lamb from becoming *notar* (left-over, prohibited from being eaten after the permissible time). If he drinks too much he may forget to eat the lamb in time and thus convert it into *notar*, in violation of a biblical injunction. This comment explicitly assumes that the four cups were already part of the Seder at the time the Temple was still in existence. As to the substance of his comment, one may wonder why there should have been a prohibition against additional wine after the third cup in the time of the Temple. Since the paschal lamb was eaten between the second and third cups (when he was sober), there was nothing left of the lamb to become *notar*, even if he did get intoxicated between the third and fourth cups.

The obligation to drink four cups of wine, to a people not given to drinking, must have appeared indeed as a most unusual distinctive feature which highlighted the extraordinary character of the celebration. Rabbi Joshua b. Levi (early 3rd cent.), who had his brushes with the Roman authorities for his sympathies for the young Jewish freedom-fighters of his day, made the mitzvah of the four cups obligatory for women as well as men, in order to publicize more extensively the miracles of the exodus (*Pesachim* 108a). It was for a similar reason that he made the reading of the *Megillah* and the kindling of the Chanukah menorah obligatory for women.

The child's four questions were inserted in the Haggadah after the filling of the second cup because the drinking of wine after Kiddush and prior to the meal would further stimulate the child to wonder, "Why is this night different?" The educational objectives inherent in the Seder service, foreshadowed by the biblical pattern of questions by the young and answers by the elders, were the incentive for the ultimate inclusion in the

Haggadah of educational material culled from midrashic sources. In addition to midrashic material, some liturgical poems were also included. Efforts to remove some of these passages in the post-talmudic period were met with strong resistance by the Geonim of Babylonia. As a result, some new material was occasionally added to the Haggadah in the course of time. Such material, however, was not universally adopted by world Jewry. An outstanding example is the popular *Chad-Gadya*, which was printed for the first time in a Haggadah published in Prague in 1590. It has been reprinted ever since in all European Haggadot, but it was never included in the Yemenite Haggadah.

V.
THE EVOLUTION OF THE FOUR SONS

We have attempted heretofore to discuss the impact of history upon the Passover rituals and their adaptation to changing conditions. A similar study of the midrashic passages of the Haggadah might be equally useful and enlightening. In this area we may feel free to indulge in speculative interpretation as we are not restrained by fixed legal concepts. Generally speaking, most aggadic statements admit more than one correct exposition. One may suggest that the ambiguity of midrashic expression is purposeful so that each generation may read into it the most meaningful message designed to meet the needs of any particular period.

The bulk of the midrashic passages of the Haggadah were culled from *Mechilta* and *Sifri*. Most of them were copied verbatim from these and other sources, with minor stylistic changes introduced by the editors of the Haggadah for the sake of greater clarity. There are a few passages which have several talmudic sources. These have perpetuated conflicting versions which present a challenge to the historically minded student. The passage which describes the four types of children (*K'neged arbaa banim*) falls into this category.

The character of each child is judged by the question posed by him. The substance of three of these questions is mentioned in the Bible: "What is the meaning of the testimonies, and the statutes, and the ordinances, which the Lord our God has commanded you?" (Deut. 6:20); "What does this service mean to you? (Exod. 12:26); "What is this?" (Exod. 13:14). To all these questions the text provides answers. There is also an answer given without a corresponding question (Exod. 13:8). This suggests a fourth child who asks no questions but to whom an instructive explanation should be offered.

The phraseology of each question offers a clue for the motive of each child. The one who is able to grasp the distinction between "testimonies, statutes, and ordinances" is labeled a "wise boy." Apparently he is motivated by a quest for wisdom. The question in Exodus 12:26 reflects hostility, and the child is labeled a *rasha* ("wicked"). The third question (Exod. 13:14) is somewhat ambiguous, concealing the real intent of the questioner. This boy is called a *tam*, a term which we will attempt to define later.

Unlike the biblical texts, which apparently deal with the reaction of the young or future generations to the Passover rituals, the rabbinic comments did not relate to the character of young children. No minor, however mischievous, is a *rasha*. In the context of the midrash, the passage seems to refer to well-defined classes of people whose ideology is reflected in the questions. This explains why the midrash did not follow the sequence of the questions as they appear in the Bible. The midrash seems to have preferred to follow the historical sequence of the emergence of the various ideological groups of that period. The midrash also failed to follow the order of the answers as they appear in the text because it felt that a reshuffling of the answers would better serve the purpose of refuting the false ideology of a particular group.

The primary source of the Haggadah passage of the four sons is a *Mechilta* (chap. 18). The *Mechilta* is assumed to have been compiled in the second century and edited in the third century. Some rabbinic authorities are of the opinion that the Babylonian sage Rav was its editor. There is another fragmentary source in the *Mechilta* (chap. 17) which discusses only the *rasha*. It seems to be an excerpt from an old, possibly the first, version of this passage. A third source is found in the Jerusalem Talmud (*Pesachim* 10). The statement is credited to Rabbi Chiya, the editor of the *beraitot*. Rabbi Chiya is not to be taken as the author of the statement but rather as the editor who had probably included it in his edition of the *beraitot*.

ANTI-RABBINIC MOVEMENTS

The Jerusalem Talmud generally preserves the earlier versions of the oral law and folklore, and it is to that source that we look for the original intent of the midrash. We must first review the religious pattern of the Jewish community and the divisive forces which threatened its stability before and after the common era. The earliest threat was posed by the Samaritans, who claimed to be the "genuine" Jews. Due to their frequent conspiracies against the security of the Jewish people, they constituted a serious menace to the physical welfare of Palestinian Jewry. Their brand of Judaism, however, never presented a challenge to traditional Judaism. They were regarded as non-Jewish enemies and treated as such. We may therefore rule them out as one of the four groups, symbolized by the four sons, with whom the rabbis had to contend.

Hellenism was the first force to threaten Judaism from within. It began its slow infiltration of the Jewish scene soon after the conquest of Palestine by Alexander the Great. It picked up momentum in the Hasmonean era, and in its forward strides swept up many pagan customs and beliefs. In Palestine it became an open antagonist of Mosaic law, and it enlisted a very considerable number of Jews in its cause. Outside of Palestine, particularly in Egypt, a peaceful synthesizing process brought about a fusion of cultures which superimposed Hellenism upon Judaism. Philo the Alexandrian was the chief spokesman of Hellenized Jewry. He admitted the validity of the biblical laws but freely employed allegorical interpretations to explain some of the laws as well as the historical accounts of the Bible. This led to a distortion of the literal sense of the text and opened the way to the ultimate creation of new sects within the Jewish fold.

Early Christianity was another force which posed a threat to

Judaism during a brief period in the first century. In the first decades of its existence, it was a Jewish sect which professed allegiance to the Torah. It recruited most of its followers from the Jewish community and consequently presented a challenge to the rabbinic leadership. However, it was as yet numerically too small to constitute a real threat. In the year 50 C.E., at the time of the alleged Apostolic Council meeting at Jerusalem, Mosaic law was declared not binding upon heathen converts to Christianity. With the beginning of this drift away from the mother religion, the threat of Christianity to Judaism began to decline. The triumph of Paulinian theology established Christianity, by the middle of the second century, as a non-Jewish church, totally divorced from Judaism. This development removed Christianity as a threatening force from within the Jewish community.

Sadduceanism, which had many adherents among the aristocracy and the priestly families was another Jewish movement antagonistic to rabbinic Judaism. Though it antedated Christianity, it also outlived it as a Jewish movement, continuing to claim the attention of the rabbis after Christianity ceased being of serious concern to them. The Sadduceans insisted on a literal interpretation of the Torah and rejected the oral traditions by means of which the rabbis were able to broaden the concise biblical text to cover the exigencies of an ever-changing society. They refused to. accept the "fences" built by the rabbis as safeguards for the preservation of the ancient law, and they contested such basic tenets of rabbinic Judaism as reward and punishment in the hereafter, the coming of the Messiah, and resurrection.

The Essenic sects (the Qumran cave dwellers were apparently such a sect) promoted a separatist, anti-priestly, and anti-rabbinical movement. They, too, constituted a challenge to rabbinic Judaism. Ignorance was another problem which the rabbis had to solve. It presented a threat no less formidable than the four anti-rabbinical forces mentioned before. The fight against ignorance called for the use of the combined weapons of piety and enlightenment.

The midrashic passage about the four sons seems to reflect the structure of the Jewish community in the first and second centuries of the common era. It mirrors the conflicting currents which disturbed the religious pattern of that time. As the scene changed from time to time, the symbolic reference of the four sons also assumed new meaning, keeping pace with the changing situation.

CHACHAM: A HELLENIST

The classification of the first son is based on the question quoted from Deuteronomy 6:20: "What is the meaning of the testimonies and the statutes and the ordinances, which the Lord our God has commanded you?" He is labeled in the Jerusalem Talmud *ben chacham* ("a wise son") and in the *Mechilta* and Haggadah simply *chacham*. The "wise son" has been commonly assumed to be the most perfect of the four sons. He has been taken to be bright, scholarly, eager to learn, and pious. This is undoubtedly the result of an association of *chacham* with the term *talmid-chacham*, the universal title of a Torah scholar. One hesitates to disagree with a unanimously accepted interpretation. However, we may suggest the possibility of another construction, at least insofar as the earliest version of this passage is concerned. That the *chacham*'s attitude is not wholly positive can be deduced from the concluding phrase of the question, "which God has commanded you." It seems that some rabbi sensed the flaw in this phraseology. In our text of the Jerusalem Talmud, the *chacham* is made to ask for the meaning of the statutes "which God has commanded us." This, however, represents an amendment by a copyist of the biblical text which we cannot accept. The adjective *chacham*, furthermore, does not mean only "wise." It may also mean "shrewd," in the uncomplimentary sense of the term. This is illustrated by the talmudic expression: *ish chacham l'risha*—"a man wise in the ways of wickedness" (*Sanhedrin* 21a). Philosophy and allegory are mentioned in the Talmud under the name of *chachma*. Gentile philosophers are called *chachme umot ha-olam* (*Berachot* 58a), and Greek philosophy is translated *chachma yevanit* (*Menachot* 99b).

The son who asks for the meaning of "statutes" (chukim), whose purpose is not disclosed in the Torah, is most likely looking for an allegorical interpretation to provide the answer to his question. He is a chacham, i.e., a philosopher or a Hellenist influenced by Greek philosophy. We may assume that he was singled out by the rabbis as the representative of Hellenism, which had made serious inroads into Jewish life. The answer indicated in the early version which appears in the Jerusalem Talmud is as follows: "And you, too, shall tell him: 'By strength of hand the Lord brought us out from Egypt.' " On the surface this answer is hardly responsive to the question. Yet it conveys the method employed by the rabbis in combating Hellenic influences. The rabbis did not enter into debate with the Hellenists nor did they attempt to refute Hellenic philosophy. Rabbinic Judaism recognized the fact that Hellenism was undermining piety. The strengthening of piety was, therefore, considered the most effective means for counteracting Hellenic influence. Traditionalism automatically excluded all allegorical rationalization of the Bible. It was therefore important to stress the fact that God had revealed himself to the Jewish people in Egypt through his might and strong hand. One will therefore implicitly follow his statutes even if the reason for them is not apparent.

Palestinian Hellenism ceased being a threat to Judaism as soon as it aligned itself with the Roman pagan brand of Hellenism. In the rebellion against Rome, the Jewish Hellenists sided with the Romans and were regarded by most Jews as enemies of their people. The destruction of the Temple and the growing deep antagonism to Rome ended the existence of a Hellenist sect within the Jewish community. The Alexandrian brand of Hellenism, even though not identified with Romanism, also lost its momentum due to Roman systematic extermination of Alexandrian Jewry. In the period between 66 and 117 C.E., the bulk of the largest Jewish community in the diaspora was eradicated as a result of violent massacres. A substantial number of Hellenized Jews in Asia Minor converted to Christianity.

The disappearance of Hellenism removed it as a force capable of challenging rabbinic Judaism. However, its philosophic influences lingered on for a long time. Rabbinic attitudes toward it reflected two schools of thought. The majority opinion did not favor any probing into the motivation of biblical statutes. It discouraged the study of secular sciences and specifically prohibited the study of Greek philosophy (*Sota* 49b). It prohibited speculation about the *merkavah* (cosmogeny) unless one had attained the status of a *chacham*, i.e., a Torah scholar (*Chagigah* 11b). On the other hand, there was a minority liberal opinion which did not consider any of the foregoing activities inimical to Judaism. Rabbi Simon deemed it proper to examine the motivation of the biblical statutes (*Sota* 8a). The house of the *nasi* permitted its youth to study Greek philosophy (*Baba Kama* 83a). Rabbi Ishmael, too, permitted his nephew to study Greek philosophy on condition that such study should not encroach upon the time devoted to the study of the Torah (*Menachot* 99b). Rabbi Elazar b. Chisma (2nd cent.) proclaimed that "astronomy and geometry are the *"prifriot* [in our version, *parpperaot*] of wisdom" (*Avot.* chap. 3). The term *prifriot* is assumed by many scholars to be derived from the Greek, meaning "dainties," "after-course," or "dessert." The use of a Greek term was probably deliberate in its application to Greek sciences, which he considered permissible, but only as an after-course to the main course of Torah.

The *Mechilta* version of the four sons reflected the prevailing rabbinic attitude to Hellenism in the post-Temple era. There the *chacham* is not to be translated "philosopher" but "Torah scholar," in the traditional sense of the word. This version expresses the majority opinion, which opposed philosophic discourses by rabbis. The answer given to the inquiring scholar includes a Passover legal maxim which is skillfully converted into an educational principle. The Mishnah prohibits the eating of dessert after the paschal lamb (*Ein maftirin achar hapesach afikoman, Pesachim* 119b). The use of the Greek *afikoman* lends greater weight to the symbolic message to be conveyed to the scholar—the Greek dessert (philosophy) is not to follow the paschal lamb (religious studies). One should note, however, that the refusal was not categorical. In deference to the persisting liberal school, the author merely said: *af ata ptach lo,* open up with an argument which may dissuade him from further philosophic research. The final Haggadah version, which copied the *Mechilta*, introduced (ca. 8th cent.) a minor change. Instead of *ptach lo* it inserted *emor lo*, the peremptory "tell him!" This, too, reflected a period in Jewish history when philosophic influence had all but vanished from the scene. The author intended to keep it so.

RASHA: A JUDEO-CHRISTIAN

The classification of the second boy is based on the question attributed to him in Exodus (12:26): "What does this service mean to you?" This son is labeled in the Jerusalem Talmud, a *ben rasha* ("wicked son"), and in the *Mechilta* and Haggadah, *rasha*. Originally the term *rasha* was confined in the Bible to individuals guilty of social crimes (*bein adam la-chavero*). It was used in this sense in the Pentateuch (Gen. 18:23, Exod. 2:13, Deut. 25:1). Later the term was broadened to include individuals guilty of offenses against God (*bein adam la makom*, Ps. 10:4, 13). The talmudic rabbis applied this label to enemies of the Jewish people, such as Nimrod (*Pesachim* 94b), Esau (*Yoma* 38b), Balaam (*Sanhedrin* 105b), Nebuchadnezzar (*Sanhedrin* 92b), Haman (*Megillah* 10b), and Titus (*Gittin* 56b). We have every reason to believe that the Talmud also labeled a member of the new Judeo-Christian group a *rasha*, as soon as the sect's enmity to the Jewish people became evident.

The hostility of the early Judeo-Christians to rabbinic Judaism was soon translated by the early Gentile Christians into hostility to Jewry. They therefore came to be regarded by most Jews as enemies of the Jewish people. The friendship professed by some Christians was viewed as a subterfuge to ensnare thereby Jewish converts. This explains the apparent use by the Talmud of the name Balaam as a code name for a Christian. Balaam had proclaimed his submission to the will of the Lord and he sang the praises of Israel. Yet he belied his mission by his schemes of deception, whereby he hoped to lead Israel back to idolatry. He also secretly desired the destruction of all synagogues (*Sanhedrin* 105a). Jesus was charged with having "deceived Israel and leading them astray" (*Sanhedrin* 43a, uncensored text). The talmudic passage discussing the death of Balaam (*Sanhedrin* 106b) undoubtedly points to Jesus. Since Balaam earned the epithet *rasha*, the same identification was most likely attached to the members of the new sect, who were equally guilty of heresy and deception. A parallel equation is expressed in another talmudic passage (*Gittin* 56b), in which three enemies of Judaism are listed: Titus, Balaam, and a "Jewish transgressor" (*poshea yisrael*). The three were asked by a prospective proselyte to give him their opinions of the Jewish people. Titus, a personifier of pagan hostility, expressed opposition to the Torah as a burdensome theology. He also offered pragmatic information about the expediency of anti-Semitism as a vehicle to political power. Balaam, in this passage, is cast in the role of the early Gentile church, which openly expressed its anti-Jewish enmity. The "Hebrew transgressor" is the code name for the typical Hebrew Christian, who professes friendship to Jews but ridicules rabbinic Judaism. He, too, is labeled a *rasha* (*Sanhedrin* 105a).

The so-called Letter of Rabban Yochanan b. Zaccai refers to Jesus as a *rasha meisit* ("inciter") and to Paul as a *rasha uposhea* ("transgressor"). This letter, allegedly written by Rabban Yochanan b. Zaccai, is dated Kislev 6, 3813 (52 C.E.). The reference to historical events of the post-Temple era makes it clear that the letter in its present form is of later origin. An examination of the letter reveals that it originally based all its contentions solely on biblical verses, without resorting to rabbinic quotations. This points to the antiquity of the original document. This part of the letter was written in a lucid biblical style. We may assume that it was published by the end of the first century to counteract an intensive Christian proselytizing campaign. At a later period, possibly in the third century, numerous Cabalist passages were interpolated to lend greater emphasis to the author's admonitions. Such expression as *nachash ha kadmoni* ("the primeval serpent") and *zuhamo shel nachash* ("the impurity of the serpent"), which appear in this letter, were introduced into the Talmud by third-century Amoraim (*Sanhedrin* 29a, *Avoda Zara* 22b). The expanded letter could have been republished in the third century, due to the continued spread of Christianity in Palestine and the diaspora. With the adoption of Christianity as the official religion of the Roman Empire at the beginning of the fourth century, the circulation of such a letter would have been too risky an undertaking. It is possible, of course, that the letter was first republished in the Islamic era, in the seventh century or later, when it was safe for Jews in Moslem countries to urge their fellow Jews in Christian countries to resist missionary blandishments and threats. The epithet *rasha meisit* appears in the original part of the letter and dates the application of this term to the early part of the Christian era.

In the post-talmudic literature a new name for the founder of Christianity was widely adopted—*oto ha-ish* ("that man"). This name was popularized by a book entitled *Maase shel Oto ha-Ish*. The book is assumed to have been written in the tenth century. The origin of the name may possibly be traced to the passage in *Gittin* (56b) which was quoted above. In that passage the *poshea yisrael*, like the two other enemies of Israel, is addressed as *hahu gavro*, the Aramaic version of the Hebrew *oto ha-ish*. However, the latter term is specifically mentioned in the Jerusalem Talmud, in the answer to the second of the four sons. I believe that here, too, the reference was to the Hebrew Christians. It is a legitimate assumption that the second son, labeled a *rasha*, represented the new force threatening Judaism—Christianity.

The various versions of the answer to be given to the *rasha* reflect different periods in Jewish history. I believe that the earliest version of the answer is to be found in the seventeenth chapter of *Mechilta*. The interrogating son is called *ben rasha*. This passage states that "this one is a wicked son who has excluded himself from the Jewish community. Inasmuch as he has excluded himself from the community, you, too, must exclude him from the community. . . . Due to your self-exclusion from the community; if you had been there [in Egypt] you would not have been redeemed." This version most likely dates from the first century, when the Judeo-Christians still considered themselves Jews. Most Jews regarded them in the same light. The author, however, asserts emphatically that the Judeo-Christians had excluded themselves from the Jewish community by embracing Christianity and urged all Jews to exclude the members of this sect and not to regard them any longer as Jews.

The later version of the answer to the second son's question is found in the Jerusalem Talmud (*Pesachim* 10). By this time the breach between Judaism and Christianity had widened to a point where it could no longer be bridged. Old Testament laws were dispensed with for Gentile converts, and even Jewish converts could join the Gentile branch of the Church. Paul had shed the *Torah mitzvot* for fear that they might prove too burdensome an imposition for pagans to accept. The new position of Christianity made it clear to everyone that it could no longer be considered a Jewish sect. Christianity's objective was no longer the search for a synthesis with Judaism but the gaining of adherents away from Judaism. The burden of the appeal for the missionary was spelled out in the Jerusalem version: "What does this service mean to you? Why all these impositions with which you burden us every year? . . . Inasmuch as he has excluded himself from the community, you, too, tell him that if that man [*oto ha-ish*, the reference might be to the missionary, or, as I suggested before, to Jesus] had been in Egypt, he would not have been redeemed."

A still later version is found in the eighteenth chapter of *Mechilta*. This reflects the victorious emergence of Paulinian theology in the second century. The divinity of Jesus became a basic tenet of the new creed. Any Jew subscribing to such a view would be a *kofer b'ikar* (a denier of the very essence of monotheism). Paulinian doctrine also proclaimed that mankind was doomed by the sin of Adam. This was contrary to the views of Judaism, which declared that no son is to suffer for the sins of his parents. The answer to the *rasha* in this version reads as follows: "Since he excluded himself from the community and has denied the very essence of monotheism [*kofer b'ikar*], you set his teeth on edge and tell him . . . if you were there you would not have been redeemed." The expression "set his teeth on edge" is rarely used and is clearly an allusion to a similar expression in Jeremiah (31:30): "but every man shall die for his own sin, 'every man who eats sour grapes, his teeth are set on edge.' " This refutes one of the basic doctrines of the Church.

(The expression *kofer b'ikar* is also used in the Jerusalem text of *Sanhedrin* [chap. 6] in what appears to be an allusion to Christ.)

The reference to Jeremiah's prophecy assumes even greater meaning in view of Paul's claim that the old covenant had been terminated and a new covenant was entered into with the Christians. Jeremiah followed his refutation of inherited sin with the prophecy of a new covenant between God and the children of Israel, who will not be held accountable for the sins of their fathers (31:31). The *rasha* who subscribes to the Paulinian theology is a heretic and sinner whose "teeth will be set on edge." No innocent people, however, will be doomed by the sins of the guilty.

The second of the two versions in *Mechilta* was incorporated into the Haggadah with only minor stylistic changes. A discussion of the true interpretation of this passage was undoubtedly suppressed due to the general atmosphere of fear beginning with the fourth century.

TIPESH: A SADDUCEE

The classification of the third boy was based on the question quoted in Exodus 13:14: "What is this?" There is no self-exclusion implied in the wording of this question. However, its ambiguity allows for two constructions. It could express a challenge: Is this multiplicity of Passover laws and rituals ordained by the rabbis really important? On the other hand, it could convey the desire of a truly pious man to learn the entire code of Passover laws so that he could follow them implicitly. He therefore asks: What laws are included in the Passover ritual?

In the Jerusalem Talmud the third boy is labeled a "fool" *(tipesh)*. This reflects the attitude of the rabbis to the Sadduceans, whose scholarship they held in low regard. As a matter of policy the rabbis preferred not to enter into any serious discussion with the Sadduceans on the merit of any rabbinic interpretation. This policy is understandable in light of the Saducean denial of the validity of the oral law. The rabbis frequently introduced a satirical note into their replies to show their contempt for their adversaries. Rabban Yochanan b. Zaccai

(1st cent.) joined many a Sadducean in debate. His favorite salutation was: *shotim* ("fools," *Baba Batra* 115b).

In response to the Sadducean objection to the rabbinic "fences" built around the biblical laws, the father was instructed to point to some of the Passover laws to illustrate the need for such "fences." "Teach him the laws of the paschal lamb—'One may not invite the group in whose company he had eaten the paschal lamb to join in the festivities of another group.' " The object of this rabbinic law was to prevent an individual from sharing in the *karban pesach* of two distinct groups. This rabbinic "fence" was essential for the prevention of a violation of a biblical statute.

In the *Mechilta* version a different construction was put on the third boy's question. The Sadducees were no longer a threat in the second century. The epithet *tipesh*, which identified the Sadducees, was dropped, and in its place was substituted the label *tam*. It has been commonly assumed that a *tam* is a simple fellow or even a simpleton. This interpretation was most likely the result of an association of the *tam* with its Jerusalem counterpart, the *tipesh*. Yet neither the biblical nor the talmudic usage of the term *tam* and its various derivations bear out such an interpretation. A more accurate translation of the *tam* in the Haggadah would be a "sincere lad," one who asks "What is the Law?" rather than "Why this law?" This boy represented the generation of young people who had set out to acquire a Jewish education. The response to the third boy in the *Mechilta* version presents a basic rabbinic principle of education: "Tell him that the Almighty took us out of Egypt with a mighty hand." A new student is to be instilled with piety before he is taught knowledge. This principle is stressed frequently in the Talmud and is expressed in the biblical phrase: "The fear of the Lord is the beginning of wisdom" (Ps. 111:10).

ONE WHO DOES NOT ASK QUESTIONS

The unquestioning boy epitomizes ignorance and indifference, the persisting problem which faces Jewish leadership in every generation. The answer is the same in all the versions: *At ptach lo* ("you open with the information"). When a Jewish child does not come to receive a religious education, we must find the way of bringing it to him. The Jerusalem version does not conclude the answer with the quotation from Exodus (13:8). There is a valid reason for this omission in view of the use of the same verse in the response to the *rasha*.

One should not rule out, however, the possibility that even the fourth boy originally reflected an ideological group which abstained from questioning not for lack of interest but out of a deliberate refusal to communicate with the rest of Jewry. The older version of *Mechilta* (chap. 17:108) labels the silent boy (Exod. 13:8) a "wicked son" and places him in the same category as the *rasha* previously alluded to in Exodus 12:26. The sect which made its headquarters at Qumran, the repository of the Dead Sea Scrolls, was the only schismatic community which imposed a discipline of self-isolation upon its membership. In its rebellion against the sacrificial ritualism of the priestly hierarchy in Jerusalem, and the rationalistic legalism of the Pharisaic leadership, the sect preached the reestablishment of prophetic Judaism, centered upon social justice. To strengthen its influence, the sect founded tightly-knit and isolated communities whose members were bound by a rigorous, narrow ritualism of its own. They were strictly enjoined to "keep apart from all perverse men who walk in the path of wickedness" (*Manual of Discipline* 5). In the Qumran terminology, all Jews outside the sect walked in the path of darkness. Another regulation provided: "No one is to engage in discussion or disputation with men of ill-repute; and in company of perverse men everyone is to abstain from disclosing the meaning of the Law" (*Manual of Discipline* 9). The Qumran sect was the only doctrinaire community to outlaw any dialogue with other Jews. They were indeed the original "unquestioning sons" who in the last century and a half prior to the destruction of the Temple posed a threat to rabbinic Judaism. They thus earned the epithet *rasha* a century before it was applied to the Hebrew Christians. Unlike the later version of *Mechilta* (chap. 18:125), there is no claim that this *rasha* denied monotheism, because the Qumran cave dwellers could not be charged with such heresy. However, they are charged with having excluded themselves from the household of Israel, and the reader is admonished to treat them as outsiders.

8

Lag B'Omer

A PRECEDENT FOR A CELEBRATION OF HITLER'S DOWNFALL

THE HITLER ERA has produced two tentative commemorative days—the twenty-seventh of Nisan, in memory of the fighters of the ghettos, and the tenth of Tevet, in memory of the six million Jewish martyrs. No parallel festival has been set aside to mark the end of Hitlerism. One may argue that the fall of Nazism should be permanently noted in the religious and secular calendars of the Jewish people no less than its rise and tragic expansion. Purim, admittedly, could not be regarded as a precedent for a post-Hitlerian festival. Did not Hitler succeed in destroying a third of world Jewry? Yet when we ponder the potential consequences of a German victory, we find ample justification for a festival. The original Nazi plans called for the extermination of eleven million Jews. The fate of the surviving third in a world dominated by Fascism is easily imagined. Furthermore, the creation of Israel could never have taken place if the Nazis had emerged victorious. Surely a religious Jew should feel impelled to express his gratitude in song and prayer on a special day dedicated to that end.

Jews have faced many mortal crises in their long history. On a number of occasions our enemies succeeded in inflicting serious losses on our ancestors. The period of acute persecution would generally last for a few years and then taper off, bringing a breathing spell and respite to the afflicted. On one such occasion

167

a festival was set aside to mark the salvation of the survivors. This celebration could serve as a precedent for a post-Hitlerian festival. Better still, the old festival may be broadened by giving it a new significance in the same manner as the tenth of Teveth was linked with the Nazi Holocaust.

The historical persecutions referred to above took place under the rule of the Roman governor Tineius Rufus in the second century. His oppression led to the Bar Kochba uprising, which cost the lives of a few hundred thousand Jews, according to some historians. The defeat of Bar Kochba was followed by the Hadrianic persecutions, which added many honored names to the roll of Jewish martyrs. A hardening of Rome's anti-Jewish attitude could have endangered the security of all the Jews scattered throughout the Roman Empire, in addition to the harassed Palestinian Jewish community. Only Jews living in Babylonia under Parthian rule were not exposed to imminent danger. One discovers here a striking parallel to the situation of world Jewry in the heyday of Nazidom.

The fortunate end of Hadrian's rule, and the successful intercession of a rabbinic delegation sent to Rome, brought about a more tolerant attitude on the part of the government, leading to the restoration of freedom of religion. It is commonly assumed that the traditional mourning period of Sefirah, between Passover and Shavuot, and the semi-festival of Lag B'Omer reflect the momentous events of that generation. Since we propose to designate Lag B'Omer as the festival of the downfall of Hitlerism, it is important to examine at greater length the history and development of this festival.

IN THE TALMUDIC PERIOD

The Talmud makes no mention of a mourning period in the days of Sefirah, or of any special significance attached to Lag B'Omer. We do know that Rabbi Akiva supported Bar Kochba (Jer. *Taanit* 4). We also have an account of the death of Rabbi Akiva's disciples, all of whom are alleged to have died within the period between Passover and Shavuot. We quote from one source: "Rabbi Akiva had twelve thousand pairs of disciples from Gabat to Antipatris [according to *Breishit Rabba*, chap. 61, "from Acco to Antipatris"], and they all died within a short period of time because they were not respectful of each other. . . . It was alleged that they died between Passover and Shavuot. Said Rav Cahna Bar Abo: 'They all died a cruel death.' What was it? Said Rav Nachman: 'It was the croup' " (*Yevamot* 62b).

A superficial reading of the above passage fails to indicate any rabbinic intent or even justification for the establishment of a mourning period in memory of Rabbi Akiva's disciples. Further analysis, however, reveals many puzzling aspects. What is the significance of the information that the disciples came from an area bounded by "Gabat and Antipatris"? Why was the number of the disciples given as "twelve thousand pairs" instead of twenty-four thousand? How can this number be reconciled with twelve thousand indicated in another source (*Breishit Rabba*, chap. 61) and the three hundred given in still another source (*Tanchuma, Chaye Sarah* 8)? What was the motive behind the talmudic effort to destroy the reputation of these disciples? If we examine this passage against the background of Bar Kochba's rebellion, we may find an answer to all these questions.

The expression "from Gabat to Antipatris" came into use in the third century, in addition to the older geographic demarcation of "from Dan to Beersheba" (*Shir HaShirim Rabba* 4:11, *Sanhedrin* 94b). The later designation was apparently used to describe the shrunken Jewish area of Palestine, resulting from the practical depopulation of the province of Judea of its Jewish inhabitants following Bar Kochba's rebellion. Rabbi Horowitz, author of the geographic encyclopedia *Eretz Yisrael Ushchenoteha* (s.v. "Gabat"), rightly concluded that the area between Gabat and Antipatris encompassed primarily the Samarian lowlands, where the bulk of the Jewish population was concentrated in talmudic times. Antipatris is situated on the boundary line between Judea and the northern province of Samaria. Gabat was situated to the north of Samaria in the lower Galilee. Both outposts are associated with the history of Roman assults upon Palestine. Josephus relates (*Life* 24) that the Roman decurion Ebutius procured the assistance of the inhabitants of Gabat in his attack upon the Jewish forces under Josephus' Galilean command. Antipatris was an important Roman garrison fortress used by Cestius and later Vespasian in their assaults upon Jerusalem. By tracing the place of origin of Rabbi Akiva's disciples, the authors make a subtle allusion to their background, thus explaining the motivation behind their ultimate role in the Judeo-Roman conflict.

The thousands of young men who were influenced by Rabbi Akiva are referred to in the talmudic text as *talmidim*. We may assume that this term is not to be given its literal translation—"students" or "scholars." Even allowing for a chronicler's exaggeration, it is impossible for one man to instruct thousands of students. A more logical translation of *talmidim* in this instance is "followers," men who looked to the sage for guidance and inspiration. The actual number of Rabbi Akiva's students is most likely indicated in the source which limits them to three hundred. These were augmented by thousands who followed their lead. There seems to have come down a tradition which described the number of these followers to have totaled twelve thousand. Another source clarified the organizational make-up of these twelve thousand, stating that they consisted of *zugot*—"pairs" or "teams." This term was apparently used in a reference to Bar Kochba's initial military strategy, which called for guerilla-type underground warfare, carried out by teams (*zugot*) which infiltrated behind Roman positions throughout the land.

The same technical and unique connotation of *zugot* is also implied in a talmudic reference to the last Jewish rebellion against Rome, which broke out more than two centuries after Bar Kochba's uprising. The Talmud quotes from a secret note which was sent to Rava in Babylonia, containing the following coded message: "A team came from Reket and they were seized by the eagle. In their hands was a product made in Luz (and what is it? The blue dye called *techeilet*). Thanks to the mercies of the Almighty and their own virtue, they escaped unharmed . . . " (*Sanhedrin* 12a). This enigmatic message was undoubtedly sent during the anti-Roman uprising in Palestine against the oppressive policies and religious repressions of the

Christian emperor Gallus, in the years 351–52. The cities of Tiberias, Sepphoris, and Lud spearheaded the rebellion. Once more there were *zugot* abroad, harassing in guerilla fashion the movement of the Roman legions stationed in Palestine, in anticipation of an attack upon the Parthians. The renascent Jewish nationalist party was mercilessly crushed and the patriots were hunted down. The latter sought to escape their Roman hunters by fleeing to the Jewish community of Babylonia, which was under Parthian rule. The Persian king, Shapur II, was not overly friendly to the Jews. However, Rava, the outstanding Babylonian Amora of his generation, was able to secure protection for the Jewish community through the influence and friendship of the king's mother. The coded message informed Rava that a *zug* (a patriotic team) from Reket (Tiberias, one of the three rebelling cities) had been seized by the Romans (the eagle). The message continues that "in their hands was a product of Luz." The sentence which follows was put by me in parenthesis because it is obviously a later interpolation. Since it purports to decode one of the items in the message, it could not have been part of the original text. This interpolation interprets the "product of Luz" to mean a blue dye, used in producing the blue strands which were attached with some white strands as fringes (*tzitzit*) on the four corners of a garment. The significance of the blue dye or blue strand which they carried in their hands is somewhat obscure. However, the answer may be found in the association of the blue and white strands with the pursuit of freedom. The biblical passage which commands the attachment of fringes links this injunction with the exodus from Egypt: "bid them that they make throughout their generations fringes in the corners of their garments, and that they put with the fringe of each corner a thread of blue. . . . I am the Lord, your God, who brought you out of the land of Egypt . . ." (Num. 15:38, 41). The blue strands were possibly carried by the *zugot* as an insignia, disclosing to their fellow Jews their affiliation with the patriotic freedom-fighters. A strikingly similar code was used by Marranos in the sixteenth century. An official of the synagogue used to attach a piece of cloth to his finger and walk through the town. This was a signal to the Marranos to assemble in the synagogue for prayer. We may note, incidentally, that the blue and white of the fringes might have been regarded, even in the fourth century, as the colors of the Jewish nationalist movement. The message further informed Rava that the *zug* had slipped out of the Roman trap thanks to the mercies of the Almighty (who thus indicated his approval of the rebellion) and their own great virtue (the patriotic cause was considered a virtuous cause).

RABBINIC ATTITUDE TO BAR KOCHBA

The commendation of the activities of the *zugot* expressed in the message to Rava is absent from the passage which describes the death of Rabbi Akiva's *zugot*, who were involved in the Bar Kochba rebellion. The uprising itself was played down by the Talmud. There were historical reasons for the rabbinic disapproval. Rabban Yochanan b. Zaccai, in the days of Titus, had indicated his opposition to useless bloodshed. Rome's overwhelming might ruled out the possibility of a Jewish victory. The venerable rabbi favored a peaceful coexistence with Rome in return for a guarantee of freedom of religion. The rabbis of Bar Kochba's generation similarly preferred a peaceful coexistence with Hadrian. The tragic end amply justified their stand. To discourage any future rebellion, which was foredoomed to defeat, the rabbinic editors glossed over Bar Kochba's rebellion and denied to Rabbi Akiva's followers the status of heroes. They quoted a tradition which noted that these followers had perished in the period between Passover and Shavuot. To further disassociate their death from martyrdom, they were said to have died from the croup, which had decimated them within a short period of time (*Yevamot* 62b). One may note an ironic bitterness in the nature of the sickness which allegedly caused their deaths. It is called *askero*, a choking death due to difficulty of breathing. It was considered the most painful of deaths (*Berachot* 8a). This sickness was probably singled out because of the relation of the term *askero* to a biblical verse: *Ki yisacher pi dovre sheker*—"the mouth of them that speak lies shall be stopped" (Ps. 63:12). Rabbi Nachman, the author of the *askero* statement, had good personal reasons for the denunciation of futile rebellions. His native city. Nehardea, was destroyed, and he became a refugee, as a result of an uprising in which Jews had taken a prominent part.

The distinguished rabbi of the fourth century confirmed rabbinic policy adopted in the first century. Surrender of political freedom was the price of religious freedom. The appalling loss of life suffered in the rebellions of the first and second centuries, without any compensatory gains, brought the realization that the restoration of Jewish national independence was to remain a basic aspiration to be proclaimed in a daily prayer, but its implementation was to be deferred to a more propitious moment in the distant future. The collapse of the Roman Empire was deemed a precondition to the revival of a Jewish state (*Megillah* 6a). Messiah himself was alleged to be imprisoned at the gates of Rome (*Sanhedrin* 98a). No Roman province had ever succeeded in regaining its independence. Rome could not afford the stigma of a defeat by Judea. Only a Parthian victory could bring hope of a renewed Jewish state. Until such time as conditions warranted a national revival, Jewish energy and all the resources of the people were to be used in defense of religious freedom even unto death. The prospects for victory in this struggle were much more promising.

Rabbi Akiva and his followers defied the majority opinion of their colleagues and thus earned rabbinic censure. The moral justification for the sudden death of the students was said to have been their arrogance. This, too, is an indirect reference to their part in the rebellion. Young fighters, imbued with a sense of patriotism and self-confidence, generally possess an exuberance bordering on arrogance. Such arrogance was attributed by the Talmud to Bar Kochba himself (*Sanhedrin* 93b). He was even accused of blasphemy (Jer. *Taanit*, chap. 4). As a result, a great epoch in Jewish history and its prime movers were relegated to practical oblivion. Only Rabbi Akiva's reputation was spared due to his immortal contributions to Judaism.

In justice to the rabbinic appreciation of the importance of history in the development of the people, we must add that they did not completely erase the memory of Bar Kochba's rebellion from national consciousness. They attempted to perpetuate it through an association with an old traditional fast and a feast. The fall of Betar, the last stronghold of Bar Kochba, was said to have taken place on Tisha B'Av (*Taanit* 26b). Thus Jews were requested to bewail this tragedy even as they mourned the loss of the Temple and independence. The permission to bury the dead of Betar, marking the termination of the Hadrianic persecutions, is alleged to have been granted on the fifteenth of Av (*Taanit* 31a). The end of the slaughter of Jewish youth was to be observed on a traditional social festival dedicated to youth. It was on that day, at the end of an agricultural season, that young men and maidens were introduced to each other at huge outdoor parties for the purpose of matrimony (*Taanit* 26b).

GEONIC REVISION

The Geonic period (7–11th cent.), far removed from the stirring passions which had rocked Jewry in the first two centuries of the common era, witnessed an objective reevaluation of Jewish history. The military exploits of the Hasmoneans, played down by the Talmud, were given new prominence in the eighth-century prayer of *Al HaNisim*. The same pattern is discernible in the evolution of the historical account of Bar Kochba's rebellion. The heroic stature of Rabbi Akiva's students was restored in acknowledgement of their participation in the fight against Rome. Bar Kochba himself, however, still remained under a cloud, probably as a result of the blasphemous arrogance attributed to him in one talmudic source. With the rise of secular nationalism in modern times, Bar Kochba regained his heroic place in Jewish history. This process was further enhanced by the discovery of a rich treasure of Bar Kochba documents by Israeli archaeologists in 1960 and 1961. These portray the leader as a man deeply concerned with the religious needs of his soldiers. This is hardly compatible with the traditional image of a warrior given to blasphemy.

The rehabilitation of the Maccabees came early in the Geonic period. The rehabilitation of Rabbi Akiva's disciples came toward the end of the Geonic period. Rav Shrira Gaon (d. 1001) was the first rabbinic authority to attribute their death to the "persecutions," thus ignoring the traditional story of the plague (*Iggeret Rav Shrira Gaon*). The first authority to mention the prohibition of marriage ceremonies in the Sefirah period was Rabbi Isaac b. Judah Ibn Ghayyat (d. 1098), who quoted Rav Hai Gaon as his source (Rav Hai, son of Rav Shrira, d. 1038). Rabbenu Yerucham (14th cent.) also quoted Rav Hai Gaon as the source for the prohibition of work from sunset to sunrise, in the Sefirah period, in commemoration of the death of Rabbi Akiva's disciples. The suggestion by some modern scholars that the prohibition of marriage during Sefirah was a superstition borrowed from the Romans which forbade marriages in May (Abrahams, *Jewish Life in the Middle Ages*, chap. 9) need not be taken seriously. Roman influence affected Palestinian Jewry first and then spread to Babylonia. The Sefirah restrictions originated in Babylonia.

EMERGENCE OF LAG B'OMER

The earliest-known rabbinic authority to mention Lag B'Omer was Rabbi Zerachiah b. Isaac Halevi Gerondi (d. 1186, quoted in *Tur, Orach Chaim* 493). He did not attach any special significance to Lag B'Omer nor did he consider it a semi-holiday. He was quoted as saying that the Sefirah restrictions continue in force only until Lag B'Omer and are discontinued thereafter. The basis for this opinion is an alleged midrash which states that Rabbi Akiva's disciples died between Passover and "midway" to Shavuot (*ad prosat ha-Atzeret*).

Rabbi Menachem b. Solomon Meiri (d. 1306) stated that the tradition of Lag B'Omer had come down from the Geonic period. He mentioned that it was customary not to fast on Lag B'Omer (Commentary on *Yevamot* 62b). He was thus the first authority to indicate the festive aspect of Lag B'Omer.

Rabbi Jacob b. Moses Halevi Mohlin (d. 1472) listed Lag B'Omer in his popular work, *Minhagim*, as a semi-festival. He stretched some historical facts in his search for a basis for this festival. His contribution to its development, however, was significant as a result of his introduction of a positive note to the festive character of Lag B'Omer. In addition to refraining from fasting on Lag B'Omer, he stated that "one should rejoice on the thirty-third day." Rabbi Mohlin's influence on the customs and traditions of European Ashkenazi communities was far-reaching.

The great cabalists of the sixteenth and seventeenth centuries contributed further to the evolution of Lag B'Omer as a festival and day of religious ecstasy. Due to their interpretation, a new historical perspective was incidentally brought into focus. This was accomplished by the fusing of two distinct traditions—the tradition of Lag B'Omer, and the tradition of the yahrzeit of Rabbi Simon b. Yochai, which falls on the same day. Rabbi Chaim Vital (d. 1620) stated that Rabbi Simon b. Yochai was one of Rabbi Akiva's disciples who died in the Sefirah period. Another cabalist work (*Nofet Tzufim*) stated that Rabbi Simon b. Yochai was the last of these disciples to die. His death on Lag B'Omer, it alleged, was an atonement for his generation, and thereafter the harsh divine decree was suspended.

The cabalists' view that Rabbi Simon b. Yochai was one of the students who had perished in the plague (or in the war) is hardly in keeping with the talmudic statement that after the death of his disciples, Rabbi Akiva moved to southern Palestine, where he ordained five students. Rabbi Simon b. Yochai was one of them (*Yevamot* 62b). The fact remains, however, that the cabalists made Rabbi Simon, the traditional author of the Zohar, the central figure of Lag B'Omer. Rabbi Simon had been condemned to death by the Romans. He succeeded in eluding his pursuers and survived the Hadrianic persecutions. He later headed the delegation which went to Rome to intercede with the authorities for the abrogation of Hadrian's anti-Jewish decrees. Lag B'Omer thus became indirectly a holiday marking the end of an ancient persecution which had cost the lives of hundreds of thousands of Jews and the survival of the Jewish people.

In summation, we may conclude that Lag B'Omer was introduced in the eleventh century, in the days of Rav Hai Gaon. At the outset it was not a semi-festival but merely the first day when the restrictions of mourning which had been imposed after Passover were lifted. The day gradually assumed a festive character to mark the suspension of mourning which had preceded it.

What was the real reason for the Geonic conclusion of the mourning period by Lag B'Omer? It is hardly plausible that an obscure midrash quoted by Rabbi Zerachiah Girondi to the effect that Rabbi Akiva's students died in the period "between Passover and midway to Shavuot" was the real basis for this limitation. Our talmudic version contradicts the midrashic text, omitting the qualifying phrase "and midway" to Shavuot. The true answer to this question is still shrouded in mystery. A possible clue to this puzzle may be found in the history of the first rebellion against Rome in the year 66. The first Jewish reprisal against a Roman legion took place on the seventeenth of Iyar, when the Roman governor of Syria, Cestius Gallus, came to Jerusalem to loot the Temple (Josephus, *Wars* 2. 15:6). The surprise attack caused him to retreat from the city. Professor Klausner considered this attack the opening of the rebellion against Rome (*Hist. shel Bayit Sheni*, vol. 5, chap. 11). Rav Hai Gaon, like his father, Rav Shrira, was well versed in Jewish history. In reinterpreting the role of Rabbi Akiva's disciples in the struggle against Rome, Rav Shrira adopted the objective view of a historian. It is plausible to assume that the Geonim felt that the mourning for Bar Kochba's defeat should terminate on the eighteenth of Iyar, which was the anniversary of the outbreak of the initially victorious first rebellion of the Jews against Rome.

Lag B'Omer, the festival of the survival of the Jewish people despite the Roman persecutions, is also the proper day for celebrating the survival of the Jewish people despite the Nazi persecutions. What is most remarkable is the coincidental historical significance of this day in the story of the collapse of the Nazi tyranny. The close of the Hitlerian era symbolically came with the end of Hitler's physical existence. Adolf Hitler committed suicide, according to reliable testimony received by the Allies, on April 30, 1945 at 3:30 P.M. This corresponded to the seventeenth of Iyar, 5705. His body was set aflame in the late afternoon, and it burned until dusk. The eighteenth of Iyar, which is Lag B'Omer, therefore marks the end of the Hitlerian era.

It is not within the purview of this essay to discuss the manner of celebrating such a festival. Only time and tradition can fix a meaningful ritual. At the outset, it should present an educational opportunity to link the great historical events which are associated with the eighteenth of Iyar, the first rebellion against Rome in the post-Temple era, the survival of the Jewish people after the defeat of Bar Kochba, and the most recent Jewish survival of the Nazi Holocaust. The celebration should also serve as an occasion of thanksgiving for the fortunate turn of events, leading to the termination of a catastrophe which, but for the providential manifestations, could have ended in total disaster.

9

Shavuot

AN APPENDAGE OF PASSOVER

THERE IS AMPLE evidence in the Bible supporting the rabbinic view that Shavuot marks the concluding phase of Passover (*Pesikta* 30:163). In the first place, we must note the absence of a fixed date for Shavuot, which one would normally expect in the case of an independent holiday. Prior to the establishment of a permanent rabbinic calendar, Shavuot used to fall on the fifth, sixth, or seventh of Sivan, depending upon the number of days in the months of Nisan and Iyar. The only fixed element in the date of Shavuot was the interval of time between it and Passover. Shavuot was always on the fiftieth day after the first day of Passover. Thus there was established a chronological link between the two festivals.

In the second place, we must note the absence of a substantive name for Shavuot. The Bible designated it once as the Festival of the Harvest (Exod. 23:16). This merely identified it with an agricultural season. It was also called the Day of the First Fruits (Num. 28:26). That, too, was not the name of the festival. Indeed, it was never labeled the Festival of the First Fruits. The text merely specified the time by pointing to the day on which the first fruits are offered.

The same verse, however, does mention the name by which the holiday is commonly known, Shavuot ("weeks"). This name is not descriptive of the character and substance of the festival. It is a chronological tag which addresses itself to the time lapse between Passover and Shavuot and thus emphasizes the relationship and interdependence of the two holidays.

It may be helpful to draw a parallel to the structure of the festival of Sukkot. This holiday has a total number of eight days, seven days of Sukkot (Lev. 23:34) and an added distinct festival, Atzeret, appended to the festival as an eighth and concluding day. On Passover, too, we have the seven days of Passover. The eighth day was not appended to the festival but is celebrated on the fiftieth day after the Omer. Consequently, it could not technically be designated Atzeret, a name reserved for the last day of a holiday, although it was that in substance. The Bible refers to the seventh day of Passover as Atzeret (Deut. 16:8). In rabbinic terminology, however, beginning with *Targum Onkelos* (Num. 28:26), Shavuot became known as Atzeret.

The parallel between Passover-Shavuot and Sukkot—Shmini Atzeret seems to be indicated in the twenty-third chapter of Leviticus, which lists the rituals of all festivals. It begins with the Festival of Matzot (v. 6) and then enjoins the counting of fifty days and "there shall be a holy convocation (*mikra kodesh*) unto you" (v. 21). The text fails to designate the festival by any name whatever, as if it were still part of the previously mentioned holiday of Passover. A similar phrase is used in connection with Sukkot. "On the fifteenth day of the seventh month is the festival of Sukkot, seven days unto the Lord" (v. 34). This is followed in the thirty-sixth verse by the statement, "On the eighth day shall be a holy convocation unto you."

The reason for the postponement of Shavuot was apparently related to the fact that Passover, like Sukkot, has a dual motif—historical and agricultural. The historical phase of Passover is the commemoration of the end of Egyptian bondage (on the evening of the fourteenth of Nisan) and the exodus (during the balance of the festival). Passover was also a spring festival, linked to the beginning of the harvest season. The agricultural aspect of the holiday began on the second day of Passover (the first day was dedicated exclusively to the theme of the exodus). It was the ritual of the Omer, the offering of a measure of barley, the earliest of the new cereal crops, that marked the harvest season. Wheat did not ripen until fifty days later. The beginning of its harvest was marked on Shavuot with the offering of *lechem habikkurim*. This concluded the celebration of the grain harvest, which had started on the second day of Passover.

Accordingly, the historical and agricultural phases of Passover were each celebrated for seven days. The exodus theme was marked during the seven days of Passover. The ripening of the harvest was marked on the last six days of Passover and on Shavuot (*sfirat haOmer* was a reminder that the celebration of the agricultural phase would be completed on Shavuot).

On Sukkot, too, the historical and agricultural phases were marked for seven days each. The theme of the exodus was marked for seven days by the Sukkah (Lev. 23:43), and the gathering of the harvest was simultaneously celebrated for seven days with the ritual of the etrog and lulav. The festival of Sukkot, therefore, came to an end after seven days. To equalize the length of both major festivals, an additional day was added to Sukkot, Shmini Atzeret. It was declared a holiday, though no longer associated with the dual themes of Sukkot.

The opinion that the relationship of Shavuot to Passover parallels that of Shmini Atzeret to Sukkot is expressed in rabbinic literature (*Pesikta D'Rav Kahana, B'Yom HaShmini Atzeret; Shir HaShirim Rabba 7; Daat HaZekenim MiBaale Ha Tosafot*, Num. 28:25): "The holiday of Shmini Atzeret should have been observed fifty days after Sukkot in the same manner as Shavuot is observed fifty days after Passover. However, a special Pilgrimage Festival in the summer season is not an inconvenience for pilgrims, whereas, an additional Pilgrimage Festival in the rainy season would entail much hardship. For that reason the Almighty appended it to Sukkot." The rabbinic author failed to note that the deferment of Shavuot was dictated by an agricultural schedule and that a similar delay of Shmini Atzeret would serve no religious purpose.

It is quite clear that the rabbinic name for Shavuot, Atzeret ("concluding festival"), rests on a very sound biblical basis. Josephus, too, mentions Atzeret as the name by which Jews identify the festival of Shavuot (*Antiquities* 3. 10). The translator of Josephus erroneously equated the Hebrew Atzeret with the Greek Pentecost.

THE LENGTH OF FESTIVALS

The conclusion that Shavuot is the seventh day of the agricultural spring festival, and that the celebration of the exodus was also spread over seven days (the same being true of Sukkot), leads us to the question why these observances were set apart from the observance of Rosh HaShanah and Yom Kippur, which were limited to one day. The answer to this question may likely lie in the fact that the agricultural festival was a thanksgiving for the creation of the earth, a process which took seven days. Similarly, the exodus period encompassed the seven days between the departure on the fifteenth of Nisan and the crossing of the Red Sea on the twenty-first day of Nisan.

The observance of eight days of Chanukah had been attributed by the author of II Maccabees to an analogy with Sukkot. This explanation is obviously erroneous inasmuch as Chanukah commemorates neither the creation nor the exodus. The rabbinic story of the miracle of the oil offers the only traditional explanation of the length of Chanukah.

An analysis of the dual aspects of Passover and Sukkot still leaves one question unanswered. Were the two phases related to each other, or was it pure chance that the exodus and agricultural celebrations fell together because of the coincidence of Passover and Sukkot with the spring and fall seasons of the year? There is no doubt that there is a substantive link between the two. The fact that the biblical text demands that Passover be celebrated in the spring (requiring an adjustment of the lunar calendar to the solar year) and that the exodus be also commemorated during the agricultural fall festival (for which there is no historical basis at that time of the year) clearly indicates a close association between the two phases.

What was the nature of this link? The Abrahamitic covenant spelled out a divine commitment that the exodus would culminate in the restoration of the Jewish people in Palestine, where they would enjoy the bounty of the land (Gen. 15:13–16).

The bounty of the harvest was an annual affirmation of the covenant and the fulfillment of an important objective of the exodus. The two phases were therefore intertwined on Passover and Sukkot. Shavuot, too, played a similar role in its relation to Passover.

PASSOVER AND SHAVUOT

In what sense does Shavuot complement Passover? It completes the celebration of the exodus by rejoicing in the great bounty which the land, blessed by the Almighty, had given. On Passover one dwelt on the oppression and slavery of the past. In the seven weeks which followed, one was busy harvesting barley and wheat. On Shavuot the Jewish farmer could pause to give voice to his joy in his current prosperity. The emphasis was on the present rather than the past. The true character of Shavuot was set by the text in Deuteronomy: "Seven weeks shalt thou number unto thee from the time the sickle is first put to the standing corn . . . and thou shalt keep the feast of Shavuot unto the Lord thy God . . . and thou shalt rejoice before the Lord thy God, thou . . . and thy slave . . . and thou shalt remember that thou wast a slave in Egypt . . ." (Deut. 16:9–12).

There were two distinct Shavuot rituals by means of which the religious objective of the holiday was given symbolic expression. The first ritual provided for the bringing of the wave-loaves of bread (*lechem tnufah*), which were to be baked from the new crop of wheat (Lev. 23:17). Thus one expressed his gratitude to God for the new crop. We must call attention to a specific requirement—the two loaves of bread had to be leavened (*chametz*). This is in complete contrast to the Passover bread, which had to be unleavened. The latter was symbolic of poverty, the former was to be the symbol of wealth and abundance. Philo, too, noted that "leavened bread is an emblem of the most perfect and entire food."

The second distinct ritual was the *bikkurim*, the choicest first-fruits were to be brought to the Sanctuary, beginning with Shavuot. This presented another opportunity for recalling the adversity of the Egyptian period and rejoicing in the happy state which followed the conquest of Palestine. The recitation which accompanied the presentation of the basket of first-fruits to the priest is very enlightening: "And thou shalt come unto the priest that shall be in those days, and say unto him, 'I told [*higadti*] unto the Lord thy God, that I came into the land which the Lord swore unto our fathers to give us' " (Deut. 26:3). The bearer of the *bikkurim* thus affirmed in the introduction to this ritual that God had kept his promise to the patriarchs that he would bring their children back to Palestine. The Hebrew verb *higadti* ("I told") appears anomalous in the context of this affirmation. What was the occasion for this telling? Does one "tell" God? Is "telling" the equivalent of prayer? Most exegetes render *higadti*, "I thanked." Rabbi Abraham Ibn Ezra mentions this translation, but he suggests that it might be translated literally—I told, "so that the young children may understand." One may recall the previous biblical injunction where the same verb was used: *ve higadta l'bincha* (Exod. 13:8), "and you shall tell your son." At that time he told his son the tale of slavery and redemption. On Shavuot he continued in the same spirit—I told my son today that we owe all this bounty to God.

After the presentation of the basket to the priest, the bearer of the *bikkurim* recited as follows: "A wandering Aramean was my father, and he went down into Egypt. . . . and the Egyptian dealt ill with us, and afflicted us . . . and we cried unto the Lord, the God of our fathers, and the Lord heard our voice. . . . and the Lord brought us forth out of Egypt with a mighty hand . . . with signs and with wonders. And he hath brought us into this place, and hath given us this land, a land flowing with milk and honey . . ." The text concludes with the injunction: "And thou shalt rejoice in all the good which the Lord thy God hath given unto thee and unto thy house, thou and the Levite and the stranger that is in the midst of thee" (Deut. 26:5–11). Thus the wandering of Jacob and the enslavement of his children are given as the background for the joy which followed the exodus and the conquest of Palestine.

The significance of the rituals of the paschal lamb and

bikkurim, as the two sides of the same coin, was greatly enhanced by the fact that they had to be performed in the Sanctuary at a time when the presence of all Jewish males was required. This is the implication of two nearly identical passages in the Bible, Exodus 23:14–19 and 34:18–26. At first the text commands the observance of these festivals. This is followed by an explanatory verse that marks them as Pilgrimage Festivals. Following this verse only two rituals are singled out: "Thou shalt not offer the blood of my sacrifice with leavened bread. . . . The choicest first fruits of the land thou shalt bring into the house of the Lord thy God." The common significance that linked the two rituals was the Passover theme.

THE DATE OF THE GIVING OF THE LAW

In the course of time a new theme was added to the festival of Shavuot, the celebration of the giving of the Law on Mount Sinai. This celebration originated in the exilic period of Jewish history. The destruction of the Temple in the year 70, and the abolition of the *bikkurim* ritual and other sacrificial rites, created a need for a new contemporary motif, not related to the agricultural season. Shavuot was the only one of the three Pilgrimage Festivals which had no distinctive ritual. By stressing the anniversary of the Law, the rabbis linked Shavuot with the survival of Judaism rather than with the Jewish land, and thus gave the festival a new and broad perspective.

The adjustments which were made in Jewish religious life after the destruction of the Temple were, of necessity, slow and gradual. A substantial area of our customs and ceremonies had to be adapted to new conditions. All practices dependent upon a functioning Temple had to be abolished. The Jewish credo, its hopes and aspirations, had to be restated. A formal order of prayers had to be created and given a place of centrality in the rebuilt structure of Jewish existence. A nation had to be converted into a religious brotherhood, without extinguishing entirely its national memories and vestiges. One can readily understand why all the exilic innovations were not introduced immediately after the destruction of the Temple. The process of adaptation was a continuous one, frequently hampered by Roman persecutions, spread out over many centuries.

When did Shavuot acquire its new motif as the anniversary of the giving of the Law? The earliest source to indicate a link between Shavuot and the covenant was the Book of Jubilees. It refers specifically to the covenants with Noah, Abraham, and Moses. It does not, however, extend this link to the Sinaitic revelation. It is assumed that the Book of Jubilees was written in the first century B.C.E. Since its author was not a member of a rabbinic school, and his method of calculating the lunar (ecclesiastic) calendar was inconsistent with the traditionally accepted calendar, this book had no impact upon the religious life of the people. Philo and Josephus, writing in the first century C.E., made no mention of the link between Shavuot and the Law. Indeed, we may assume that few people were aware of the date of the revelation on Mount Sinai, and those who were might have considered the identical anniversaries as coincidental.

What is most likely the earliest talmudic statement on the date of the revelation on Mount Sinai may be found in the tractate *Shabbat* (86b). According to the calculations of the Rabbanan, the Jews left Egypt on Friday, the fifteenth of Nisan. The Torah was given on Saturday, the sixth of Sivan. If we examine the latter date, we discover that it was the equivalent of the fiftieth day of the Omer, the day on which Shavuot was permanently fixed in the Scriptures.

Rabbi Jose (2nd cent.) offers a dissenting view. He states that the Jews left Egypt on Thursday, the fifteenth of Nisan, and that the Law was given on Saturday, the seventh of Sivan. It is interesting to note that the ecclesiastic calendar of the Book of Jubilees corroborates Rabbi Jose's date of the giving of the Law. This calendar is divided into thirteen months of twenty-eight days each. The seventh day of every month always falls on the Sabbath. The first Saturday in the month of Sivan in the Exodus year fell on the seventh of that month. The calendrical calculations of the Qumran sect are also in agreement with Rabbi Jose's date of the giving of the Law. According to Professor Yadin, the ecclesiastic calendar of the Qumran sect is in accord with the solar calendar of the Book of Jubilees, twelve months of thirty days each, with an intercalary day at the end of every three months. Following his reconstruction of the Qumran calendar, the Jews left Egypt on Wednesday. Nisan 15, and received the Law on Saturday, Sivan 7.

The author of *Magen Avraham (Orach Chaim* 494) points out that the seventh of Sivan was the equivalent of the fifty-first day of Omer, one day after the fixed day of Shavuot. Consequently Shavuot could not mark the anniversary of the Law. It seems rather obvious that at the time of Rabbi Jose, a survivor of the Hadrianic persecution following the defeat of Bar Kochba in 135 C.E., there was not yet a clearly established tradition linking Shavuot with the Law. Indeed, neither Rabbi Jose nor the Rabbanan mention Shavuot in the context of their discussion of the date of the Law.

The preliminary step in the development of the exilic Shavuot was the official establishment of the date of the revelation on Mount Sinai. It was the date indicated by the Rabbanan (Sivan 6) which was accepted by the majority of the rabbis. The first major rabbinic historical work, *Seder Olam,* of which the aforementioned Rabbi Jose is said to have been the editor (*Yevamot* 82b), adopted the view of the Rabbanan. This work thus placed an authoritative stamp of historical authenticity upon the date of the sixth of Sivan. However, even the *Seder Olam* seems to have attached no special significance to the coincidence of this date with Shavuot.

The publication of the *Seder Olam* made the date of the Law common knowledge. The linking of the Torah with Shavuot was a logical development that followed shortly thereafter. The first official connection of the two is quoted in a passage in *Midrash Shmot Rabba* (chap. 31), attributed to Rabbi Meir. Mention is made of the "Festival of the Harvest on which the Torah was given to Israel." It appears that this sentence is part of Rabbi Meir's statement.

Rabbi Meir, a contemporary of Rabbi Jose, had also witnessed the disastrous consequences of Bar Kochba's defeat. The hope for a speedy restoration of Jewish national independence was completely shattered. Many Jews must have left Palestine during the Hadrianic persecutions to join the growing diaspora. Rabbi Meir was among the sages who were members of the Sanhedrin in Usha, convoked in 140 C.E. under the leadership of Rabban Simon b. Gamliel. This Sanhedrin, like its predecessor in Yavneh headed by Rabban Gamliel, had to promulgate many new decrees to ameliorate Jewish life and give it new hope. We may assume that the exilic Shavuot, commemorating the giving of the Law, was sanctioned at Usha. The festival was thus given a universal motif of equal importance to the Jews of Palestine and the diaspora.

The growing supremacy of Torah scholarship in Jewish life gradually enhanced the festive aspects of Shavuot. Rabbi Elazar and later Rabbi Joseph, both sages of the third century, emphasized the need for feasting and rejoicing on this day (*Pesachim* 68b). However, the extraordinary feasting associated with Shavuot was somewhat played down in post-talmudic times, with the emergence of Simchat Torah as the occasion for intense joy and festivity. Characteristically, Jews found greater cause for rejoicing on a festival marking the study of the Torah than the one marking the giving of the Torah.

FALASHA DATE OF SHAVUOT

The Falashas observe Shavuot on the twelfth of Sivan because it is the fiftieth day after the conclusion of Passover. Thus they agree with the rabbinic interpretation of the term *shabbat*, mentioned in the biblical injunction to count fifty days (Lev. 23:15), as a reference to the festival of Passover rather than the day of the Sabbath. However, according to the Falasha tradition, the counting is to begin on the conclusion of the festival of Passover and not at the end of the first day of the festival.

The Falashas observe Shavuot as the day of the giving of the Law. In this respect, too, they follow rabbinic tradition. Their source, however, is not the Talmud, with which they were not familiar. It is undoubtedly the Book of Jubilees. They did not adopt, however, the Shavuot date established by the Book of Jubilees, the fifteenth of Sivan. The author of Jubilees followed a special ecclesiastic calendar, consisting of thirteen months of twenty-eight days each. As a result, each of the three Pilgrimage Festivals falls on a Sunday on the fifteenth of the month. The Falashas follow the traditional lunar calendar.

The talmudic date of the giving of the Law is Sivan 6 or 7 (*Shabbat* 86b). This is the date of the proclamation of the Decalogue. There may be some basis also for the date of Sivan 12 if we consider the giving of the Law, not the proclamation of the Decalogue, but the date of the commencement of instruction in the Torah, which Moses received, according to tradition, while on Mount Sinai. The biblical text reads as follows: "And Moses went up into the mount . . . and the cloud covered it six days; and the seventh day He called unto Moses" (Exod. 24:15–16). According to Rabbi Jose Haglili's interpretation (*Yoma* 4a), Moses was isolated for six days following the proclamation of the Decalogue. On the seventh day he began to receive instruction. That day was the twelfth of Sivan.

10

The Second Festival Day of the Diaspora

INTRODUCTION

RABBINIC SCHOLARS HAVE questioned the need for an additional day of Shavuot (Zevin, *HaMoadim BaHalacha*, Shavuot). The question is based on the fact that Shavuot must always fall on the fiftieth day of the Omer. The considerable period of time between Passover and Shavuot provided ample opportunity to ascertain the date of Passover as it was fixed by the Sanhedrin in Jerusalem, and hence one could easily calculate the true date of Shavuot. This would obviate the need for a second day. In answer to this question, scholars have pointed to a passage in the code of Maimonides: "And in order to avoid differences between festivals, the sages decreed that every locality too distant to be reached by messengers [dispatched by the Sanhedrin], an additional day is to be observed, even in the case of Shavuot" (*Kiddush HaChodesh* 3:12). The expression "even in the case of Shavuot" indicates clearly that Maimonides felt there was no basic reason for an additional day of Shavuot. It was only for the sake of uniformity that a second day was added to all holidays.

The source for Maimonides' statement is a talmudic text (*Rosh HaShanah* 21a) which quotes a decree of Rabbi Yochanan that every community which must add a day to Sukkot, due to a lack of information from Jerusalem, must similarly add a day to

191

Passover, even if the required information is then available. This text does not specify whether a day is to be added to Shavuot as well. Maimonides obviously interpreted Rabbi Yochanan's decree to cover all festivals. There are indeed other talmudic sources which mention the "second day of the festival of Shavuot (*Pesachim* 52a).

The reason for an additional day of Shavuot is, in reality, not as obscure as the original question would make it out to be. In Palestine and in the countries contiguous to it, within reach of the messengers from Jerusalem, no festival (with the exception of Rosh HaShanah) required an additional day. The distant communities, not linked to Jerusalem by regular communications, were not likely to discover the dates of Rosh Chodesh Nisan and Tishri (i.e., whether Adar and Elul had twenty-nine or thirty days). The Sanhedrin made every effort to inform even the furthest community of the intercalation of a second Adar, but it could never hope to transmit the date of every Rosh Chodesh to them. Such communities were compelled to add one day to Passover and also, for the same reason, to Shavuot. There are, of course, many obscure areas in the development of the "second festival day of the diaspora" (*yom tov sheni shel galuyot*). When, by whom, and in which countries was it instituted? To answer this question we must explore the history of the early diaspora itself and the extent to which it depended upon the religious leadership of Palestinian Jewry. We must also examine the laws which regulate the fixing of the calendar and the identity of the person or body vested with the authority to fix the calendar.

INTERCALATION

For the purposes of our study, it is not necessary to complicate this note by a detailed account of the rules of the calendar. It is sufficient to state that the problems inherent in determining our calendrical dates stem from the biblical injunctions which connect the dates of the major festivals to both the lunar and solar calendars. In view of the substantial discrepancy between these two calendars, periodic adjustments are required to prevent Passover, for instance, from falling prior to the spring season. This adjustment is achieved by assigning twenty-nine days to some months ("incomplete") and thirty days to others ("complete"). It is also necessary to insert a thirteenth month at certain intervals in a given cycle. Prior to the publication, in the fourth century, of the rules which established the permanent calendar, there was no way for the people to know in advance which month would be complete and which incomplete, which year would have twelve months and which thirteen. The proclamation of Rosh Chodesh was of momentous importance to ancient Jewry because it determined the date of a festival or fast falling within that month. Furthermore, Rosh Chodesh itself was a popular semi-festival, and special rituals were performed at the Sanctuary on that day. The proclamations of Rosh Chodesh Tishri and Rosh Chodesh Nisan were of particular importance. Rosh Chodesh Tishri determined the dates of Rosh HaShanah, Yom Kippur, and Sukkot. Rosh Chodesh Nisan determined the dates of Passover and Shavuot.

THE FIRST COMMONWEALTH

The prerogative of proclaiming Rosh Chodesh originally belonged to the high priest, the supreme religious authority of the nation. In the First Commonwealth, when the bulk of Jewry was concentrated in Palestine, it was easy to transmit to the nation the information emanating from Jerusalem. This was particularly true later on in Judea, where the Jewish population lived in a comparatively small area close to the capital.

There are some talmudic statements which seem to contradict the assumption that the high priest was the sole ancient authority who had the power to fix the calendar. Thus it is stated that the prophet Elisha performed this function in the northern kingdom. King Hezekiah is alleged to have done the same in Judea (Sanhedrin 12a). One may, of course, dismiss these statements as being merely aggadic in character, without any historical basis. On the other hand, they may reflect a historical fact. The prophet Elisha was active in the northern kingdom, where there was no high priest. King Hezekiah succeeded his father, Ahaz, after an interlude of predominant paganism, during which time the doors of the Temple had been shut and the priesthood had degenerated. Normally, however, it was the high priest who exercised the powers of the highest religious authority. Thus the Bible describes the religious reforms under King Jehoshaphat (874 B.C.E.), who set up a judicial tribunal which was constituted as the supreme religious and administrative council of the nation: "And behold Amariah, the chief priest, is over you in all matters of the Lord; and Zebadiah, the son of Ishmael, the ruler of the house of Judah, in all the king's matters . . ." (II Chron. 19:11).

There is another talmudic source (Tosefta, *Sanhedrin*, chap. 2) which apparently seems to deny that the high priest had the prerogative of fixing the calendar. It states that no king may be a member of the Sanhedrin and that both the king and the high priest are enjoined from participating in the intercalation of the calendar. If we remove this Tosefta from its historical perspective, it would appear to be inconsistent also with the tradition that King Hezekiah exercised this right. However, the Talmud indicates that the exclusion of royalty from membership in the Sanhedrin dates from the Hasmonean period, following the death of King Jannai (*Sanhedrin* 19b). The restriction was probably introduced by Rabbi Simon b. Shatach upon the restoration of the Pharisees to power (76 B.C.E.). The second limitation on the right of kings and high priests was undoubtedly enacted at the same time. It was designed to prevent interference by the Hasmoneans, who had served in the dual capacity of king and high priest. The rabbis opposed them because of their Saducean affiliation, dating back to the closing years of Yochanan b. Hyrcanus.

In the opinion of many historians, the Jews in the period of the First Temple used a solar calendar, similar to the calendar of the Book of Jubilees or the one used by the Qumran sect. This would have obviated the need for intercalation and an additional festival day. It is claimed that it was the Babylonian diaspora which adopted the Babylonian lunar calendar, resulting in the need for intercalation to keep pace with the solar calendar.

The fact that David and Jonathan knew in advance the date of

Rosh Chodesh (I Sam. 20:5) does not support the view that there was a fixed calendar in existence. The high priest, no doubt, announced the date in advance to give the people sufficient time to prepare the monthly feasts. It is relatively certain that the ancient Hebrew month was a lunar month, as is evident from the term *chodesh*—the renewal of the moon. It is equally clear that the year coincided in length with the solar seasons, as evidenced by the term *shanah*, a repetitive cycle. It was natural for ancient man to measure time by visible signs, hence the lunar months and the solar year. The Bible, therefore, linked the two major festivals of Passover and Sukkot to the lunar and solar calendars. The preservation of a link between the two systems would require either intercalation at regular intervals or a fixed calendar. The Qumran calendar is divided into solar months and therefore would have been unacceptable to the ancients. The ecclesiastic calendar of the Book of Jubilees is permanently divided into thirteen months. Had there been such an arrangement, it surely would have been reflected in the biblical literature. Furthermore, the Bible would have indicated a fixed date for the festival of Shavuot.

The talmudic tradition that Hezekiah intercalated the calendar indicates a belief that there was no fixed calendar even prior to the Babylonian diaspora. There was a similar tradition about Jeremiah (Jer. *Sanhedrin* 1). It is likely, however, that a fixed calendar was introduced by distant Jewish communities of the post-exilic era, who were out of touch with the religious leadership of the Babylonian diaspora.

THE EARLY DIASPORA, 586–538 B.C.E.

After the destruction of the First Temple, the religious and cultural center of the Jewish people shifted to Babylonia. A resurgence of faith produced an influential leadership which provided guidance in all religious matters. The outstanding leader of the early Babylonian diaspora was the prophet Ezekiel, who had been taken to Babylonia with the first captivity in 597 B.C.E. He settled in Tel-Aviv on the river Chebar, where he began his prophetic career in 592 B.C.E.

Some of the prerogatives of the high priest, whose office had been suspended with the destruction of the Temple, were taken over by the prophet. According to a talmudic tradition, it was Ezekiel who had fixed the calendar for Babylonian Jewry (Jer. *Sanhedrin* 1). Another rabbinic source (*Pirke D'Rabbi Eliezer*) denies that Ezekiel performed this function, claiming that only the Palestinian sages could fix the calendar. While it is true that the Palestinian rabbis were given exclusive authority over the calendar in the talmudic era, this was not the case in the pre-talmudic early diaspora, during which time there were no sages left in Palestine.

After the death of Ezekiel, the authority to fix the calendar was undoubtedly transferred to his disciples. Was there any need for a second festival day of the diaspora at this early period? It does not appear likely. The religious leadership and the bulk of the people were concentrated in Babylonia and Syria. The proclamation of Rosh Chodesh could easily be communicated to all the Jews throughout the land.

There was, however, one innovation which can be traced to the early diaspora, an additional day of Rosh HaShanah. A talmudic tradition attributes this innovation to the "early prophets" (Jer. *Eruvin* 3). Most historians assume that this phrase is to be interpreted merely as an expression of the antiquity of the second day of Rosh HaShanah, and that it was introduced by some early religious authority. This is a rash assumption. If the Talmud had merely sought to convey an impression of great antiquity, it would have attributed the second day of Rosh HaShanah to the prophets. By attributing it to the "early prophets" (*neviim harishonim*), the rabbis indicated a definite effort to offer a more precise timing to the introduction of the additional day of Rosh HaShanah.

By talmudic definition, the term "early prophets" embraces all the prophets, with the exception of the three post-restoration prophets—Haggai, Zechariah, and Malachi (*Sota* 48b). These are known as the "later prophets." It is obvious that the Talmud clearly asserted the fact that the second day of Rosh HaShanah was introduced prior to the restoration of Judea and the rebuilding of the Temple.

Were there any grounds for the introduction of an additional day of Rosh HaShanah in Palestine prior to the diaspora? There were neither historical nor theological reasons for such an innovation during the First Commonwealth. We may discover the key to the second day of Rosh HaShanah, however, in the replacement of the high priest by the prophet and scholar as the religious head of the community in the Babylonian diaspora. The authority of the high priest was inherent in his position. He was the repository of knowledge transmitted by generations of high priests. He was authorized to proclaim Rosh Chodesh by virtue of his knowledge and the power vested in his office. On the other hand, the prophet and scholar, acting as religious heads of the community, had no such hereditary powers. They acted in their capacity as judges and interpreters of the law. A proclamation of Rosh Chodesh by the high priest was an administrative act. A proclamation of Rosh Chodesh by the prophet or scholar was a judicial act, the pronouncement of a verdict of a court of law (*Sanhedrin* 11b). The high priest could announce in advance the date of Rosh Chodesh Tishri, obviating the need for a second day of Rosh HaShanah. The prophet and scholar were bound by judicial rules which require all judgments to be based on legal evidence. We may assume that the practice of hearing the testimony of a witness who had seen the new moon, as a prerequisite to the proclamation of Rosh Chodesh, was first introduced in Babylonia. This practice led to an occasional additional day of Rosh HaShanah in anticipation of the arrival of witnesses, whereupon the day was proclaimed the first day of Tishri. In the event the witnesses failed to arrive before the end of the day, the following day was proclaimed the first day of Tishri, and it, too, was observed as Rosh HaShanah.

A text in Nehemiah (8:13) seems to imply that two days of Rosh HaShanah were observed in Palestine in the period of Ezra and Nehemiah (ca. 444 B.C.E.). It conveys the impression that the additional day was not a novel experience but a practice with which the people were familiar. If this interpretation is correct, it would seem to corroborate our assumption that the additional day of Rosh HaShanah was instituted in Babylonia and was brought to Palestine by Zerubbabel after the proclamation of Cyrus (537

B.C.E.). The restoration of the high priesthood did not affect the new practice. The fixing of the calendar had become a judicial procedure in Babylonia, and the high priest of the Second Temple could no longer claim it as a personal prerogative. (For a detailed examination of the history of the second day of Rosh HaShanah, see Zevin's *HaMoadim BaHalacha*, Rosh HaShanah, chap. 1.)

EXTENT OF DIASPORA IN THE SIXTH CENTURY B.C.E.

The Babylonian Jewish community was not the only diaspora in the period of 586–538 B.C.E. There were a few more Jewish communities in the diaspora, without any regular contacts with the new religious center in Babylonia. There were substantial remnants of the "ten lost tribes" who had been exiled by the Assyrian King Sargon in 721 B.C.E. Some had settled in Halah, near Nineveh, the capital of Assyria. Others were moved to Habor, on the border of Media. Still others had settled in Media (II Kings 17:6). Within one century after their removal from Palestine, these Jews came under the rule of the kingdom of Media and Persia. Many of them may have assimilated and disappeared, but a considerable percentage must have retained its identity. Their numbers might have increased by a gradual influx of Babylonian Jews. We know very little about the life of the early Jewish settlers in Media. We must assume, in view of their origin, that they lacked a knowledgeable leadership and that their religious customs were confused and peripheral. In light of what we know of the life of other distant and isolated Jewish communities, we may doubt whether the early Jewish community of Media even retained a knowledge of the Jewish calendar. The situation undoubtedly changed after the conquest of Babylonia by Cyrus, when large numbers of Babylonian Jews moved to Persia and Media.

There was another early Jewish diaspora about which we know a little more, the Egyptian diaspora. This community was also unable to maintain contacts with Babylonian Jewry due to unsettled political conditions. The Egyptian diaspora was not only smaller in numbers than its Babylonian counterpart, but it failed to develop the necessary qualifications to enable it to survive in the diaspora. Babylonian Jewry early manifested the genius of Judaism to adapt itself to changing conditions by laying the groundwork for the establishment of the synagogue and the scholarly academy and by perpetuating the hope for the ultimate restoration of Zion as a fundamental aspect of Judaism. Early Egyptian Jewry, on the other hand, lacked an imaginative and creative leadership, capable of charting a new course for a Judaism deprived of the sacrificial rituals based on the Temple. They did not envision the synagogue nor did they produce scholars who could interpret the law and point to it as a guide for diasporic Jewry. Instead of the synagogue they created a small replica of the Temple at Jerusalem. Instead of the scholarly leader they clung to the leadership of priests, who were preoccupied solely with Temple rituals. These priests, headed, no doubt, by a high priest, continued to exercise all priestly functions formerly performed in Palestine. The proclamation of Rosh Chodesh continued to be a priestly prerogative, and there was no need for any additional festival days. Even Rosh HaShanah remained, as it had been in the First Commonwealth, a single day.

The Egyptian diaspora began in the last stormy years of the Judean kingdom. A substantial number of Jews, most likely members of the pro-Egypt party, fled to Egypt in anticipation of Nebuchadnezzar's invasion òf Palestine. They were part of Judea's aristocracy, which had supplied officers for the king's army. It was probably this group of immigrants which had provided the Jewish soldiers for the army of King Psamtik (594–589 B.C.E.) in his war against Ethiopia. The aristocracy had always leaned toward paganism, and their removal to Egypt was not likely to revive their interest in Judaism.

The destruction of the Temple (586 B.C.E.) sent a new wave of immigrants into Egypt. These were mainly patriots who had fought Nebuchadnezzar to the bitter end. They were traditional Jews who needed a Temple for their continued existence as Jews. The prophet Jeremiah, now elderly, was forced to accompany them into Egyptian exile.

Jeremiah did not live long enough in Egypt to lay the

foundation of a viable Jewish community. He left a transcript of his stirring appeal to the heathen Jews of Migdol (on the northeastern border of Egypt) and Patros (Upper Egypt). The paganized Jews who had scorned Jeremiah in Jerusalem also rejected his leadership in Egypt. The prophet thereupon predicted their ultimate extinction. He held out hope, however, for the faithful remnant who would some day return to Zion (Jer. 44). Like Ezekiel in Babylonia, he confirmed the basic belief of Judaism in the restoration of Zion. He undoubtedly provided religious leadership to his followers. According to a talmudic tradition, he also fixed the calendar for the Egyptian diaspora (Jer. *Sanhedrin* 1). This tradition indicates clearly that the Jewish community of Egypt did not receive calendrical information from Babylonian Jewry.

The prophet Jeremiah would have strenuously opposed the building of a Temple in Egypt. Traditionally, its legality was questionable; psychologically, it was undesirable as a potential deterrent to the hopes for the restoration of the Temple at Jerusalem. After Jeremiah's death, the leaderless Jewish community yearned again for the only religious institution they had known, the temple. The Elephantine papyri reveal that a temple was built (ca. 468 B.C.E.) in the fortress town of Yeb, where a substantial Jewish community, doing military guard duty, had settled shortly after the destruction of Jerusalem. The priest performed the traditional rituals and undoubtedly fixed the religious calendar. They obviously had no need of any additional festival days. This fact is corroborated by a later Elephantine document dated 419 B.C.E. It appears that the Jews of Yeb had become the victims of the heathen priests of Khnub, who also resided at Yeb. As a result of their conspiracy the Jews were forbidden to practice their religion. Special permission was ultimately secured from the Persian king, Darius, permitting the Jews of Yeb to observe the Passover. Chananiah, who was in charge of Jerusalem, transmitted the king's orders and instructed the Jews of Yeb "to keep the Passover, and from the fifteenth day to the twenty-first day of Nisan, seven days of unleavened bread. . . . Do not work on the fifteenth day and on the twenty-first day." Thus the biblical number of days was preserved.

We may conclude the account of the early Egyptian diaspora with the destruction of the Elephantine temple in 411 B.C.E. Thereafter the Jewish community entered a period of stagnation and assimilation. It was not until a little over a century after the destruction of the Elephantine temple that a new and vibrant Jewish Egyptian community came into being. We will discuss that phase a little later.

THE PERSIAN ERA

The conquest of Babylonia by Cyrus in 538 B.C.E. led to profound changes in the Jewish diaspora. The incorporation of Babylonian Jewry into the Persian Empire opened new avenues for rapid expansion to the Jews who had been crowded into Babylonia and Syria. They moved in large numbers into Media, Persia, and other provinces of the empire. The Book of Esther, which sheds light on conditions in the fifth century B.C.E., describes the Jews, in the words of Haman, as a "people scattered abroad and dispersed among the peoples in all the provinces of the kingdom" (3:8). This widespread dispersion was not a figment of Haman's fantasy. Mordecai, we are told, sent letters to all the Jews who were in all the provinces of the King Ahasuerus, both nigh and far (9:20). The phenomenal dispersal of Jews through-out the Persian Empire, initiated with the reign of Cyrus, was concurrent with another event of transcendent importance, the resettlement of the Jewish community in Palestine. In 537 B.C.E., Zerubbabel and Joshua, the high priest, led a group of 42,360 Jews back to Jerusalem. Under the inspiration and persistent urging of the prophets Haggai and Zechariah, the construction of the Second Temple began in 520 B.C.E., and the dedication took place in 516 B.C.E.

Who assumed the religious leadership of the ever-expanding diaspora of the sixth century B.C.E.? The presence of two prophets in Jerusalem lent the new Palestinian community great prestige. A Babylonian Jewish deputation was sent in 518 B.C.E.

to inquire from Zechariah about the future status of exilic fasts (Zech. 7:3, Kimchi). A much later rabbinic tradition preserved Mordecai and Esther's appeal to the religious leadership of Palestine for their sanction of the festival of Purim (Jer. *Megillah,* chap. 1). We may assume that the Palestinian community had gained a temporary position of religious leadership due to the presence of the prophets. They undoubtedly provided guidance to the Palestinian community and to the diaspora. The Talmud attributed to the prophets Haggai, Zechariah, and Malachi laws regulating the intercalation of the calendar (*Rosh HaShanah* 19b). However, the prestige of Palestinian Jewry declined with the passing of the prophets. Pressing problems and inner dissension weakened the community. When Ezra arrived in 458 B.C.E., he found the people in a state of decadence and discouragement. Ignorance was the rule, and intermarriage was rampant. Babylonian Jewry, on the other hand, had continued to produce, throughout this period, an active religious leadership. The all-important prerogative of fixing the religious calendar was unquestionably exercised by the Babylonian leaders for their local communities, even though the Jews of Palestine looked to the priests at Jerusalem for guidance. The bulk of diasporic Jewry of the sixth and fifth centuries B.C.E. lived within communication distance of the large Babylonian Jewish centers and was able to avail itself of the calendar established by the Babylonian leaders. The distant communities had to rely on their own calculations. This, no doubt, resulted in a divergence of festival dates in the diaspora. Seven centuries later we still find a record of a Yom Kippur which was observed in Babylonia a day ahead of its observance in Palestine (*Rosh HaShanah* 21a).

Is there a probability that some Jewish community of the Persian era (6th-5th cent. B.C.E.) introduced the additional festival day? This is unlikely. There was no regular system of communication between the religious leaders of Babylonia and the far-flung Jewish communities of the diaspora, as was instituted later between Jerusalem and many distant Jewries. The Jews who remained ignorant throughout the year of the dates of Rosh Chodesh fixed in Babylonia would find no need for an additional festival day. The accumulated discrepancy in the dates of Rosh

Chodesh was at least four days and possibly more. Under these circumstances, the addition of a single day to a festival would not solve the problem (see Tosafot, *Veal Elul; Rosh HaShanah* 18a). Palestinian Jewry never resorted to the addition of a festival day (with the exception of Rosh HaShanah). The same was true of the early Egyptian diaspora.

With the coming of Ezra to Palestine (457 B.C.E.), Judea was restored to its prominence as the second independent center of Jewish religious leadership. Ezra introduced the school of scribes, who gave great impetus to the development of rabbinic Judaism. These constituted themselves into the Men of the Great Assembly, forming thus an important link in the chain of Jewish leadership. For the remainder of the Persian era, both religious centers coexisted in a friendly relationship. We may assume that both centers acted independently in the fixing of the calendar, though they cooperated in many respects to avoid discrepancies. According to a talmudic tradition, the month of Elul was generally limited to twenty-nine days from the days of Ezra and on (*Rosh HaShanah* 19b). This regulation helped in the establishment of uniform dates for Rosh HaShanah and the other Tishri festivals in Palestine and the diaspora. The two centers also cooperated in the intercalation of an added month. This prevented a big gap in the dates of Passover and Shavuot. The Babylonian sphere of influence included Persia and Media. Palestine's sphere of influence included Syria. The mandate given by King Artaxerxes to Ezra bestowed upon him theological and juridical jurisdiction "to appoint magistrates and judges who may judge all the people that are beyond the river" (Ezra 7:25). The text is vague on the precise demarcation of the territory "beyond the river." I Esdras is more specific: "And thou Esdras, according to the wisdom of God, ordain judges and justices, that they may judge in all Syria and Phoenicia . . ." (chap. 8). Josephus' version of Artaxerxes' mandate is based on I Esdras and also contains the phrase "in all Syria and Phoenicia" (*Antiquities* 11:5). There is no doubt that the Syrian Jewish communities, due to their proximity to Palestine, followed the lead of Jerusalem.

THE HELLENISTIC ERA

The turmoil and chaos of the declining period of the Persian Empire despoiled many of its provinces. Palestine was happily spared the ravages of interminal civil wars. As a result, Palestinian Jewry was able to raise its cultural level. Babylonian Jewry, on the other hand, entered a period of stagnation. It was natural, therefore, for Palestine to assume the role of dominant leadership of the diaspora and to adopt a protective attitude toward the Jews in foreign lands. The shift in leadership became apparent with the Hellenistic epoch, which enfolded Palestine and most of the Jewish diaspora with great speed, in a short period of time. In the historic meeting between Alexander the Great and the Jewish representatives in 332 B.C.E., the latter petitioned the king for freedom of religion for the Jews of Babylonia and Media. Thus Jerusalem became the spokesman for world Jewry. The supremacy of Jerusalem's religious leadership over the diaspora would have matured early in the Hellenistic era had it not been for the untimely break-up of Alexander's empire and its division into several parts. Beginning with the year 301 B.C.E., Palestine and the southern provinces of Syria were taken over by Ptolemy I, founder of the Ptolemaic dynasty in Alexandria, Egypt. Throughout the following century, regular communication between Jerusalem and Babylonian Jewry was interrupted. The Seleucid dynasty, which ruled over Babylonia, was challenged at the same time by the Parthians, who succeeded in detaching parts of Media. Thus some remote Jewish communities found themselves isolated from both the Babylonian and Jerusalem centers of religion. Here, too, an autonomous religious leadership must have developed to regulate the religious life of these communities.

The third century B.C.E. witnessed an accelerated expansion of the diaspora throughout the Hellenistic world. Ptolemy I is alleged to have carried 100,000 Jews from Jerusalem into captivity in Egypt. These, together with some Babylonian Jews who had come to Egypt with the Persian armies, laid the foundation of a flourishing new Jewish community. A prosperous colony of Egyptian Jews was also established at Cyrene,

North Africa. Communication between Egypt and Palestine was good and uninterrupted throughout the third century B.C.E. Indeed, the Egyptian governor of Palestine ruled the province from his residence in Egypt. We may assume that many Egyptian Jews visited Jerusalem regularly and that the religious authorities were able to transmit through them the exact dates of all festivals. This obviated the need for an additional festival day in Egypt. The very close relationship between the two Jewish communities continued through most of that century. However, Hellenistic influences spread among the Jews living under the Ptolemaic dynasty. These encroached upon Jerusalem's authority and ultimately were to destroy the close link between the neighboring communities.

Just before the close of the century, the Jewish diaspora reached out into Asia Minor. Antiochus III (210–203 B.C.E.) transferred two thousand Jewish families from Mesopotamia and Babylon to Lydia and Phrygia. The Hellenization process of Babylonian Jewry was as yet ineffectual. The Jewish religious authorities of Babylonia continued to provide religious leadership for the Jews living in the Seleucid kingdom. Here, too, there was no need for a second diasporic festival day. However, as the movement toward Asia Minor gained momentum, many distant communities must have lost contact with the Babylonian centers and begun to rely upon their own calculations in fixing the lunar calendar.

The second century B.C.E. witnessed a further expansion of the diaspora in Greece, Macedonia, the island of Rhodes, Cyprus, Rome, etc. Most of these communities were too distant to have regular contacts with Jerusalem. They were more likely to follow the lead of the Egyptian diaspora due to the busy Mediterranean shipping routes to Alexandria. The Alexandrian Jewish community had become thoroughly Hellenized and independent of Jerusalem's religious dominance. The Temple of Onias was built at Heliopolis approximately in the year 175 B.C.E. by the high priest Onias and other refugees from Seleucid persecution in Palestine. Though this temple apparently attempted to counteract Hellenistic influence in Egypt, it became a rival to the Jerusalem Temple. The priests who officiated at

Heliopolis were of the family of Boethus, who had leaned toward the Sadducean sect. The Boethusians had opposed the calendrical rules instituted by the Sanhedrin in Jerusalem and no doubt followed their own rules. In this they were aided by their own Sanhedrin, which had its seat at their temple (Tosefta, *Sukkah* 4:6).

In the year 200 B.C.E. Palestine was annexed to the Seleucid kingdom. This led to the eventual emergence of its supremacy over the Jews of the Seleucid kingdom (Media, Babylonia, Syria, and Asia Minor). The inroads of Hellenism weakened the leadership of the Babylonian Jewish community. The triumphant conclusion of the Hasmonean rebellion (141 B.C.E.) left the Palestinian Jewish community and the administration of the reconsecrated Temple in Jerusalem in a position of undisputed leadership in that part of the world. This assumption of leadership over a vast area of the Jewish diaspora cast upon the Palestinian rabbis the obligation to keep the Jews of the Seleucid kingdom apprised of the dates of Rosh Chodesh. Babylonian Jewry was no longer in a position to exercise this prerogative.

THE KINDLING OF FLARES

The Talmud preserved a record of the early method used by the Palestinian leadership to transmit calendrical information to the diaspora. Unfortunately, this record does not include the date when this method was introduced. The Mishnah describes the method as follows: "At first they used to kindle flares, but after the misleading deeds of the Samaritans it was decided that messengers go forth. . . . And where did they kindle the flares? From the top of the Mount of Olives [they signaled] to Sarteba, and from Sarteba to Agrippina, and from Agrippina to Hauran to Bet Baltin [a Babylonian city near the Euphrates]. They did not go beyond Bet Baltin, but there the flare was waved to and fro and up and down until a man could see the whole diaspora before him like a sea of fire" (*Rosh HaShanah* 22b).

Upon the abolition of the flare signals the rabbis instituted a courier system. This method is described as follows: "In six months do messengers to out [to announce the date of Rosh

Chodesh]. In Nisan, to determine the time of Passover; in Av, to determine the time of the fast; in Elul, to determine the time of Rosh HaShanah; in Tishri, to determine the time of the feasts; in Kislev, to determine the time of Chanukah; in Adar, to determine the time of Purim. When the Temple was in existence they went out also in Iyar, to determine the time of the minor Passover" (*Rosh HaShanah* 18a).

When were the flares instituted? When was the courier system substituted? The fact that the flare signals were directed toward Syria, Babylonia, and Asia Minor (see Israel S. Horowitz, *Eretz Yisroel Uschenoteha*, s.v. Bet Baltin) seems to point to the second century B.C.E. as the date of the origin of these flares. There was little contact between Palestine and the Seleucid kingdom in the third century B.C.E. Had the flares been used in the third century, they would have been directed toward the Egyptian Jewish communities. Babylonian Jewry did not become dependent upon religious guidance from Palestine until the second century. By that time Egyptian Jewry had asserted its religious independence of Palestinian Jewry. That is the reason why the flare signals were directed solely toward Babylonia and the other provinces of that kingdom.

The high priest in Jerusalem was primarily concerned with Temple rituals. It was the rabbinic leadership that instituted the flares to carry its message to the diasporic Jewry. Palestine gained its independence under Simon the Hasmonean. Scholars assume that the powerful institution of the Sanhedrin had its inception at the same time (Sidney B. Hoenig, *The Great Sanhedrin*, chap. 4). The preoccupation of Simon, the high priest, with the political affairs of the nation and the safeguarding of its newly won independence strengthened the authority of the early Sanhedrin in all religious matters. The Sanhedrin soon preempted the right of intercalation and the fixing of the calendar. As a result of the conclusion of a treaty of friendship between Simon and the Seleucid kingdom, the doors were open for the Palestinian leadership to exert a religious influence over the Jewish communities of that kingdom. A similar treaty with Rome was also helpful, except for the fact that the Jews under Roman domination were geographically removed from regular intercourse with Palestine's rabbinic leadership. There is no doubt, however, that every effort was made to inform the Jews in the Roman Empire of the intercalation of a month. Unquestionably, the independence of Palestinian Jewry greatly enhanced its prestige and lent valid substance to its claim of leadership over diasporic Jewry.

It is a sound assumption that the flare signals were instituted shortly after the year 141 B.C.E., after the establishment of the Sanhedrin. How long was this system maintained? The Mishnah relates that the abolition of the flares was due to the mischief of the Samaritans. The latter were in control of Mount Gerizim and consequently were in a position to send up misleading flares, in keeping with their own calendrical calculations. The Samaritan temple on top of Mount Gerizim was destroyed by John Hyrcanus in 129 B.C.E. The final rout of the Samaritans came in 109 B.C.E., when their capital of Samaria was razed. The Jews took over control of Mount Gerizim and were surely in a position afterwards to prevent any sabotage by the Samaritans. There would have been no need to abolish the flares after 109 B.C.E.. We must conclude that they were abolished sometime prior to 109 B.C.E., when the Samaritans were still able to interfere with their operation. We may consequently limit the early flare-signal period to the years between 141 and 109 B.C.E..

In the period when the flare signals were used, the Jews of Syria and Babylonia were apprised of the date of Rosh Chodesh within twenty-four hours of the proclamation. Thus there was no discrepancy in the festival dates of Palestine and the most substantial part of the Asian diaspora. It may be properly assumed that the second festival day of the diaspora had not yet been introduced in this period (with the exception of Rosh HaShanah, according to most rabbinic scholars).

Josephus quotes an account of a battle waged by Antiochus against the Parthians in 131 B.C.E. The account was written by the ancient historian Nicolaus of Damascus. John Hyrcanus and a Jewish army participated in this battle. Nicolaus wrote as follows: "When Antiochus had erected a trophy at the river Sycus, upon his conquest of Indates, the general of the Parthians, he stayed there two days. It was at the request of Hyrcanus the Jew, because it was such a festival derived to them from their forefathers, whereon the law of the Jews did not allow them to travel" (*Antiquities* 13. 8). Josephus tried to identify the two-day holiday and suggested that it was the festival of Shavuot. He adds the explanatory note that Shavuot of that year fell on a Sunday, which accounts for the two-day festival—the Sabbath followed by Shavuot. It is clear that in the view of Josephus even the Jews beyond the Tigris River had not yet added a second festival day at that time.

SUBSTITUTION OF MESSENGERS

The substitution of messengers for the flares created a problem which had not existed heretofore. It took a long time to transmit the proclamation of Rosh Chodesh by courier, and many large Jewish communities in Babylonia could not get the information in time for the holidays. The time problem was not the only problem the diaspora had to face. By the time the flares were discontinued, or shortly thereafter, John Hyrcanus was engaged in a bitter conflict with the Pharisees. His son, Alexander Jannaeus (104–76 B.C.E.), instituted a reign of terror against the Pharisaic leadership and banished them from the Sanhedrin. Was the proclamation of a Sadducean Sanhedrin acceptable to the diaspora? The Sadducean faction was composed mainly of the aristocracy and the priesthood. Since neither of these two elements predominated in the diaspora (with the possible exception of the Egyptian diaspora), it is certain that observant Jews overwhelmingly leaned toward the Pharisees. We may assume that the rabbinic leaders who fled Palestine went not only to Egypt, as we know from talmudic accounts, but also to Babylonia. They were in a position to provide religious guidance during this period of confusion and tensions.

With the death of Alexander Jannaeus in 76 B.C.E. and the return of Rabbi Simon b. Shatach from exile, the full authority of the Sanhedrin, now controlled entirely by the Pharisees, was restored. This Sanhedrin would surely be expected to cope with the problem of the many communities located beyond the reach of the messengers. Yet we find no record of any action taken by this Sanhedrin or its successors. There is apparently a simple answer to this dilemma. Contrary to the common belief that the flares had been abolished completely due to Samaritan interference, they were merely temporarily suspended. The courier system was a poor substitute for the flares. The area serviced by the messengers was necessarily limited. The constant wars beyond the northern borders of Judea, frequently embroiling Judea itself, must have seriously hampered their activities. It is therefore logical to assume that the flares were resumed after the defeat of the Samaritans and used concurrently with the messengers. The resumption of flares is indicated in the Jerusalem Talmud, where it is stated that it was Rabbi Judah HaNasi (d. ca. 220 C.E.) who abolished flares (*Rosh HaShanah* 2). The final abolition of the flares came about three centuries after the temporary suspension in the Hasmonean era. There were good reasons for continuing the messengers even after the resumption of the flares. They provided a personal contact between the Sanhedrin and the diaspora. They could be directed toward new settlements outside the range of the flares. They were particularly valuable in periods of religious persecution (as under Trajan, 98–117 C.E.; Hadrian, 135–140 C.E.), when they were sent out secretly to inform the diaspora of the intercalation of a month (for a report of a similar secret mission in the fourth century, see *Sanhedrin* 12a).

Why did Rabbi Judah HaNasi abolish the flares? It is probable that his efforts to avoid conflict with the Romans, who might have viewed with suspicion the possible use of flares in the anti-Roman activities of the Jewish nationalists, led to their abolition. The only exception was the city of Tiberias, one of the seats of the patriarchate, where the flare signals were not discontinued. The reason for this exception is not indicated. It is possible that the warm baths of Tiberias attracted many Jews from the diaspora. It was important that all visitors be informed immediately of the proclamation of Rosh Chodesh so that they might start out in time to get to their homes for the festival.

THE NEED FOR AN ADDITIONAL FESTIVAL DAY

The abolition of the flares by the rabbis created the need for the second festival day of the diaspora. There were many large Jewish centers in Babylonia which could not be reached by the messengers before the festival. The Jews of Media and Persia, who depended upon Babylonia, were naturally also deprived of the necessary information. Although many great scholars who were competent to fix the religious calendar had come to the fore in Babylonia by the end of the second century, they deferred to the Palestinian patriarchate and refrained from exercising this prerogative. The introduction of the additional festival day was, therefore, the only answer to their problem. We may definitely conclude that it was introduced sometime during the patriarchate of Rabbi Judah HaNasi (ca. 165–230 C.E.). The likelihood is that it was inaugurated in the latter period of his term of office. This accounts for the fact that no Tanna ever discussed or even mentioned the second festival of the diaspora, with the exception of the second day of Rosh HaShanah. On the other hand, the leading Amoraim of the first generation—Rav (ca. 175–247), Samuel (ca. 165–257), and Rabbi Yochanan (ca. 200–270)—stressed the importance of this new festival and provided a number of rabbinic regulations to bring uniformity in its observance throughout the diaspora.

In the few decades immediately following the abolition of the flares, no central rabbinic authority imposed or enforced the observance of the additional festival day. It was, rather, a spontaneous innovation which different people in different localities adopted voluntarily (*Betzah* 4b). The sole factor which determined whether any given festival was to have an additional day was the availability of information from the Palestinian patriarchate. If the messengers arrived in time, there was only a single festival day. If they failed to arrive, a second day was added. One area was within reach of the Nisan messengers but not of the Tishri messengers (they had two days less of travel time). As a result, the Jews of that area observed single Passover days and double Sukkot days. The need for a second day of

Shavuot was similarly determined by the availability of information. If Passover messengers had reached a community in time, or if the proper information had come through other channels even after Passover, then Shavuot was observed one day only, the fiftieth day of the Omer. In the absence of the required information, an additional day was added to Shavuot. This practice was changed by Rabbi Yochanan, who decreed that all communities beyond the reach of the Tishri messengers (and therefore required to observe an additional Sukkot day) must add a day to all festivals, even if the information for those festivals was available (*Rosh HaShanah* 21a).

The strict rabbinic regulations of the second festival day was at first resisted by some local communities. Two of Rabbi Yochanan's students spent the holiday in a community which defied their teacher's decree, and they did not protest this lack of compliance. This aroused their master's anger. Apparently they did not sympathize fully with the rigid new policy (*Rosh HaShanah* 21a). Another student of Rabbi Yochanan's went to Alexandria and reported to the local Jews the exact date of Rosh Chodesh. Even though he was not an official messenger of the patriarch (none was sent to Alexandria), he felt that the community should follow the Palestinian ritual (Jer. *Eruvin*, chap. 3). The fact that Rav and Samuel punished violators of the second festival day with excommunication (*Pesachim* 52a) indicates that there must have been a considerable degree of resistance which had to be overcome by threat of severe punishment. However, we find no record of any opposition in the next generation (by the end of the third century), and the additional day was happily accepted and practiced in most of the diaspora, except for the Jews of Palestine and the adjoining provinces of Syria, where the messengers could arrive prior to the festival of Sukkot.

The prerogative of fixing the calendar was retained by the Palestinian patriarchate until the middle of the fourth century, when Hillel II published, in 359, the rules which were to enable every Jewish community to determine the date of each Rosh Chodesh. Theoretically, therefore, there was no longer any need for a second festival day. However, the additional day had already been observed in the diaspora for at least 150 years, and it was felt that its abolition would no longer be desirable. The Jews in the diaspora were therefore cautioned: "Take care to preserve the custom of your ancestors" (*Betzah* 4b). The Jerusalem Talmud implies that a similar message was sent to Alexandrian Jewry (Jer. *Eruvin* 3). This indicates that Alexandrian Jewry had joined the rest of the diaspora in accepting the second day after the rabbis decreed its compulsory observance.

11

The Festival of the Fifteenth of Av

ANCIENT ORIGIN

THE MULTIPLE REASONS mentioned in the Talmud for the celebration of the festival of the fifteenth of Av reflect its antiquity and evolution through the ages. According to one sage, the festival dates back to the days of Moses (*Baba Batra* 121a). Another opinion fixes its origin in the post–Bar Kochba period (*Baba Batra* 121a). Still others point to dates in between. The earliest Tanna to mention the festival of the fifteenth of Av is Rabbi Simon b. Gamliel, who had saved his life by escaping from the fortress of Betar. In his statement he refers to the dances of the maidens of Jerusalem which were held on the fifteenth of Av. It is very likely that the occasion for Rabbi Simon b. Gamliel's reference to the dances in Jerusalem was the reinstatement of the festival of the fifteenth of Av, under his patriarchate, by the Sanhedrin which had convened at Usha in the year 140.

An examination of talmudic sources (biblical texts do not allude to the fifteenth of Av) reveals four facets of the festival: (1) an agricultural holiday, (2) a matrimonial holiday for youth, (3) a Temple holiday, (4) a national holiday.

215

AGRICULTURAL AND MATRIMONIAL HOLIDAY

The agricultural and matrimonial holidays were closely related and most likely date back to the period of the Judges. Climatic conditions forced the cessation of the felling of trees on the fifteenth of Av (*Baba Batra* 121b). The conclusion of the wood-chopping season freed many young people from their chores in the forest and provided the occasion for turning their attention to the more pleasant task of bride-hunting. The dance of the maidens was designed to meet that end. The dances in Shiloh (Judg. 21:21), the religious capital of Palestine at that period, were, according to the text, an annual event. Most modern historians assume that the dances had a religious character and were part of the celebration of the three Pilgrimage Festivals. This view conforms to the opinion of Josephus that the Shiloh dances took place on a Pilgrimage Festival (*Antiquities* 5. 2, 12). Talmudic tradition, however, considered the fifteenth of Av as the date of this annual event (*Baba Batra* 121a). The objective of the ancient dance of the maidens was undoubtedly matrimonial. This was the reason for the advice given to the survivors of the tribe of Benjamin to go to Shiloh and to seize some of the dancing maidens for wives. The matrimonial character of the dances was spelled out in greater detail in later talmudic traditions. Because of the centrality of the religious capital, the dances were held there. When Jerusalem subsequently became the religious capital of the nation, the dances were moved from Shiloh to Jerusalem.

The destruction of Solomon's Temple brought to an end Jerusalem's dance festivals. Apparently these dances were not revived in the Second Commonwealth. Some historians assume that Rabbi Simon b. Gamliel referred to contemporary dances held at that time. This appears to be an erroneous assumption. A dance festival would normally require supervision to prevent improprieties. The rabbis of Jerusalem would have taken special precautions, as they had done in the case of the merriment connected with Simchat Bet HaShoava (*Sukkah* 51b). We find no record of such safeguards mentioned by any of the contemporary rabbis. Josephus makes note of the festive character of th fifteenth of Av, but he does not mention any dances (*Wars* 2. 17). Furthermore, the talmudic elaboration upon Rabbi Simon b. Gamliel's statement could hardly fit the period of the Second Temple. It was the custom, according to Rabbi Simon, for the participants in the dance to borrow dresses from their friends in order to avoid embarrassing the poor girls, who had no dresses of their own. Some rabbis subsequently added the information that the king's daughter used to borrow a dress from the high priest's daughter (*Taanit* 31a). There was no royalty in the Second Commonwealth until the Hasmoneans renewed the kingdom. The Hasmonean kings, however, retained also the high priesthood. One may also rule out the turbulent period of King Herod, even though he was not a high priest. He did not participate in the national and religious events celebrated by the people of Jerusalem. The same is true of the period of forty-four years following the reign of Herod, when the Romans usurped the right of appointing the high priests. That right reverted to King Agrippa II during the last twenty years of the Temple's existence. However, that was too short a period to establish a precedent. We are, therefore, led to conclude that Rabbi Simon b. Gamliel referred to the First rather than the Second Temple.

THE WOOD-OFFERING RITUAL

When the fifteenth of Av was reinstated in the Second Commonwealth as a festive day, it was no longer a youth festival but a Temple holiday, associated with the offering of wood for the altar. The practice of wood-offering began with Nehemiah, who had assigned the duty of providing wood in successive months of the year to some prominent families (Neh. 10:35). According to a talmudic tradition, all Jews not specifically charged by Nehemiah with the duty of providing wood could volunteer their contribution on the fifteenth of Av (*Taanit* 26a). This date was selected by design because it marked the end of the wood-cutting season. *Megillat Taanit* mentions this wood-offering festival (chap. 5). Josephus too records this festival and calls it by its popular Greek name, Xylophory, an indication that this custom dated back to the Greek-speaking Syrian era. The

ancient tradition that King Hosea had restored free access to
Jerusalem on the fifteenth of Av (*Baba Batra* 121a) might have
provided an additional reason for fixing the wood-offering
festival on that date.

The destruction of the Second Temple brought the wood-
offering to an end, and the practice of bringing wood to
Jerusalem was discontinued. Only the families specifically
charged with the duty of procuring wood on specific dates
continued to observe their own date as a private festival for some
time following the destruction of the Temple (*Taanit* 12a;
Tosafot, *Hatam*).

The festival was apparently briefly reinstated by the Sanhedrin of Usha under the patriarchate of Rabbi Simon b. Gamliel
(ca. 140), in commemoration of the termination of the Hadrianic
persecutions. To avoid a hostile reaction by the Roman
authorities to any festival which might glorify the heroism of Bar
Kochba and his followers, Rabbi Simon b. Gamliel referred to
the ancient youth festival of the fifteenth of Av (*Baba Batra* 121a).
The action of the Sanhedrin was thus given the appearance of a
restoration of a traditional holiday.

The revival of the festival of the fifteenth of Av was very likely
also motivated by reason of public policy and morale. The
observance of a prolonged period of sorrow and mourning,
culminating on Tisha B'Av, required a balancing day of joy to
offset the sadness and to reassert Jewish hope and faith in a
brighter future. Just as Sabbath Nachamu became, in a later
period, the antidote to Shabbat Chazon, so the fifteenth of Av
was to give expression to the belief that "out of sorrow will come
joy." The concluding months of the year were not to end on the
doleful Tisha B'Av note. The last message was that of the
fifteenth of Av, when Jewish youth used to meet in ancient times
to fill the streets of Jerusalem with nuptial joy and to assure a
posterity for Israel. The end of the Roman carnage and the
specter of death which had stalked Jewish homes popularized
once again the ancient tradition that the death which had
decimated the wandering desert generation had at last spent its

force on the fifteenth of Av. The new generation was now ready to resume its task of building a normal and healthy Jewish life.

The renewed festival of the fifteenth of Av shared the fate of ·most of the festivals mentioned in *Megillat Taanit*. It fell victim to resurgent pressures and oppressions of the time.

12

The Fast of Esther

REPLACEMENT OF THE FESTIVAL OF NIKANOR

THE THIRTEENTH OF Adar was alternately a holiday and a fast-day. Although the story of Esther antedated by several centuries the Hasmonean Festival of Nikanor, which was celebrated on the thirteenth of Adar, no fast had been ordained in that early period in commemoration of Esther's plight. The text of *Megillat Esther* merely records the assumption of an obligation to "keep these two days" of Purim (9:27). The letter dispatched by Mordecai and Esther to the Jewish communities of Persia does mention the phrase "the fasts and their outcry" (9:31). To Rashi is attributed the opinion that the letter did not intend to impose a commemorative fast upon the Jews. It merely exhorted them to remember the tribulations of Mordecai's generation, "the fasts and their outcry," and their ultimate salvation. The succeeding generations were, therefore enjoined to observe these events with festivity and joy (*Shvile Haleket* 194).

After the designation of the thirteenth of Adar as the Festival of Nikanor, any fast on that day would have been considered incompatible and illegal. This applies even to the initial years of the festival, when it was primarily a secular holiday, marking a Maccabean military victory.

II Maccabees (ca. 75 B.C.E.) relates Nikanor Day chronologically to the date of Purim by indicating that the festival of Nikanor precedes Purim by one day (chap. 15). II Maccabee is the earliest postbiblical work to mention Purim. It was written in Egypt or Syria. It does not allude to any fast, nor is there any implication of a possible conflict between the new Festival of Nikanor and any previously established fast-day.

The next important historical source, Josephus' *Antiquities*, was written about 165 years later. Here, too, we fail to discover any mention of a fast-day. In describing the observance of Purim he merely states: "even now all the Jews that are in the habitable earth keep these days festival and send portions to one another" (2. 6).

After the inclusion of Nikanor Day in *Megillat Taanit*, the official rabbinic compendium of legal holidays (completed ca. 120), the festival definitely assumed a religious character, and a fast on that day was expressly prohibited. In fact, neither the Talmud nor the appendix to *Megillat Taanit* ever mentions the fast of Esther on that day or on any other day.

One may parenthetically note at this point a historical curiosity. The Bene Israel of India, who are assumed to be descendants of the captivity of Sargon of Assyria in 722 B.C.E., are ignorant of the fast of Tisha B'Av and of Chanukah, but do observe a fast on the thirteenth day of Adar and celebrate a festival on the fourteenth. The festival, which they call Shila San, has no relation to the story of Esther, and the same is true of the fast. It is possible that some itinerant rabbi who had visited, according to a Bene Israel tradition, in the tenth century, introduced them to the Purim rituals. They might have been impressed with the fact that the ancient Jews of India were involved in the story of Purim and therefore continued to observe the ritual even after its origin and reason had been forgotten.

With the exception of the few isolated Jewish communities, such as the Bene Israel, all other Jews celebrated Purim, and we may definitely state that they did not fast on the thirteenth of Adar before the proclamation of the Nikanor Festival and surely not after its proclamation.

EARLY SOURCES

The first record of Nikanor Day is found in I Maccabees (chap. 7). The account relates the defeat of Nikanor's large army and his death on the field of battle. Nikanor's threats to burn the Temple had caused much anxiety to the Jews. His sudden death brought joy to everyone, including those who had not been partisans of the Maccabean cause. "The people rejoiced greatly, and they kept that day a day of great gladness. Moreover, they ordained to keep yearly this day, being the thirteenth of Adar."

In view of the fact that Nikanor Day was ordained by the same Maccabean court which had a few years earlier ordained the Festival of Chanukah, it undoubtedly met with the same degree of acceptance as Chanukah. In the parts of Palestine dominated by the Maccabees, it must have been promptly accepted. In all other places it most likely came up against some resistance, which was gradually overcome with the spread of Chanukah.

The Maccabean decree establishing the Festival of Nikanor is mentioned again in II Maccabees (chap. 15). The author fails to make it clear whether the festival was actually observed in his time (ca. 75 B.C.E.). Inasmuch as he was not a Palestinian Jew, he probably reflected the fact that the festival had not yet been widely observed in Egypt or Syria.

Josephus is the first historian to report the actual observance of Nikanor Day. In concluding the account of Nikanor's defeat he states: "And the Jews thereon celebrate this victory every year, and esteem it as a festival day" (*Antiquities* 12. 10). The *Antiquities* was published in the year 93. Josephus recorded in this instance his personal observation and experiences, and his comments must have applied to his native Palestine. This assumption is borne out by contrast with the comprehensive expression used in describing the universal observance of Purim: "even now all the Jews that are in the habitable earth keep these days . . ." (11. 6).

Nikanor Day received universal Jewish acceptance after its inclusion in *Megillat Taanit*. The official imprimatur of the rabbinic leadership made it a religious festival, and its observance became obligatory for all Jews. It also set in force the restrictive rules applicable to all the festivals enumerated in *Megillat Taanit*. The rabbis treated Nikanor Day in the same manner as they had treated Chanukah. The military phase of the Maccabean victory was minimized. They also changed the character of the festival from a "day of great gladness" and rejoicing to a commemorative festival on which day no fast was permissible. Emphasis was given to the threats which Nikanor had uttered against Jerusalem. The *beraita* interpreted his defeat as a heavenly retribution which awaits all who speak arrogantly against Jerusalem. To highlight Nikanor's punishment, the Maccabees are said to have cut off his head and placed it prominently in front of the city gates as an admonition against all future tyrants who might threaten the holy city.

This *beraita*, which presents the rabbinic interpretation of Nikanor Day, was most likely written in the same period as the *beraita* which offered the rabbinic interpretation of Chanukah (*Shabbat* 21b), during the patriarchate of Rabbi Gamliel II, 80–118). Both *beraitot* use the standard expression coined by the rabbis of that time: *Uke-shegavra malchut bet chashmonai* ("When the Hasmonean kingdom gained in strength"). The memory of a sovereign Judea was still fresh in the minds of the people. The *beraita* speaks of Nikanor, "who raised his hand against Judea and Jerusalem." A much later amoraic version of Nikanor Day (Jer. *Taanit*, chap. 2) does not mention the threat to Judea and Jerusalem but to the Temple. The fate of the Temple rather than the independence of Judea evolved as the central theme of the commemorative feasts and fasts. The scholiast (*Megillat Taanit*, chap. 12) restored the balance in the eighth century by amalgamating both rabbinic versions to read: "the hands which were raised against Judea, Jerusalem, and the Temple, etc."

The discovery of the earliest possible date of origin of the Fast of Esther will depend upon the date of the discontinuance of the Festival of Nikanor. It is commonly assumed that the *Megillat Taanit* festivals, with the exception of Purim and Chanukah, went into disuse upon the abolition of the *Megillah*. Unfortunately, it was never exactly ascertained when *Megillat Taanit* was abrogated, nor can we agree with the view that *Megillat Taanit* and all its festivals were discontinued simultaneously.

ABOLITION OF *MEGILLAT TAANIT*

The harsh Hadrianic persecution, after the suppression of Bar Kochba's rebellion, was apparently responsible for the rabbinic movement to abolish *Megillat Taanit*. The sequence of events can be followed best by an understanding of the motivation of the authors of the scroll, as it was interpreted by the rabbis of the Hadrianic era. Chananyah b. Chezkiah and his colleagues were said to have composed *Megillat Taanit* because "they cherished their troubles" (*Shabbat* 13b). This explanation did not reflect a masochistic tendency. *Megillat Taanit* only chronicled the tragedies with a happy ending, leading to a commemorative festival. The authors apparently had a religious moral in mind. They sought to stress the theological doctrine, spelled out in Deuteronomy (30:1–3), that sin leads to retribution, and penitence is rewarded with compassion and forgiveness. Sorrows must therefore be made to serve a good purpose. They must stimulate man to self-correction so that he may be worthy of atonement and happiness. The events which demonstrated the truth of this doctrine were cherished by the authors of *Megillat Taanit*, as testimonials of divine revelation. To this laudable objective Rabbi Simon b. Gamliel offered a dissenting view: "We, too, cherish our troubles, but what can we do? If we were to record all our vexations, we would be unable to find the time to do it" (*Shabbat* 13b). Rabbi Simon's statement was hardly responsive to the preceding statement. Even if we were to take his objection literally, the number of their misfortunes which had a happy ending was surely not too numerous to be recorded. The fact that two alternate versions of Rabbi Simon's statement are mentioned in the Talmud is indicative that the subsequent rabbis were baffled by his original response.

There is no doubt that Rabbi Simon b. Gamliel sympathized with the purpose of *Megillat Taanit*, but he felt that the people were no longer receptive to the observance of so many festivals. The Hadrianic persecutions, which cost the lives of countless thousands of Jews and almost succeeded in destroying Judaism, left a lasting impact upon the whole nation. Rabbi Simon himself had borne the full brunt of the oppression and barely escaped with his life. Hadrian died in 138, and the rabbinic academy of

Usha was convened in 140, at which time Rabbi Simon was elected *nasi*. He knew the temper of the people, depressed by the loss of kin and the final extinction of the glowing embers of independence. They were in a mood for fasting, which was an important phase of devotion and prayers, rather than feasting. The thirty-six festivals enumerated in *Megillat Taanit* interfered with the people's individual and public fasts. This consideration was undoubtedly responsible for the Rabbi Simon b. Gamliel's opinion that the laws restricting fasting applied only to the festive days themselves and not to the days preceding and following them (*Taanit* 18a).

Rabbi Meir, who held the rank of *chacham* in the same academy of Usha, disagreed with the views of his colleague, the *nasi*. He objected to the abolition of *Megillat Taanit* (*Rosh HaShanah* 19b). Rabbi Yosi, however, was of the opinion that the *Megillah* had been automatically invalidated upon the destruction of the Temple (*Rosh HaShanah* 19b). Rabbi Judah b. Shamua, a disciple of Rabbi Meir, followed the views of his teacher (*Rosh HaShanah* 19a).

Due to the divergence of opinion among the leadership of the academy of Usha and the scholastic preeminence of Rabbi Meir, no official stand was taken by the academy, and *Megillat Taanit* continued in force. No serious challenge to its validity was likely to have arisen during the patriarchate of Rabbi Judah HaNasi (170–220). The improvement in Judeo-Roman relations and the great prestige enjoyed by Rabbi Judah as the leader of the Jewish people helped erase somewhat the heritage of bitterness left by Hadrian's tyranny. The people could gradually resume their festive mood, and they had no reason to object to the numerous festivals of *Megillat Taanit*.

Shortly after the passing of Rabbi Judah, events took a less favorable turn. Conditions continued to deteriorate with the years. It was left to the first amoraic generation, both Palestinian and Babylonian, to take a definite stand on the validity of *Megillat Taanit*. The leading Babylonian Amora, Rav, contended that the *Megillah* had been abolished. The leading Palestinian Amora, Rabbi Yochanan, a disciple and admirer of Rabbi Judah HaNasi, disputed this view and considered the *Megillah* to be still valid (*Rosh HaShanah* 18b). The Jerusalem Talmud (*Taanit*, chap. 2) lists a considerable number of Palestinian Amoraim of the first generation who ruled that the *Megillah* was no longer .valid. Among those who subscribed to this view are included the well-known sages Rabbi Jacob bar Acha, who had the distinction of being called a *gadol hador* ("a great man of his generation," *Moed Katan* 22b), Rabbi Zeira, and Rabbi Joshua b. Levi. There are, incidentally, two conflicting statements attributed to Rabbi Joshua b. Levi. The Babylonian Talmud (*Rosh HaShanah* 18b) quotes his opinion in favor of the continuity of *Megillat Taanit*. The Jerusalem Talmud (*Taanit*, chap 2) quotes the opposite view. Considering Rabbi Joshua's stormy career as the patron of the rebels of Lud, his uncompromising enmity to the Romans, and his strong espousal of the fast of Tisha B'Av (Jer. *Taanit* 1), one is justified in assuming that he would be inclined toward the abolition of the festivals of *Megillat Taanit*. In view of the overwhelming weight of opinion of the Amoraim of the first generation in favor of the discontinuance of the *Megillah*, we may safely conclude that it was abolished, in fact, in the second half of the third century.

EFFECTS OF ABOLITION OF *MEGILLAT TAANIT*

The next question to be resolved is the effect of the abolition of *Megillat Taanit* on the festivals listed in it. Were all of them discontinued at the same time? There is considerable evidence against such a view. The Talmud mentions that Rav Nachman (d. 320) abolished Trajan Day (*Taanit* 18b). It was apparently still observed as a festival by the people of his generation.

We may parenthetically note that the eminent medieval sage Raavad wondered why Rav Nachman had to announce the cancellation of Trajan Day prior to his declaration of a public fast on the twelfth of Adar, considering the fact that the entire *Megillat Taanit* was no longer valid. He therefore concluded that public fasts, unlike private fasts, continued to be restricted when in conflict with a *Megillah* festival, even after the *Megillah* had been abolished. In order to legalize a public fast, the rabbinic authorities must specifically cancel the conflicting festival by name (see Rosh, *Taanit*, chap. 2; *Tur, Orach Chaim* 573). This conclusion might be correct if we were to assume that all festivals went out of existence at the time of the abrogation of the *Megillah*. However, if we are to accept the suggestion that individual holidays locally survived the abolition of the *Megillah*, Raavad's conclusion might have no basis.

The previously suggested view is substantiated by a number of talmudic passages. Thus Abaye (d. 338) was asked whether a student residing in the town of his teacher is permitted to render decisions in response to questions relating to the festivals of *Megillat Taanit* (*Eruvin* 62b). It is obvious that people still referred to the *Megillah* for practical guidance. There is also a statement by Rav Ashi (d. 427) which clearly indicates that Nikanor Day was observed even after the abolition of Trajan Day (*Taanit* 18b). The observance of Nikanor Day for several centuries after Rav Ashi is implied in the post-talmudic *Masechet Sofrim* (8th cent.) in its statement: "Our teachers in Palestine have instituted the custom of fasting after Purim on account of Nikanor . . . " (chap. 17).

It is evident that the primary effect of the discontinuance of *Megillat Taanit* was the end of its status as an official rabbinic document, binding on all Jews everywhere. It also terminated all the added restrictions relating to the days preceding and following the festivals. Henceforth every local community or province was free to retain or discard any of the festivals.

It is reasonable to expect that under the new permissive rule most of the festivals, whose origin was obscured by time and ignorance, went into oblivion. The festivals which commemorated the Pharisean victories over the Sadducees retained only academic interest since the latter had for some time faded from the scene. The same was true of the festivals related to the Temple rituals. The people most likely felt similarly about most of the lesser Hasmonean festivals and those dating from the Roman period. On the other hand, there were a few minor festivals which survived the abolition of *Megillat Taanit* because they commemorated events which were of special significance to a particular country or locality.

Nikanor Day was one of the minor festivals which was

voluntarily retained by the Palestinian Jewish community. There were ample reasons for its retention. The heroic stand of Palestinian Jewry under the Maccabees was a cherished memory and a source of inspiration and encouragement to the oppressed Jews of the Holy Land. There was also the consideration of its antiquity and the fact that it had been widely observed in many communities long before the publication of *Megillat Taanit*.

As a minor satellite of Chanukah, Nikanor Day attained a great momentum, which apparently kept it in orbit until the seventh or eighth century, by which time most of the Byzantine Empire had been taken over by the Moslems, bringing momentary relief to Palestinian Jewry.

Trajan Day was another minor festival, dating from the Roman period, which survived the abrogation of *Megillat Taanit*. This festival was of special significance to the Babylonian Jewish community because it commemorated their liberation from the oppressive Roman rule and their transfer to the more tolerant Persian authority. Rabbi Jacob ben Acha (3rd cent.), a Palestinian Amora, early proclaimed the abolition of Trajan Day (Jer. *Taanit*, chap. 2). The Babylonian Jews, however, continued to observe the festival until it was abolished by Rav Nachman (early 4th cent.) due to local disturbances and martyrdoms.

INTRODUCTION OF THE FAST OF ESTHER

The gradual disappearance of Nikanor Day, first in Babylonia and later in Palestine, left a vacuum on the thirteenth of Adar which was soon filled by a fast. The earliest reference to a fast on that day is found in *Sheeltot* by Rav Achai Gaon (d. ca. 761). He based this custom on a talmudic text (*Megillah* 2a) which refers to the thirteenth of Adar as *zman khilah* ("a day of assembly"). The term *khilah*, in its talmudic context, was derived from the verse in the Book of Esther which describes the counter-measures taken by the Jews in self-defense (*nikhalu haYehudim*, 9:2). Rav Achai Gaon commented: "What is the meaning of 'assembly'? A day of fast. The children of Israel had assembled to fast and to pray for heavenly mercy" (*vayakhel*). Rashi did not accept Rav

Achai's interpretation, but the majority of the great medieval scholars followed his view.

Purim fasts came into vogue in Palestine even when Nikanor Day was still considered a bar, precluding any fast. These fasts were observed on Monday, Thursday, and the next Monday, following Purim (*Sofrim*, chap. 21). The rapid spread and universal acceptance of a Purim fast was due, to some extent, to a desire to commemorate the biblical fast of the Persian Jews (Maimonides, *Yad HaChazakah, Hilchot Taaniyot* 5:5). The deciding factor, however, was the implication of the ambiguous verse in Esther 9:31, which mentions "the fasts and their outcry." Both *Targumim*, in their translations of this verse, reflect an old tradition that Mordecai and Esther enjoined a commemorative fast as well as a feast.

The name Taanit Esther did not come into use at the inception of this fast. *Masechet Sofrim* designated the three Palestinian fast days as *yemei tzom Mordecai VoEsther* ("the fast days of Mordecai and Esther"). The Babylonian custom of a one-day fast prevailed, however, soon after its inception, and it became known as the fast of the thirteenth of Adar, in the same manner as the fast of the seventeenth of Tammuz and the fast of the ninth of Av. Ibn Ezra (12th cent.) mentions the name Taanit Esther (Esther 9:31). *Shvile HaLeket* (13th cent.) identifies the fast as Taanit Esther VMordecai (194). When the Tur (14 cent.) included the phrase Taanit Esther in his code (*Orach Chaim*, chap. 686), it gained wide circulation and became permanently attached to the fast.

13

The Fast of the Seventeenth of Tammuz

FOUR COMMEMORATIVE FASTS

THE FAST OF Tammuz is one of four fast days which was established after the destruction of the First Temple. The four are mentioned in the Book of Zechariah (8:19): "Thus says the Lord of Hosts: The fast of the fourth month, and the fast of the fifth, and the fast of the seventh, and the fast of the tenth, shall be to the House of Judah joy and gladness and cheerful seasons . . . "

The basic talmudic comment on these four fasts is found in tractate *Rosh HaShanah* (18b). Rabbi Akiva identified the four fasts as follows: the ninth of Tammuz—the capture of Jerusalem by the Babylonians; the ninth of Av—the burning of both Temples; the third of Tishri—the assassination of Gedaliah; and the tenth of Tevet—the beginning of the Babylonian siege of Jerusalem. According to Rabbi Simon, the "fast of the tenth" was observed by the Babylonian diaspora on the fifth of Tevet (the day when the report of the burning of the Temple reached Babylonia—Ezek. 33:21) and therefore should continue to be observed in the diaspora on the fifth. The opinion of Rabbi Akiva prevailed.

The four fasts were ostensibly observed by the Babylonian diaspora until the prophet Zechariah ordered their suspension

231

(ca. 518 B.C.E.). According to Rav Papa (4th cent.), the commemorative fast days were converted into festivals and observed as such throughout the Second Temple era (516 B.C.E.–70 C.E., *Rosh HaShanah* 18b).

It is generally assumed that even Tisha B'Av was suspended during that period. Indeed, the query put to Zechariah by the Babylonian Jews mentioned only the fast of Tisha B'Av (7:3). His response was obviously addressed to that specific question. One talmudic text seems to imply otherwise (*Taanit* 12a). Rabbi Elazar b. Zadok, who lived at the time of the destruction of the Temple, reminisces about a delayed Tisha B'Av which he had observed only part of the day due to a private holiday connected with the Temple service. A Tosafist, however, places this incident after the destruction of the Temple (*Taanit* 12a). Furthermore, according to a Jerusalem version, the name of the rabbi who related this experience is Rabbi Elazar b. Jose, a Tanna of the post-Temple era (Jer. *Taanit,* chap. 4).

Upon the destruction of the Second Temple (70 C.E.), the four commemorative fasts theoretically reverted to their original status of fast days (see Ritva, *Taanit* 26b). However, more than half a century was to elapse before they were restored into practice. Tisha B'Av was the only exception. It gained wide acceptance, probably shortly after the destruction of the Second Temple, because the end of both Temples was associated with the same date. It became, therefore, a commemorative day for the First as well as the Second Temple.

The earliest Tanna to mention the fast of Tisha B'Av was apparently Rabban Gamliel of Yavneh, a senior colleague of Rabbi Akiva. He died approximately three decades prior to the Bar Kochba rebellion. Rabbi Meir's interpretation of a statement by Rabban Gamliel (*Taanit* 15b) implies that the latter had discussed the laws of Tisha B'Av. Another statement on Tisha B'Av attributed in our Babylonian text to Rabbi Akiva (*Taanit* 30b) is quoted in the version of Alfasi in the name of Rabban Gamliel. We may therefore assume that the fast of Tisha B'Av was reintroduced in Yavneh under the presidency of Rabban Gamliel II and made compulsory for all Jewry.

A passage in the Mishnah corroborates the view that for a

period of time Tisha B'Av was the only commemorative fast in the calendar. The Palestinian rabbinic court, we are told, used to send messengers to announce the date of Rosh Chodesh Av to distant Jewish communities so that they might be informed when to observe the fast of Tisha B'Av. No messengers were dispatched, however, in the months of Tevet and Tammuz because such information would be of no practical importance (Rosh HaShanah 18a).

It was not until the Roman persecutions of the Bar Kochba period that all the commemorative fasts became popular, although with the exception of Tisha B'Av, their observance was optional. The mere fact that the exact date of the fast of Tevet was still in issue between Rabbis Akiva and Simon indicates that the fast had not been observed prior to that time.

The dates of the fasts of Av, Tishri, and Tevet were fixed at the very outset of their reinstatement in the second century and were retained unchanged thereafter. There is ample reason to believe, however, that the fast of Tammuz was originally set by Rabbi Akiva for the ninth of Tammuz, as it had been observed by the Babylonian diaspora after the destruction of the First Temple. In the Babylonian version of Rabbi Akiva's statement, he is quoted as follows: "The 'fast of the fourth month' is the ninth of Tammuz because on that day the city was captured" (Rosh HaShanah 18b). Rabbi Akiva's designation of the dates of the four fasts was intended for the guidance of the people of his generation in their observance of the fasts. He did not engage in a purely academic discussion of a historical event. His failure to mention any change in date from the ninth to the seventeenth of Tammuz is conclusive proof that he did not contemplate such a change. Rabbi Akiva merely reactivated the four diasporic commemorative fasts.

The Tosefta quotes an old beraita (Taanit, chap. 3) which supports our conclusion that the fast of Tammuz was observed on the ninth of Tammuz when it was reintroduced in the second century. The beraita alleges that "on the ninth of the month the city was captured in the Second [Temple] and in the First." This reflects an early attempt to broaden the fast of Tammuz (like Tisha B'Av) into a memorial day for both Temples. We may incidentally note that the Karaites have retained the ninth of Tammuz as the commemorative fast-day of the month (Nemoy, *Karaite Anthology*, Samuel Al Magribi).

CHANGE FROM THE NINTH TO THE SEVENTEENTH OF TAMMUZ

The change in date from the ninth of Tammuz to the seventeenth apparently took place after the fall of Betar, a climactic tragedy which put the finishing touch to the disastrous post-Temple era. A review of the historical events of that day led to a shift of emphasis from a commemoration of the First Temple to a commemoration of the Second Temple. A mishnaic passage (*Taanit* 26a) cites five historical events which occurred on this day: the Tablets of the Law were broken, the Karban Tamid was suspended (in the Second Temple), the Torah Scroll was burned (in the Second Temple), a graven image was placed in the Temple (in the First), Jerusalem was captured (in the Second Temple). A *beraita* elaborates upon the latter event by stating: "In the First [Temple] the city was captured on the ninth of Tammuz. In the Second [Temple] the city was captured on the seventeenth (*Taanit* 28b). The list of the five events of the seventeenth of Tammuz is paralleled by a list of five events on the ninth of Av. Both were unquestionably edited at the same time. The latest historical event in the Tisha B'Av list is the destruction of Betar. It appears, therefore, that following the tragedy of Betar the fast of Tammuz was shifted to the seventeenth.

The Jerusalem Talmud records a tradition which was in conflict with the historical account of the Babylonian Talmud. According to the Palestinian version, Rabbi Akiva is quoted as follows: "The fast of the fourth [month] is the seventeenth of Tammuz, the day on which the Tablets were broken, the offering of the Tamid was suspended, and the city was captured, etc." (Jer. *Taanit*, chap. 4). It is thus alleged that Rabbi Akiva designated the seventeenth of Tammuz as a fast-day (not the ninth of Tammuz, as indicated in the Babylonian version) and that it was on that day that the city was captured. In view of the fact that his statement was a commentary on the Book of Zechariah, he obviously referred to the capture of the city by the Babylonians. The Amoraim questioned that statement by pointing to the biblical verse which states that the city was captured on the ninth of Tammuz (Jer. 52:6). This inconsistency was resolved by the explanation that due to the chaotic conditions during the siege, the people had erroneously assumed that the city was captured on the ninth. The biblical verse recorded the mistaken date in order not to upset the people by revealing their error. We thus arrive at a new tradition, according to which the city was in reality captured by the Babylonians on the seventeenth of Tammuz and that the fast was ultimately set for that day. Unlike the Babylonian version, the Jerusalem Talmud does not allege that the Romans captured Jerusalem on the seventeenth of Tammuz. This explains the omission in the mishnaic passage of a comment that both the Babylonians and the Romans had captured the city on the seventeenth of Tammuz, as was done in the case of the ninth of Av. We may note another difference between the two talmudic traditions. According to the Babylonian version (*Rosh HaShanah* 18b), Rabbi Akiva mentioned only the captivity of the city on the ninth of Tammuz as the reason for the fast. We must conclude, therefore, that he had originally reinstated the fast solely as a memorial to the First Temple. In the Palestinian version, Rabbi Akiva cited the five historical tragedies of the seventeenth of Tammuz as the reason for the fast. Some of these occurred in the Second Temple. We may, therefore, conclude that Rabbi Akiva initially designated the seventeenth of Tammuz as a memorial to both Temples.

How can one explain the Palestinian tradition, which on its face is contrary to a biblical verse? The answer may be found in another tradition which gained wide currency among the Palestinian Amoraim. According to that tradition, the period of time between the Babylonian capture of the city and the destruction of the Temple was exactly twenty-one days (Jer. *Taanit*, chap. 4). Since the date of the ninth of Av was firmly established everywhere, it became the anchor which determined the date of the fast of Tammuz. The seventeenth of Tammuz is twenty-one days before the ninth of Av.

The Jerusalem tradition seems to have lingered on in some quarters for many centuries. It was apparently preserved by the author of *Josippon*, Joseph b. Gorion, who is assumed to have lived in Southern Italy in the ninth or tenth century. In his account of Pompey's capture of the Temple (63 B.C.E.), he mentions the seventeenth of Tammuz as the date of this tragedy. The information in *Josippon* is based primarily on Josephus. The latter stated that Pompey had captured Jerusalem "in the third month, the day of the fast" (*Antiquities* 14. 4). Modern historians disagree about the identity of the fast. *Josippon*'s assumption that it was the fast of the seventeenth of Tammuz indicates a belief that that day was observed as a fast even prior to the destruction of the Second Temple. It may also indicate an opinion that according to the Jerusalem tradition the five commemorative fasts were never suspended by the prophet Zechariah. The Palestinian Talmud does not include in its text any statement similar to the one expressed by Rabbi Simon Chasida and Rav Papa (*Rosh HaShanah* 18b) that the four commemorative fasts were suspended and converted into festivals upon the restoration of the Temple.

Rav Saadia Gaon (d. 942) is alleged to have stated that Daniel's three-week period of fast and mourning (Dan. 10:2) began on the seventeenth of Tammuz and ended on the ninth of Av (*Shvile Haleket* 263). Thus he, too, seems to have preserved the tradition that even in the Babylonian Diaspora the seventeenth of Tammuz was a day of fast. A similar opinion was apparently subscribed to by Maimonides (*Pirush HaMishnayot, Rosh HaShanah*, chap. 1, third mishnah).

DATE OF THE CAPTURE OF JERUSALEM BY THE ROMANS

The historical basis of the assertion in the Babylonian Talmud that the Romans captured Jerusalem on the seventeenth of Tammuz requires some clarification. The Talmud provides the historical sources for four out of the five tragic events which are alleged to have taken place on that day. Some sources are found in the Bible. Two sources are attributed to oral traditions (the suspension of the Tamid and the burning of the Torah). No source is given for the date of the capture of the city (*Taanit* 28b).

The date of the capture of Jerusalem by the Babylonians was properly indicated as the ninth of Tammuz. The invaders entered the city on the ninth, when all resistance by the Jewish defenders came to an end. King Zedekiah was captured on the night of the tenth (Jer. 39:4–5). The Temple was apparently occupied on the same day (See Josephus, *Antiquities* 10. 8). The fate of the Temple awaited Nebuchadnezzar's decision, which was dispatched with Nebuzardan. Upon his arrival he ordered the burning of the Temple (Jer. 52:12).

The capture of Jerusalem by the Romans was a piecemeal operation which lasted nearly three months. Josephus was with the Romans throughout this period, frequently addressing the defenders to urge their surrender. He was undoubtedly in a position to get first-hand information on the progress of the war. According to Josephus, the Romans breached the first wall of Jerusalem on the fifteenth of Iyar and captured the northern part of the city (*Wars* 5. 7). The second wall was taken and lost on the twentieth of Iyar. It was retaken on the twenty-fourth. One of the formidable obstacles barring the Romans from the Temple Court was the Tower of Antonia. The wall at the Tower of Antonia fell to the Romans on the first day of Tammuz. The Tower itself was captured on the sixth. Desperate fighting, however, continued to rage, with the defenders confined to the Temple Court. On the seventeenth of Tammuz the Romans demolished the Tower of Antonia. This was probably done to give the Roman legions greater access to the Temple Court and also to prevent the Jews from recapturing the Tower. The demolishing of the fortress did not actually affect the course of the fighting. One may therefore wonder why the seventeenth of Tammuz was designated as the day of the capture of Jerusalem in preference to the fifteenth of Iyar (the breaching of the first wall), the sixth of Tammuz (the capture of the Tower of Antonia), or the twenty-fourth of Tammuz (the capture of the northwestern wall of the inner court)? There are two possible answers to this question. There may be some merit to the assertion in *Josippon* that the original capture of Jerusalem by the Romans under Pompey, who put an end to Jewish independence, took place on the seventeenth of Tammuz, 63 B.C.E. At least this assertion may have reflected an ancient tradition to that effect. The allegation in the *beraita* that the city was captured by the Romans on the seventeenth might have originally been a reference to Pompey and then later was applied to Titus.

THE SUSPENSION OF THE TAMID

There is some evidence of the existence of an ancient tradition that the suspension of the Tamid also took place during Pompey's siege of the Temple in the year 63 B.C.E. Rabbi Levi (3rd cent.) provided, in the Jerusalem Talmud, the historical background to the mishnaic allegation that the Tamid was suspended on the seventeenth of Tammuz. Rabbi Levi said: "Also in the days of this wicked government [Rome], they [the besieged] used to lower two baskets of gold coins, and they [the besiegers] used to send up two lambs. In the end they lowered two baskets of gold, and they sent up two pigs. Before they reached midway to the top, the swine pushed against the wall and jumped forty miles out of Palestine. At that moment the sins led to the suspension of the Tamid, and the Sanctuary was destroyed!" (Jer. *Taanit*, chap. 4). Thus Rabbi Levi linked the ancient account of the swine with the fateful seventeenth of Tammuz, during Titus' siege of Jerusalem, several weeks prior to the destruction of the Temple. However, the original account of the story of the swine, which is recorded in a *beraita* and quoted in several Babylonian tractates (*Sotah* 49b, *Menachot* 64b, *Baba Kama* 82b), placed this incident in a much earlier period. It fails to associate this temporary suspension of the Tamid with the destruction of the Temple. The *beraita* reads as follows: "When the Hasmonean kings besieged each other, Hyrcanus was on the outside [of the Temple] and Aristobulus was on the inside. [The version in *Baba Kama* erroneously reads: "Hyrcanus was on the inside and Aristobulus on the outside."] Every day they used to lower *dinarim* in a basket, and they used to send up the *Tmidim*. There was an elder who was conversant in Greek science. He lectured to them Greek science. He said: 'So long as they continue to offer the sacrificial rites they will not be conquered by you.' On the following day they lowered *dinarim* in a basket, and they sent up pigs. Thereupon they [the rabbis] said: 'Cursed is the person who raises swine, and cursed is the man who teaches his son Greek science.' "

Aristobulus II, who had usurped the royal title from his brother Hyrcanus, was besieged twice by the latter. The first siege occurred in the year 66 B.C.E. Antipater, the champion of Hyrcanus' cause, persuaded Aretas, king of Arabia, to besiege Jerusalem. According to Josephus, this happened during the Passover season. Aristobulus and the priests confined in the Temple needed animals for the festival sacrifices. They arranged with the Jewish followers of Hyrcanus for the supply of animals, agreeing to pay a very high price. The priests lowered the money, but the Jews outside the Temple failed to deliver the animals, thus causing the suspension of the sacrifices (*Antiquities* 14. 2). Josephus does not mention any delivery of swine. Indeed, such an outrageous act would never have been perpetrated by Hyrcanus or his Pharisaic followers. The Jerusalem Talmud, too, has preserved a record of two occasions when the besieged and the besiegers traded money for animals. The first occasion was "in the days of the Greek government," i.e., prior to the Roman occupation of Palestine. In that case the besiegers are said to have cheated the defenders by sending up goats instead of lambs, thus preventing the offering of the Tamid. This incident compares to the one described by Josephus in which the besieged were cheated by not getting delivery of the needed animals. The second incident in the Jerusalem text, involving the service, is alleged to have taken place during the Roman rule and therefore must have happened after the first siege.

The second siege of the Temple in the civil war between Hyrcanus and Aristobulus took place in the year 63 B.C.E. The besieging army consisted mainly of Roman legions led by Pompey. The account of the swine mentioned in the *beraita* and alleged to have taken place in the civil war between the Hasmonean brothers could only have reference to the second siege. The Romans were capable of such a sacrilegious act. It is inconsistent with the Jerusalem text, which states that the swine incident took place when the Romans were in control.

We may conclude that there were several distinct oral traditions in the post-Temple era. One tradition designated the seventeenth of Tammuz as the day of the suspension of the Tamid (*Taanit* 28b). It is also confirmed by Josephus (*Wars* 6. 2). Another tradition linked the suspension of the Tamid with the incident of the swine (Jer. *Taanit*, chap 4). Still another tradition placed the incident of the swine in Pompey's siege of the Temple in the year 63 B.C.E. Those who followed this last tradition must have regarded the fast of the seventeenth of Tammuz as a memorial to the siege of Pompey. They most likely assumed that the capture of the Temple by Pompey took place on the same day.

Rabbi Levi, on the other hand, accepted the first two traditions mentioned before but disagreed with the third. He placed the swine incident in the siege of Titus, in the year 70. In this opinion he was supported by the mishnaic allegation that the ban on the study of Greek sciences was proclaimed in the War of Titus (*Sotah* 49a). According to the *beraita*, the ban on Greek followed the swine incident. This leads to the inevitable conclusion that the swine incident also occurred in the War of Titus.

A more likely explanation of the allegation that the city was captured on the seventeenth of Tammuz is probably the fact that the real reason for the designation of the fast was the suspension of the Karban Tamid, which marked the end of sacrificial rituals at the Temple. The seriousness with which the Jews viewed this tragedy is reflected in Josephus (*Wars* 6. 2) and the Talmud (Jer. *Taanit*, chap. 4). It was impossible to assert formally that the suspension of the Tamid was the main reason for the fast as that would have given it merely rabbinic status. In order to continue the old prophetic status of the fast of Tammuz, it was necessary to restore the ancient fast which had commemorated the capture of Jerusalem. It was now claimed that the seventeenth of Tammuz was the date of the capture of the city by the Romans. The demolition of the Tower of Antonia might have lent a slender historical basis to this claim, though it was hardly the true reason for the fast.

According to Maimonides, the Tamid was suspended in the First Temple during the Babylonian siege of Jerusalem (*Hilchot Taaniyot* 5:2). A statement by Rabbi Levi in the Jerusalem Talmud (Jer. *Taanit,* chap. 4) clearly indicates that it was suspended in the Second Temple. Josephus, too, stated that the daily sacrifice was suspended on the seventeenth of Tammuz, the very day on which he had been summoned by Titus and ordered to transmit to the defenders an offer for the continuation of the sacrifices in return for their withdrawal from the Temple grounds (*Wars* 6. 2).

Why did Maimonides associate the suspension of the Tamid with the First Temple? A possible explanation may lie in his assumption of the historical origin of the fast of the seventeenth of Tammuz. We quote from his *Hilchot Taaniyot* (5:4): "The 'fast of the fourth' is the seventeenth of Tammuz, which is in the fourth month." Commenting on this statement, the author of *Lechem Mishnah* alleges: "Even though the biblical 'fast of the fourth' was on the ninth [of Tammuz] because the city was captured on the ninth, nevertheless now we fast on the seventeenth because the destruction of the Second Temple is more distressing to us, and the city was captured on the seventeenth." This comment follows the Babylonian version of the sequence of events in the history of both Temples (*Rosh HaShanah* 18b). According to this version, the fast was originally observed by the Babylonian diaspora on the ninth of Tammuz but was postponed to the seventeenth following the destruction of the Second Temple.

Rabbi Jacob b. Asher's code, the *Tur* (*Orach Chaim* 549), parallels Maimonides' phraseology: "The 'fast of the fourth' is the seventeenth of Tammuz." It is quite apparent that the talmudic text used by both of them conformed to the Palestinian version of the *beraita* in which Rabbi Akiva is quoted as saying that "the 'fast of the fourth' is the seventeenth of Tammuz" (Jer.

Taanit, chap. 4). The *Tur* follows, however, the Babylonian tradition that the fast was originally observed on the ninth of Tammuz. Maimonides, on the other hand, makes no such distinction (the author of *Lechem Mishnah* is attempting to read this view into his words). It seems that Maimonides accepted the apparent conclusion of the Palestinian Talmud that the fast was always observed on the seventeenth (see Maimonides, *Pirush HaMishnayot, Rosh HaShanah,* chap. 1, third mishnah). He also seems to have accepted another implied conclusion of the Palestinian Talmud that the commemorative fasts were never discontinued during the existence of the Second Temple but had became optional (ibid.). The verse in Zechariah (8:19) in which the prophet predicts that the commemorative fasts "shall be to the house of Judah joy and gladness and cheerful season" was not applied by Maimonides to the time of the Second Temple, as indicated in the Babylonian Text (*Rosh HaShanah* 18b), but to a future messianic era. It is with this interpretation of the verse that he concluded the chapter on fasts (*Hilchot Taaniyot* 5:19). One may compare the conclusion of this chapter with the concluding passage in the *Tur.* The latter applied Zechariah's prophecy to the Second Temple, in keeping with the Babylonian tradition that the fasts were converted into festivals (*Tur, Orach Chaim* 550). He, too, ends the chapter with the comforting promise of joy in the messianic era. Unable to quote Zechariah in this context because Zechariah, according to him, had referred to the era of the Second Temple, he quotes instead from Jeremiah (31:12): "For I will turn their mourning into joy and will comfort them and make them rejoice from their sorrow."

Maimonides did not agree with all the conclusions of the Palestinian tradition. He did not go along with the statement that the Babylonians had captured the city on the seventeenth of Tammuz, in view of the contradictory statement in the Bible. In an apparent attempt to provide the reason for the fast of the seventeenth of Tammuz even in the Babylonian diaspora, he mentions the suspension of the Tamid in the First Temple. As was stated before, the weight of evidence indicates that the Tamid was suspended on the seventeenth of Tammuz in the Second Temple.

THE PERIOD OF STRESS

The term *bein hametzarim*, embracing the three-week period between the seventeenth of Tammuz and the ninth of Av, is taken from the Book of Lamentations (1:3): "All her pursuers overtook her within the straits [*bein hametzarim*]." *Midrash Eicha Rabati* pointed out the special character of these three weeks: "in the 'days of anguish,' when the deadly pestilence [or the demon] prevails." The midrashic comment did not designate this period a time of mourning. It merely called attention to the historic tragedies which had occurred at that time and drew the conclusion that one may consider these three weeks a period of bad luck. One should therefore take special care to avoid unfortunate mishaps. Rabbi Yochanan is alleged to have ordered all schoolteachers to refrain from administering corporal punishment at that time for fear of serious consequences. Some mildly restrictive mourning laws were instituted by the tannaic rabbis, but these were limited to the first nine days in the month of Av (*Taanit* 26b, *Yevamot* 43b).

Despite the absence of officially imposed mourning laws for the entire three-week period, there were apparently individuals who voluntarily assumed mourning, beginning with the seventeenth of Tammuz. *Machzor Vitri* (twelfth cent.) quotes a passage from the Jerusalem Talmud, according to which some women are alleged to have abstained from eating meat and drinking wine from the seventeenth of Tammuz to the ninth of Av. Some medieval rabbis attributed such abstention to the suspension of the Tamid and the libation of wine.

It was not until the latter part of the Geonic period that semi-mourning was officially prescribed for the three weeks. The Geonim reevaluated many of the old Jewish customs and traditions, and the period of *bein hametzarim*, too, did not escape their attention. Rav Saadia Gaon (10th cent.) is quoted as the author of the statement that Daniel's three-week period of fasting and mourning (Dan. 10:2) covered the three weeks between the seventeenth of Tammuz and the ninth of Av (*Shvile HaLeket* 263). Rav Hai Gaon (11th cent.), the earliest authority known to have considered the Sefirah days a period of mourning, is also quoted as the author of the ban on meat and wine during the first nine days of Av (*HaManhig* 49a). The author of *Shiboleh HaLeket* (13th cent.) mentions a similar optional ban for the full three weeks. Rabbi Judah HaChasid (13th cent.) mentions a prohibition against the eating of new fruits during the three weeks (*Sefer HaChasidim* 840). The ban on marriages during this period was not observed until it was incorporated by Rabbi Moses Isserles (16th cent.) into the code (*Orach Chaim* 103).

SUMMATION

The four commemorative fasts were suspended by the prophet Zechariah in 518 B.C.E.

According to the Babylonian Talmud, they were converted into holidays. A source in the Jerusalem Talmud, however, indicates that they were retained on an optional basis.

The observance of Tisha B'Av was made obligatory by the end of the first century C.E., and the remaining fasts, after the Hadrianic persecutions (135 C.E.).

The Babylonian fast of the ninth of Tammuz was restored by Rabbi Akiva in commemoration of the First Temple. The date was changed to the seventeenth of Tammuz after the Hadrianic persecutions in commemoration of the breach of the walls of Jerusalem by the Romans (Babylonian Talmud).

According to the Jerusalem Talmud, the fast was initially decreed by Rabbi Akiva for the seventeenth of Tammuz in commemoration of both Temples.

The talmudic assertion that the walls of Jerusalem were breached on the seventeenth of Tammuz is not confirmed by other sources. According to Josephus, it was the Tower of Antonia, overlooking the Temple Court, that was demolished on the seventeenth of Tammuz.

It appears that the real reason for the fast of the seventeenth of Tammuz was the suspension of the Korban Tamid (daily offering) during Rome's siege of Jerusalem.

14

The Fast of Tisha B'Av

A DAY PREDESTINED FOR DISASTER

A MISHNAIC PASSAGE lists five major tragedies which occurred on the ninth of Av. On that day it was decreed that our ancestors (of the exodus) could not enter Palestine, both Temples were destroyed, Betar was captured, and the site of Jerusalem was plowed up (*Taanit* 26b).

Rabbi Yochanan (3rd cent.) traced the traditional background material which led to the designation of the ninth of Av as "a day predestined for disaster." When our forefathers in the desert heard the unfavorable report of the scouts, upon their return from Palestine, they burst out crying. "That night was the night of Tisha B'Av, and the Almighty said to them: You wept in vain. I will set aside this day as a day of weeping unto all generations' " (*Taanit* 29a). Folklore feeds the soul of a nation, but it does not authenticate history. The same Rabbi Yochanan, speaking with the preciseness of a historian, remarked: "If I had lived in that generation [after the destruction of the First Temple], I would have decreed the fast on the tenth of Av because the major part of the Temple was burned on that day" (*Taanit* 29a). This leaves us wondering why the ninth of Av was designated a fast-day.

Rabbi Yochanan's statement that the First Temple was burned on the tenth of Av may be accepted as a historical fact. The biblical accounts of the date of the burning of the Temple appear to be in conflict. II Kings (25:8) mentions the seventh of Av.

245

Jeremiah (52:12) mentions the tenth of Av. A careful reading of the two texts, however, reveals no inconsistency. II Kings states that Nebuzaradan arrived at Jerusalem on the seventh of Av with the king's instructions for the disposal of the city. The instructions obviously contained a detailed plan of destruction. We are told that Nebuzaradan carried out Nebuchadnezzar's orders with efficient thoroughness. "And he burned the house of the Lord, and the King's house; and all the houses of Jerusalem, even every great man's house burned he with fire. And all the army of the Chaldeans, that were with the captain of the guard, broke down the walls of Jerusalem round about." It is easily understood that it took several days to complete this major wrecking operation. The text does not necessarily convey the exact sequence of the order of destruction. The "house of the Lord" is mentioned first because it ranked first in importance and not necessarily because it was the first structure to be destroyed. The text in Jeremiah presents what might have been the climactic point of the destruction. It came on the tenth of Av, when Nebuzaradan announced Nebuchadnezzar's order to burn the Temple. This interpretation of the text leads to the conclusion that the Temple was burned, at the very earliest, on the tenth of Av.

The Talmud reconciles the conflicting biblical dates by reconstructing the following table of events. The Babylonians entered the Temple on the seventh of Av. They proceeded to desecrate it for the next two days. They finally set it aflame on the evening of the ninth of Av. The Temple burned throughout that night and the day of the tenth of Av. In view of the fact that the fire was started at the end of the ninth of Av, it was decided to commemorate the burning of the Temple on that day (*Taanit* 29a). While the talmudic reconciliation of the texts explains the reason for the designation of the ninth of Av as a fast-day, it concedes that the major part of the Temple was burned on the tenth of Av. Josephus, too, mentions the generally accepted view that the First Temple was burned on the tenth of Av (*Wars* 6. 4).

Was the Babylonian diaspora aware of the true date of the burning of the Temple? There was one Palestinian Amora (3rd cent.) who attributed to the prophet Ezekiel the erroneous belief that the Temple was destroyed on the first of Av (Ezek. 26:1–2; Jer. *Taanit* 4). Another Palestinian tradition, current at the same time, declared that the period between the capture of the city and the destruction of the Temple was exactly twenty-one days. The acceptance of the ninth of Tammuz as the date of the capture of Jerusalem led to the conclusion that the first of Av was the date of the destruction of the Temple (Jer. *Taanit* 4). It is amazing that Josephus also mentioned the latter date (*Antiquities* 10. 8), contradicting his earlier statement in the *Wars*. In spite of this unorthodox opinion, however, no one put forth the claim that Babylonian Jewry had, in fact, ever observed the fast on the first of Av. We have the unequivocal statements of Rabbi Akiva and Rabbi Yochanan that the fast was observed at its very inception on the ninth of Av. Only the Karaites, who reject all rabbinic traditions and adhere strictly to the biblical text, observe the fast on the tenth of Av.

The only biblical reference to the fast of Av is found in Zechariah (7:4, 8:19), where it is labeled "the fast of the fifth [month]." The specific date, however, is not indicated. We may assume that the fast was decreed shortly after the news of the destruction of the Temple reached Babylonian Jewry. A messenger bearing the news of the capture of Jerusalem came to Ezekiel of the fifth of Tevet, 585 B.C.E., six months after the disaster (Ezek. 33:21). The news of the burning of the Temple must have reached the prophet soon thereafter, and the fast was most likely decreed on the first anniversary. This is substantiated by the words of Zechariah addressed to the Babylonian Jewish emissaries in the year 518 B.C.E.: "When you fasted and you mourned in the fifth and in the seventh month, almost these seventy years . . ." (7:5). This statement, made sixty-eight years after the destruction of the Temple, clearly implies that the fast had been decreed shortly after the destruction of the Temple.

What sources of information were available to the Babylonian diaspora? The texts of Jeremiah and II Kings were not yet published and could not provide the necessary information to the Jews of the early period. They had to rely solely on reports brought by Palestinian refugees. Some of these might have witnessed the inception of Nebuzaradan's wrecking operations, but it is doubtful whether they had accurate information on the date of the burning of the Temple structure. Indeed there must have been conflicting reports, in view of the fact that fires had raged in the vicinity of the Temple over a period of four days, between the seventh and the tenth of Av. The leaders of Babylonian Jewry had to sift and evaluate the conflicting reports. The choice of the ninth of Av was, no doubt, based on a conclusion that the Temple was actually burned on that day. In view of the near accuracy of the date, and the possibility that the fire was, in fact, set on the evening of the ninth, it was not deemed necessary to change this date, even after the publication of the Book of Jeremiah.

It is generally agreed that the fast of Tisha B'Av was discontinued in the Second Commonwealth. It was reinstated after the destruction of the Second Temple. Josephus, who was in a position to know the exact date of its destruction, reports that it was set aflame on the tenth of Av (*Wars* 6. 4). We have no reason to doubt the authenticity of this date. However, the rabbis chose to ignore the information supplied by Josephus or any other historical source. They ostensibly relied upon the maxim: "Happy events are caused to transpire on a day ordained for happiness and tragedies on a day fated for tragedy" (*Taanit* 29a). It is obvious that they felt that for religious and historical purposes it was preferable to reinstate the ancient fast day of the ninth of Av, which commemorates the loss of both Temples, rather than to create a new fast-day on the tenth of Av. By clothing their elegies with the phraseology of the Book of Lamentations, they could give voice to their resentment of Rome without fear of retribution by the authorities.

Professor Klausner explained the choice of the ninth of Av by claiming that the fast was first instituted after the fall of Betar, which brought the Bar Kochba rebellion to an end. According to the Talmud, Betar was captured by the Romans on the ninth of Av (*Hist. shel Bayit Sheni*, vol. 5, chap. 20). It is hardly plausible that the fall of Betar rather than the fall of Jerusalem dictated the selection of the date of a national memorial day. Furthermore, there is evidence that the fast of Tisha B'Av was observed prior to the destruction of Betar.

SHABTAI TZVI AND TISHA B'AV

Shabtai Tzvi exploited the traditions associated with Tisha B'Av to promote his messianic schemes. Thus the allegation that he was born on Tisha B'Av was designed to provide a link to the rabbinic tradition that the ninth of Av is the birthday of the Messiah (*Bamidbar Rabba* 13). To further emphasize Shabtai Tzvi's messianic claims, his disciples ordained the conversion of ancient commemorative fast-days into holidays, in keeping with the prophecy of Zechariah (8:19) that the fasts would be turned into days of "joy and gladness." The fulfillment of the prophecy was an affirmation of his messiahship.

The following is a list of the sect's festivals:

Seventeenth of Sivan, Shabtai Tzvi began his prophecy in Gaza.

Twenty-first of Sivan, Shabtai Tzvi was anointed by prophet Elijah.

Seventeenth of Tammuz, Shabtai Tzvi began to radiate light.

Twenty-fourth of Tammuz, Shabtai Tzvi ordered his followers to light candles in commemoration of the day of light.

Ninth of Av, the day of sorrow, was renamed the day of solace in honor of Shabtai Tzvi's birth.

Fifteenth of Av, Shabtai Tzvi was circumcised.

Twenty-fifth of Elul, Shabtai Tzvi was summoned to heaven.

Third of Tishri.

Tenth of Tevet.

The list of festivals contains three categories of dates: one is associated with ancient festivals, the second with fasts, and the third with historical events. The seventeenth of Sivan is listed in *Megillat Taanit* as a Maccabean festival, commemorating a victory over native enemies who had harassed the Jews since the days of Joshua. They were finally expelled and replaced with Jewish settlers. The coming of Shabtai Tzvi was thus to be considered the signal for the ultimate destruction of the enemies of the Jews. The fifteenth of Av is also listed in *Megillat Taanit* as a "Wood Festival" on which day people contributed wood for the altar. According to Rabbi Jose, this festival turned into a day of mourning after the destruction of the Temple. In the pseudo-messianic era of Shabtai Tzvi, this day reverted to its original status of a festival. The ostensible reason offered by the sect for the celebration of the fifteenth of Av, the anniversary of the circumcision of the pseudo-Messiah, is inconsistent with the alleged date of his birth, the ninth of Av.

The seventeenth of Tammuz, the ninth of Av, the third of Tishri, and the tenth of Tevet are all exilic commemorative fast-days which were converted into festivals in the alleged messianic era.

The festival of the twenty-first of Sivan may be related to the biblical story of the confinement of Miriam. The confinement began, according to the *Seder Olam*, on the twenty-first of Sivan. Miriam was disciplined because of her derogatory comments about the marital affairs of Moses. Some commentators assume that she was critical of Moses' separation from Zipporah. Others assume that she referred to a legendary princess whom he had allegedly married because of her beauty. Shabtai Tzvi had a similar history. He had separated from his first two wives. The separations ended in each case in a divorce. This aroused some unfavorable comment. His third wife was an eccentric, with an unsavory reputation of an immoral past. The silencing of the unjustifiable criticism of Moses might have been pointed out by the followers of Shabtai Tzvi as a vindication of their leader's life and morals.

The twenty-fourth of Tammuz marked the extermination of Jerusalem's medieval Jewish community, which came to a fiery end in a synagogue set on fire by the Crusaders in 1099. The sad memories of this destruction, like the memories of the destruction of both Temples, were now wiped away by the coming of the pseudo-Messiah. Shabtai Tzvi ordered his followers to kindle many lights on this day. The candles were thus to symbolize the conversion of the flames of destruction into a source of light and joy.

The twenty-fifth of Elul is the traditional date of the creation of the world. On that day the heavens and the earth were created, "and the spirit of God hovered over the face of the water" (Gen. 1:2). According to the Zohar (Gen. 49:16), the spirit which hovered over the water "was the spirit of the king the Messiah." The messianic spirit descended to earth on the twenty-fifth of Elul. On this date, the followers of Shabtai Tzvi alleged, their leader was summoned to heaven.

15

Holocaust Day

IN SEARCH OF A DATE

THE NEED FOR a memorial day to commemorate the Nazi victims has been strongly felt by Jews throughout the world. A Joint Resolution by the United States Congress, signed by President Kennedy, designated April 21, 1962, as a day of commemoration of the martyrs of the Warsaw ghetto and other Nazi victims. The resolution was passed at the behest of the Jewish Nazi Victims Organization of America. A memorial day based on a civil date and promulgated under non-Jewish auspices can hardly be expected to become a permanent institution in the Jewish calendar.

There are numerous precedents in Jewish history for the commemoration of Jewish catastrophes by fast-days proclaimed by a recognized religious authority. Such was the origin of countless local fast-days and the more widespread fast-days listed in the chronicles of *Megillat Taanit*. On occasion, the rabbis utilized a long-established fast and associated it with a later tragedy by the addition of new prayers and liturgical poems.

The fast of the twentieth of Sivan was originally decreed by the famous Tosafist Rabbenu Tam to commemorate the martyrdom in 1171 of the first Jews on the European continent to be condemned for the crime of a blood ritual. After the Chmelnitzky massacres (1648–49), the same fast was adopted to commemorate the frightful bloodshed of that period. The historical basis for the choice of that date was provided by the extermination of the large Jewish community of Nemirov on the twentieth of Sivan. The adaptation of an old fast obviated the need for adding a new fast to a calendar already crowded with commemorative days. Furthermore, old elegies, hallowed by time, were invested with new meaning by associating them with more recent tragedies.

The practice of instituting annual fast-days was very popular in medieval times. It gradually tapered off in the course of the centuries and had become a rare occurrence by the nineteenth century. The rise of secularism and the diminished authority of the religious leadership made the institution of new fast-days, even on a local basis, increasingly impractical.

The establishment of a secular Jewish national government in Israel provided, for the first time since the disappearance of ancient Judea, a new authority for proclaiming a memorial day. The proclamation of a secular memorial day would constitute, however, a break with tradition, which had always assigned this task to the religious leadership.

SUGGESTED DATES

In 1941, the secular Vaad HaL'umi, representing Palestinian Jewry, proclaimed the traditional fast-day of the tenth of Tevet as a day of solidarity with European Jewry. The Chief Rabbinate of Israel subsequently adopted the same date as a memorial day for the six million martyred Jews. The Knesset, however, in 1951, designated the twenty-seventh of Nisan as Holocaust Day. The reason for this choice is obscure. The date is allegedly the anniversary of the first liberation of an extermination camp. Such an event, however, would qualify the twenty-seventh of Nisan to be a Liberation Day rather than a Holocaust Day. Another alleged reason for the Knesset's choice is the fact that the twenty-seventh of Nisan marked the end of the uprising of the Warsaw ghetto. This allegation is questionable in view of the continued active resistance until the third of Iyar.

The historical basis of the rabbinic selection of the tenth of Tevet is also questionable. The only tenuous association of that date to the Nazi era is a decree eliminating Jews from the German economy which was published on the tenth of Tevet (January 1, 1939). Yet that decree was merely an economic measure at a time when the ultimate extermination of Jews had not yet been decided. The only justification for the rabbinic designation is the widespread observance in religious circles of the tenth of Tevet as a fast-day. It was therefore expedient to identify this fast with the most recent tragedy, in the same manner as the twelfth-century fast of the twentieth of Sivan was adopted as a seventeenth-century fast in memory of the Chmelnitzky martyrs.

The twenty-seventh of Nisan, proclaimed by the Knesset as a secular memorial day for the victims of the Holocaust and the fighters of the ghetto, has even less justification than the tenth of Tevet. The most widely known anti-German uprising broke out in the ghetto of Warsaw on April 19, 1943 (Nisan 14). The uprising lasted twenty-eight days and on May 16 was officially declared by the Germans to be over. The twenty-seventh of Nisan marked the fourteenth day of the uprising, by which time it had reached its midpoint. The total number of Jews reported captured at the end of the liquidation of the ghetto was 56,065. On May 2 (Nisan 27) the number of captured Jews stood at 40,160. These figures do not include the Jews killed in action and those who perished in the flames. Whatever grounds there may be for the selection of Nisan 27 as a memorial day for the Warsaw uprising, they are not relevant to a designation of this date as Holocaust Day. Nisan 27 marked the outbreak of bloody Arab anti-Jewish riots in Palestine (April 19, 1936). There is little connection, however, between this event and the Nazi mass murders.

National secular memorial days generally tend to lose their solemnity in the course of time. The cessation of normal work routines and the closing of banks and schools present an opportunity for vacationing. A generation which is not linked to previous tragedies by personal loss and memories will readily exploit the "free day" for pleasurable ends. Such a development is unlikely in the case of religious memorial days, which must forever remain days of sorrow, dedicated to fasting and prayers. That the government of Israel became aware of the ineffectiveness of a secular memorial day is evident from the new decree passed by the Knesset in 1961. The new decree provided for an extension of the memorial day to a full period of twenty-four hours, beginning with the eve of Nisan 27. It also provided for the closing down of all theaters and places of amusement. This decree, in effect, attempted to incorporate into a secular observance some traditional aspects of a religious memorial day. However, the door was still left open for private entertainment at home, at the club, or at the beach. Furthermore, the authority of the Knesset cannot extend beyond the borders of Israel. Its decrees will be heeded neither by the religious nor by the secularist elements of world Jewry. It is obvious that the combined authority of the religious leadership of Israel and the diaspora and of the Knesset will be required to give the memorial day a substantial measure of acceptance by world Jewry. The rabbinate must decree a fast-day, and the Knesset must lend force to the rabbinic decree by proclaiming it a national Jewish memorial day, thus broadening its base by reaching out to all elements of the Jewish community.

Cooperation between the rabbinate and the Knesset will depend upon their mutual agreement on a date to be designated as a memorial day. The rabbinate is unlikely to adopt any day but one which had already been hallowed by tradition as a day of fast and mourning. The twenty-seventh of Nisan falls during the Sefirah period, traditionally associated with a tragic chapter of martyrdom in the Hadrianic persecutions. However, this date was never previously observed as a fast-day nor are fasts observed (with the exception of the Fast of the Firstborn) on any day in the month of Nisan (*Orach Chaim, Hilchot Pesach* 429). Hence the preference of the rabbinate for the tenth of Tevet. The only legitimate objection to this date is the fact that it has no historical association with either the Nazi mass murders or the ghetto uprisings. The same objection applies to the twentieth of Sivan, suggested by Dr. Levinsky as a memorial day for the Nazi victims (*Sefer HaMoadim*, vol. 7, p. 213).

ALTERNATE SUGGESTIONS

The most appropriate date for a memorial day, from the historical point of view, is the fifth of Tammuz. On that day the Jews of Xantem, Germany, committed mass suicide in the crusade of 1096. Rabbi Yom Tov Heller set aside this day in 1629 as a private fast-day for himself and his descendants. In the Chmelnitzky massacres (1648), many Jews lost their lives on this date in the province of Podolya. Numerous Jews perished in Breslau in 1649 on the same day, leading to the proclamation of a communal fast-day. In 1768 the Cossacks, under the leadership of Gunta and Zhelyeznyk, massacred close to 50,000 Jews in the Ukraine. The large Jewish community of Uman was exterminated on the fifth of Tammuz. This day was designated a fast-day, and special prayers and liturgical poems were composed in commemoration of the tragedy. This historical day of sorrow became infamous again in the annals of Nazi bestiality. The first Nazi mass extermination of Jews was carried out on the fifth of Tammuz, 1942, in the Auschwitz camp.

Nazism did not die with the collapse of the Third Reich. A Holocaust Day, in the manner of the biblical admonition against Amalek, will serve as a reminder of the need for vigilance against the resurgent spirit of Nazism. That the potential for genocide is still real was evidenced by another fifth of Tammuz tragedy. It was on this day in 1946 that the post-Nazi massacre of Polish Jews took place in Kielce.

One may justly argue that the choice of the fifth of Tammuz for a memorial day is faulted by the fact that it has not been observed as a fast-day in modern times. This would impair its acceptance by the religious segment of the Jewish community. We may therefore suggest as an alternative the ancient fast-day of the seventeenth of Tammuz. Its link to the Nazi era may be based on the execution of four thousand Jews in the ghetto of Bialystok on the seventeenth of Tammuz, 1941. The decree to liquidate the ghetto of Kovno was issued on the seventeenth of Tammuz, 1944.

Another alternative date is the fast of the ninth of Av. The decree of implementation of the Nazi program of mass extermination was issued by Goering on the seventh of Av, 1941. The Babylonian destruction of the Temple, according to II Kings (25:8), also took place on the seventh of Av, but the tragedy is commemorated on the ninth of Av. A decree expelling Jews from Hungarian Ruthenia was issued on the ninth of Av, 1941.

The commemoration of a ghetto uprising within the context of a Holocaust Day is open to serious question. It would be more appropriate to take note of it on a day when the defeat of Nazidom is celebrated. The most logical date for such a celebration is Lag B'Omer, the anniversary of the death of Hitler (see chap. 8).

Bibliography

Abraham Ibn Ezra, Commentary on the Pentateuch. Vilna: Mikraot
Gedolot, 1930.
Against Apion, by Flavius Josephus. Translated by Havercamp.
Alfasi. Vilna 1893.
Antiquities of the Jews, by Flavius Josephus. Translated by Havercamp.
Apocrypha, edited by Manuel Komroff. New York, 1936.
   The First Book of Esdras
   The First Book of Maccabees
   The Second Book of Maccabees
   The Book of Jubilees. Tel Aviv: HaSforim HaChitzonim, 1936.
Baal Haturim, by Rabbi Jacob b. Asher (commentary on the Pen-
tateuch). Vilna: Mikraot Gedolot, 1930.
Bet Yoseph, by Rabbi Joseph Caro (commentary on the *Tur* Code).
Warsaw, 1867.
Bible
   Pentateuch. Vilna: Mikraot Gedolot, 1930.
   Genesis
   Exodus
   Leviticus
   Numbers
   Deuteronomy

   The Former Prophets. Warsaw, Kitve Kodesh.
   Joshua
   Judges
   I Samuel
   II Samuel
   I Kings
   II Kings

   Later Prophets. Warsaw, Kitve Kodesh.
   Isaiah

Jeremiah
Ezekiel
Joel
Amos
Jonah
Zechariah
Malachi

Ktuvim. Warsaw, Kitve Kodesh.
Psalms
Lamentations
Ecclesiastes
Esther
Daniel
Ezra
Nehemiah
II Chronicles
Chidushe Haritva (on *Megillah*), with commentary by Rabbi Chaim I.
    Bloch. Brooklyn, 1937.
Chinuch, by Rabbi Aaron Halevi of Barcelona. Lemberg, 1889.
Daat Zekenim Baale Tosafot (commentary on the Pentateuch). Vilna:
    Mikraot Gedolot, 1930.
Dead Sea Scrolls, translated and edited by Theodor H. Gaster.
    New York, 1956.
    The Manual of Discipline
    Commentary on the Book of Habbakuk
    Megillat Milchemet B'Nai Or, edited by Yigal Yadin. Jerusalem, 1955.
Eshkol Hakofer, by Judah b. Elijah Hadasi. Eupatoria, 1836.
Falasha Anthology: Black Jews of Ethiopia, edited by W. Leslau.
Great Sanhedrin, by Sidney B. Hoenig. Philadelphia, 1953.
Haggadah.
Hamakneh, by Rabbi Pinchas b. Tzvi Halevi Horowitz. Offenbach, 1801.
Historia shel Habayit Hasheni, by Joseph Klausner. Jerusalem, 1951.
Iggeret Rav Sherira Gaon, edited by Abraham Kahane. Warsaw: Sifrut
    HaHistoria HaYisraelit, 1922.
Josippon, by Joseph b. Gorion Hakohen. Jerusalem, 1961.
Karaite Anthology, edited by Leon Nemoy.
Kimchi, David, commentary on the Prophets. Warsaw: Kitve Kodesh,
    1879.
Maase Oto Haish. Otzar HaMidrashim by J. D. Eisenstein. New York,
    1928.

Magen Avraham (commentary on code *Orach Chaim*). Warsaw, 1879.

Meiri, Menachem B. Shlomo, commentary on Yevamot.

Megillat Antiochus. Otzar Midrashim, edited by J. D. Eisenstein. New York, 1928.

Megillat Taanit. Warsaw, 1874.

Midrashim

  Mechilta. Mikrae Kodesh, Shmot. Vilna, 1891.

  Midrash L'Chanukah. Otzar Midrashim, edited by J. D. Eisenstein. New York, 1928.

  Midrash Rabba al Hatorah Vechamesh Megillot. New York, 1925.

  Shmot Rabba

  Vayikra Rabba

  Bamidbar Rabba

  Shir Hashirim Rabba

  Esther Rabba

  Midrash Shochar Tov. Jerusalem, 1960.

  Pesikta Chadata. Otzar Midrashim, edited by J. D. Eisenstein. New York, 1928.

  Pesikta DeRav Kahana, edited by Solomon Buber, 1868.

  Pesikta Rabbati. Vienna, 1880.

  Sifri. Chamishe Chumshe Torah, Bamidbar and Devarim. Warsaw, 1879.

  Tanchuma (Midrash Yelamdenu). New York, 1925.

  Yalkut Shimoni. New York, 1944.

  Yalkut Job. New York, 1944.

Mishneh Torah, by Rabbi Moses b. Maimon. Berlin, 1926.

Moadim Bahalacha, by Rabbi Shlomo J. Zevin. Tel Aviv, 1954.

Moshe B. Nachman (Ramban—commentary on the Pentateuch). Vilna: Mikraot Gedolot, 1930.

Orach Chaim, by Rabbi Joseph Caro. Berlin, 1918.

Otzar Haaggadah, by Rabbi Moses D. Gross, Jerusalem, 1956.

Philo the Alexandrian. *Works of Philo Judaeus*, translated by C. D. Younge. London, 1854.

Pirke D'Rabbi Eliezer, edited by D. Luria. Warsaw, 1852.

Pirush Hamishnayot, by Rabbi Moses b. Maimon. Babylonian Talmud.

Piske Halachot, by Rabbi Asher b. Yechiel (Rosh). Babylonian Talmud.

Post-Biblical History of the Jews, by Morris J. Raphall. Philadelphia, 1856.

Rise and Fall of the Judean State, by Solomon Zeitlin. Philadelphia, 1968.

Samuel b. Meir (Rashbam, commentary on the Pentateuch). Vilna: Mikraot Gedolot, 1930.

Seder Hadorot, by Rabbi Yechiel b. Solomon Heilperin. Warsaw, 1905.

Seder Olam Rabba. New York, 1952.

262   Bibliography

Sefer Hachasidim, by Rabbi Judah HeChasid. New York, 1953.
Sefer Hamaor, by Rabbi Zerachya Halevi b. Yitzchak (Razah, commentary on Alfasi). Vilna, 1892.
Sefer Hamitzvot, by Rabbi Moses b. Maimon. Edited by Rabbi Chaim Heller. Jerusalem, 1946.
Sefer Hamoadim, by Yom Tov Levinsky. Tel Aviv, 1954.
Shiboleh Haleket, by Zedekiah b. Abraham of Rome. Venice, 1546.
Shlomo Yitzchaki (Rashi, commentary on the Pentateuch).
Talmud (Babylonian). Vilna, 1880.

Berachot	*Sukkah*
Bikkurim	*Betzah*
Shabbat	*Rosh HaShanah*
Pesachim	*Taanit*
Shekalim	*Megillah*
Yoma	*Moed Katan*
Yevamot	*Sanhedrin*
Ketubot	*Avoda Zarah*
Nazir	*Avot*
Sotah	*Zevachim*
Gittin	*Menachot*
Kiddushin	*Erachin*
Baba Kama	*Keritot*
Baba Batra	*Niddah*

Talmud (Jerusalem). Vilna, 1926.

Peah	*Rosh HaShanah*
Maaser Sheni	*Taanit*
Eruvin	*Megillah*
Demai	*Chagigah*
Pesachim	*Ketubot*
Sukkah	*Sanhedrin*

Targum Yonatan b. Uziel. Vilna: Mikraot Gedolot, 1930.
Tosefta (appended to Alfasi). Vilna, 1893.
Pesachim
Sukkah
Rosh HaShanah
Megillah
Tur Code. Warsaw, 1863.
Wars of the Jews, by Flavius Josephus. Translated by Havercamp.
Zohar. Cremona, 1560.

Index

Compiled by Robert J. Milch, M.A.

I. Passages

1. Hebrew Bible

Genesis

1:2	251
1:5	9
2:3	1
7:13	114,116
15:6	103
15:10	104
15:13–16	183
15:14	103
15:16	6
15:18	103
17:2	5
17:7	103
17:9	5
17:10	5,103
17:13	5
17:23	116
17:26	114
18:23	159
20:17	35
31:54	106
33:17	40, 42

Exodus

2:13	159
5:1	42
5:3	102
8:18	139
8:22	103
9:16	145
10:1–2	145
10:2	117
12:1	18
12:8	101, 108, 111, 130, 140, 142
12:9	108
12:10	108, 110
12:11	106, 110
12:13	117
12:14	22, 102, 117
12:15	111, 112
12:17	6, 114, 116
12:18	101, 111, 140
12:19	43
12:22	106, 107
12:23	107, 117
12:24	117
12:26	131, 153, 159, 165
12:27	106, 107
12:34–45	108
12:41	114, 116
12:43	103
12:46	108
12:48	104, 106
12:49	43
12:51	114
13:3	102, 129
13:8	117, 118, 134, 146, 153, 165, 184
13:14	117, 131, 153, 163
14:31	144
15:25	2
15:26	3
15:27	8
16:2	112
16:13–29	1
16:23	13
16:25–30	9
16:26	9
16:30	8
19:15	10

19:16	21
20:8–11	4
23:12	4
23:14–19	185
23:16	18, 179
24:15–16	189
30:16	23
31:6	6
31:12–17	5
31:13	7
31:14	6
31:18	41
32:25	41
34:10	105
34:18	19
34:18–26	185
34:22	18
34:25	113
35:2	7
36:3	41
36:6	41

Leviticus

1:3	106
2:1	106
3:1	106
9:12	106
16:1–34	27
16:3	13
16:29	43
16:30	27
17:15	44
18:3	44
18:26	44
19:2–4	7
19:3	7
19:5	107
19:19	6
19:29–30	7
19:32	7
20:30	115
22:29	107
23:5	101
23:6	180
23:14	114
23:15	188
23:17	183
23:21	114, 180

23:27	27
23:28	114
23:30	114
23:34	180
23:39	13
23:42	43
23:43	39, 40, 42, 181
24:2	59
26:45	104

Numbers

3:10	6
9:2	105
9:7	106
9:11	141
9:13	106
9:14	43
10:10	14, 23
12:1	80
15:38	171
15:41	171
21:7	35
25:13	6
28:11–31	27
28:25	181
28:26	179, 180
29:1	13, 18
29:1–39	27

Deuteronomy

4:34	117
4:37	117
5:12	1
5:15	118
5:16	1
6:7	6
6:9	106
6:10	108
6:12	108, 118
6:20	108, 131, 153, 156
6:21	108
7:8	117
7:18	102, 117
7:19	118, 139
7:22	117
7:23	117
8:17	116
10:20–21	118
10:21	117

11:8	118
11:12	20
11:13–18	22
12:21	106
13:1	90
˙14:21	44
14:28	77
16:2	106
16:3	102, 113
16:8	180
16:9–12	183
25:1	159
26:3	184
26:5	132, 184
26:5–8	132
26:5–11	111, 184
26:8	139
26:9–10	132
29:24	104
30:1–3	225
32:48	114, 116

Joshua

1:1	48
5:3	105
5:10	105
5:11	114, 115
10:27	114, 115
17:3	85
24:2–14	119, 132

Judges

2:10–13	119
6:13	120
10:9	85
11:1	85
11:3	85
11:31	85
20:28	85
21:21	216

I Samuel

1:10	35
7:4	120
20:5	195
20:29	106

I Kings

8:2	18

8:22	47
8:30	35
38:41	35

II Kings

17:6	198
23:22	120
25:8	245, 258

Isaiah

1:1	85
1:11–12	30
1:16	30
1:18	33
9:14	21
12:3	63
27:13	21
33:15	115
56:7	35
58:1	21

Jeremiah

1:1	85
31:12	242
31:30	162
31:31	104, 163
39:4–5	237
44	200
52:6	235
52:12	237, 246
52:28	83
52:30	83

Ezekiel

2:3	114, 115
24:2	114, 116
26:1–2	247
33:11	36
33:21	231, 247
40:1	20, 114, 115
45:17	124
45:21	124
45:25	124

Hosea

14:2–3	36
14:3	34

Joel

2:11	28

Amos

9:11   39

Zechariah

7:3   202
7:4   247
7:5   247
8:19   242, 247, 249
14:16   43
14:17   43
14:19   43

Malachi

3:23   28

Psalms

10:4   159
10:9   39
10:13   159
19:2   145
21   39, 45
27:5   39
31:20   39
34:15   2
47   21
47:6   22
47:4   22
47:15–16   22
63:12   172
79:6   144
111:10   164
114   132

Proverbs

30:29   45

Lamentations

1:3   243

Ecclesiastes

11:2   59

Esther

1:10   89
2:3   86
2:5   83
2:5–6   81, 82, 84
2:6   83
3:8   201
3:12   89

4:5   86
4:16   35
5:5   90
6:1   79
6:13   84
7:1   90
9:1   79
9:2   229
9:20   201
9:27   221
9:29   88
9:31   221, 230

Daniel

1:3   83
1:6   81
9:1   82
10:1   81
10:2   236, 243

Ezra

2:2   83
2:5   83
3:1   83
3:6   15
4:1   83
4:4   84
4:5   86
4:6   79
4:24   86
5:3   86
6:7   84, 86
6:14   84
6:16   52
6:19   84
6:22   124
7:25   203
7:28   84
8:2   81
10:9   83

Nehemiah

1:2   83, 84
1:6   32
2:16   84
4:6   84
7:7   83
8:9   15, 31, 36, 128
8:13   197

8:14   31, 43
9:6–11   146
10:7   81
10:35   217
11:4   83

II Chronicles

7:8–10   31
7:9   56
19:11   194
29:10   122
29:17   52, 90
30:10   122
30:16   121
30:21   121
34:30–32   122
35:11   121
35:15   121, 124
35:18   120, 123

2. *Apocrypha and Pseudepigrapha*

I Esdras

8   203
9:54–55   16

I Maccabees

4   52, 60
7   53
11   67

II Maccabees

2   53, 57
7   223
10   57, 58
15   93, 222, 223

Jubilees

6:23   19
16   41
23:6   41–42

3. *New Testament*

Acts

27:9   28

4. *Mishnah*

Maaser Sheni

5:15   70

Bikkurim

1:6   75, 77

Shekalim

7:2   135

Rosh Hashanah

1:3   236, 242

Avot

3   158

Erachin

9:4   128

5. *Tosefta*

Pesachim

4   124
6   133
10   147

Sukkah

4:6   206

Taanit

3   233

Sanhedrin

2   194

6. *Jerusalem Talmud*

Dmai'

2   77

Maaser Sheni

5   77

Eruvin

3   15, 196, 212, 213

Pesachim

10   130, 133, 146, 149, 150, 154, 162
10:1   148

Yoma

5   32

Sukkah

3   58
3:13   45

Rosh HaShanah

1   19
2   210
4   135

Taanit

1   227
2   34, 224, 227, 229
4   168, 173, 232, 234, 235, 238, 240, 241, 242, 247

Megillah

1   50, 90, 97, 202
1:5   87
2   95, 96

Chagigah

1   53

Ketubot

8   128

Sanhedrin

1   195, 196, 200
6   163

7. Babylonian Talmud

Berachot

8a   172
9a   146
9b   104
12b   132
39b   142
48a   129
51b   129
58a   156

Shabbat

13b   225
21a   62
21b   58, 63, 64, 65, 71, 224

21–24   76
22a   59
23a   74, 98
86a   10
86b   186, 189
87b   8
118b   8
139a   36

Eruvin

40a   23
62b   228

Pesachim

52a   192, 212
53a   134
58a   101
64a   121
64b   136
66a   125
68b   188
86a   133, 149
94b   159
95a   125
95b   124
99b   146
103a   125, 129
106a   128
108a   98, 147, 148, 151
108b   74
109a   53, 148, 149
109b   148, 158
114a   125, 129, 130, 131
114b   130
115a   125
115b   146
116a   126, 130, 131, 132, 133, 138, 143, 147
116b   132, 144, 146
117a   125
117b   150
120a   102, 113, 134, 140

Yoma

4a   189
16a   51
19b   33
21b   56

26b	62
29a	73
35b	32
38b	159
41b	32
53a	32
66a	30, 32
68a	32
68b	33
81a	116
86a	37

Sukkah

11b	41
12a	129
20a	126, 127
26a	39
28b	39
41b	114
43b	46
44a	47
45a	44, 45
48b	62, 63
51a	62, 127
51b	216

Betzah

4b	211, 213

Rosh HaShanah

2a	20
6a	21
12b	20
13a	115
15a	21
16a	21, 24, 46
16b	24, 28
18a	28, 203, 207, 233
18b	66, 76, 227, 231, 232, 233, 235, 236, 241, 242
19a	226
19b	202, 203, 226
21a	191, 202, 212
22b	206
24b	51, 72
29b	16, 17
32b	20
33a	15
33b	17–18

Taanit

3a	62
12a	218, 232
15a	17
15b	232
18a	226
18b	227, 228
26a	217, 234
26b	52, 174, 232, 243, 245
28b	234, 237, 240
29a	245, 246, 248
30b	232
31a	174, 217

Megillah

2a	92, 229
3a	92, 95
3b	73
4a	73, 98
5a	97
5b	76
6a	72, 173
6b	94, 97
7a	50, 88, 90, 91, 97
10b	159
11a	60, 70, 80
11b	87, 88
13b	83
14a	63, 92, 94
15a	82, 86
15b	87
17b	74
18a	96
18b	96
19a	94
31a	47

Moed Katan

9a	31
22b	227
27b	128

Chagigah

11b	158

Yevamot

43b	243
62b	169, 172, 175, 176
82b	187

115a	128	92b	159
		93b	173
Ketubot		94b	169
65a	150	98a	173
		105a	159, 160
Nazir		105b	159
53a	125	106b	160
Sotah		*Avoda Zara*	
8a	158	22b	160
48b	129, 196	52b	51
49a	240		
49b	158, 238	*Zevachim*	
		12b	107
Gittin		62a	125
34a	128		
36a	128	*Menachot*	
56b	159, 160, 161	28b	51
57b	60	62a	45
61b	128	64b	238
		65a	83
Kiddushin		99b	156, 158
37b	9		
38a	112	*Chulin*	
		83a	16
Baba Kama			
82b	238	*Erachin*	
83a	158	13a	16
Baba Batra		*Keritot*	
9a	36	2a	105
10a	36	7a	37
15a	84, 91		
56a	135	*Niddah*	
115b	164	38a	10
121a	196, 215, 216, 218	38b	10
121b	216		
147a	20	*Sofrim*	
155b	92	21	230
Sanhedrin		**8. Midrashic Literature**	
11b	197	*Mechilta*	
12a	170, 193, 210	Exod. 13:7	135
19b	194	Exod.13:8	134, 146
21a	156	Exod. 14:31	144
29a	160	chap. 18	153
38b	24	18:125	165
43a	160	chap. 17	153
56b	1, 8	17:108	165

Sifri
Deut. 32:48   116
Deut. 26:8   139

Breishit Rabba
56:13   22
61   169

Shmot Rabba
15   69
31   187

Bamidbar Rabba
10   150
13   249
14   40
14:8   41

Vayikra Rabba
29:1   25
30   39, 45, 47, 58
30:7   41

Esther Rabba
1   80
5   84
2:3   88
7   86, 87
8   86

Shir HaShirim Rabba
3:6   82

4:1   39
4:11   169
7   111, 181

Pirke D'Rabbi Eliezer
29   41

Pesikta D'Rav Kahana
28   40
29   41

Seder Olam
5   8, 104
6   28
30   80, 87

Tanchuma
Vayero 22:13   25

Chaye Sarah   8   169

Vayishlach   10   34

Chukat   24   48

Targum Jonathan
I Kings 8:2   18

Targum Onkelos
Numbers   28:26   180

II. Names and Subjects

Aaron, 119
Aaron b. Elijah, 42
Aaron Halevi of Barcelona, 108
Abaye, 228
Abimelech, 35
Abraham, 23, 35, 40, 41, 103, 105, 114, 116, 119
Abraham Ibn Ezra, 8, 9, 42, 84, 110, 112, 184
Abrahamitic covenant, 5, 6, 7, 103, 104, 119, 186
Abudarham, David b. Joseph, 116
Acha ber Yaakov, 146
Achai Gaon, 229–30
Achashverosh, 79, 80. See also Ahaseurus
Adam, 24, 25, 162
Agrippa I, 135, 136
Agrippa II, 136, 217
Ahasuerus, 65, 79, 87, 201
Ahaz, 194
Akiva, R., 21, 97, 143, 144, 149, 168, 169, 170, 172, 173, 174, 176, 177, 231, 232, 233, 234, 235, 241, 244, 247
Al Chet, 32
Alexander Jannaeus. See Alexander Jannai
Alexander Jannai, 16, 50, 51, 54, 57, 61, 62, 63, 126, 127, 129, 194, 209
Alexander the Great, 127, 154, 204
Alexandrian Jewry, 50, 54, 135, 205. See also Egyptian diaspora
Al Hanisim, 59, 70, 71, 74, 174
Alkabez, Solomon, 88
Amalek, 257
Amariah, 194
Antiochus, 54
Antiochus III, 205
Antipater, 239
Antipatris, 169, 170
Anti-Semitism, 46, 160
Apostolic Council, 155

Arami oved avi, 132, 184
Aravot, 44, 47
Aretas, 239
Aristobulus II, 238, 239
Artachshasta, 79, 80, 87
Artaxerxes I Longimanus, 80, 82, 87, 203
Ashi, Rav, 228
Asia Minor, 205
Atzeret, 180
Auschwitz, 257
Avtalion, 61, 125
Azariah, 70
Azazel, 30

Baal HaMaor, 51, 150, 175, 177
Baal HaTurim, 42, 59, 241
Babylonian diaspora, 42, 194, 195, 196, 198, 199, 201, 204, 206, 247
Babylonian exile, 15. See also Babylonian diaspora
Babylonian New Year Festival, 20
Bacchides, 64, 66, 67
Balaam, 159, 160
Bar Kochba, Simon, 76, 168, 169, 170, 172, 173, 174, 177, 178, 187, 218
Bar Kochba revolt, 76, 168, 169, 172, 173, 174, 225, 248
Ben Zoma, 132
Bene Israel, 222
Betar, 174, 234, 245, 248
Bet Hillel, 63, 65, 97
Bet Shammai, 58, 63, 65, 97
Bialystok, 257
Bikkurim, 77, 78, 145, 183, 184, 185
Bilshan, 83
Bnai Brak, 144
Boethus, Boethusians, 206
Breslau, 257

Cahna bar Abo, 169
Calendar, Babylonian, 19, 194
Calendar, Book of Jubilees, 187

Calendar, Gezer,18
Calendar, Jewish, 186, 192–93,
    194, 195, 196, 202, 206
Calendar, Qumran, 186
Cambyses, 79, 80, 87
Cestius Gallus, 31, 136, 170, 177
Chad-Gadya, 152
Chananiah, 200
Chanukah, 49–78 passim, 97, 207,
    222, 223, 224, 229
  name, 52, 58, 61, 65, 74, 78
  date, 60, 71
  duration, 49, 52, 55, 57, 60, 71,
    72
  analogies with Sukkot, 42, 55,
    57–58, 182
  seasonal aspect, 77
  national-historical significance,
    50, 51–52, 53, 55, 58, 59, 60,
    61, 64, 78
  in I Maccabees, 51–53, 60
  in II Maccabees, 50, 51, 53–55,
    58, 59
  in Josephus, 51, 60, 61, 63
  in *Megillat Antiochus*, 51, 64–69
  in *Megillat Taanit*, 61, 64
  in Talmud, 51, 57, 61, 63, 69,
    71, 73–74
  early opposition to, 50, 76, 88
  rabbinic demilitarization of, 64,
    67, 74, 75, 224
  dedication and cleansing of
    Temple, 51, 52, 55, 57, 59, 62,
    64, 66, 67, 74, 78
  miracle of fire, 55–57, 58, 59,
    60, 61, 64, 78
  miracle of oil, 57, 63, 64, 67, 68,
    71, 72, 74
  kindling of lights, 61, 63, 71,
    74, 78, 127
Charoset, 125, 133
Chasidim HaRishonim, 10, 11, 67
Chief Rabbinate (Israel), 254
Chinuch, 108
Chiya, R., 46, 149, 154
Chmelnitsky massacres, 253
Christianity, 11 154–155, 160, 161,
    162. *See also* Judeo-Christianity;
    Paul, Paulinism

Chukim, 6, 157
Circumcision, 5, 103, 104–5. *See
    also* Abrahamitic covenant
Converts, 43
Cossacks, 257
Covenant. *See* Abrahamitic
    covenant; Sinaitic covenant
Creation, date of, 250–51
Crusades, 250
Cyrus, 79, 80, 82, 86, 197, 198,
    201
Daniel, 70, 79, 81, 82, 86
Darius I, 82, 86, 200
Darius II, 87
Darius the Mede, 79
Darius Hystaspes, 79, 80
Daryavesh, 79, 80
David, 85, 120, 194
Dead Sea Scrolls, 92, 165. *See also
    names of works*; Qumran sect
Decalogue, 1, 2, 3, 4, 7, 8, 21, 189
Ebutius, 169
Edels, Samuel Eliezer, 75
Egyptian diaspora, 198, 199, 200,
    201, 204, 205. *See also*
    Alexandrian Jewry
Elazar, R., 188
Elazar b. Chisma, 158
Elazar b. Jose, 94, 232
Eleazar b. Azariah, 37, 132, 146
Eleazer, R., 36, 68
Elephantine papyri, 200
Eliezer, R., 24, 34, 76, 144
Eliezer b. Judah of Worms, 59
Eliezer b. Tzadok, 125, 134, 232
Eliezer Maccabee, 54, 68
Elijah Gaon, 40, 41, 71
Elisha, 193
Eretz Yisroel Uschenoteha
    (Horowitz), 169, 207
Esau, 159
Esdras, Book of, 15
Eshkol HaKofer, 10
Essenes, 11, 155
Esther, 35, 70, 87, 88, 89, 90, 91,
    202, 221
Esther, Book of, 65, 84, 91, 92, 93,
    96–97, 221

Ethiopia, 80
Etrog, 62, 181
Exile, Babylonian, 40, 47
Exodus, from Egypt, 6, 42, 94,
    104, 107, 111, 171, 182
Ezekiel, 20, 36, 37, 114, 123, 195,
    196, 200, 247
Ezra, 15, 16, 31, 36, 79, 80, 81, 83,
    126, 197, 202, 203
Ezrach, 43, 44

Falasha Anthology (Leslau), 23
Falashas, 9, 14, 23, 188–89
Fast of Esther, 221–22, 229–30
Fast of the Firstborn, 256
Fasts, fasting, 52, 71, 76, 97, 123,
    222, 224, 230, 253, 254, 256. *See
    also* Tisha B'Av; Yom Kippur
Fifteenth of Av, 174, 215–19
    passim, 249
    agricultural aspect, 216
    matrimonial aspect, 216
    wood-offering ritual, 217–18,
    250
Four Cups (Passover), 73, 148–51
Four Questions (Passover), 130,
    133, 138, 147, 149, 151
Four Sons (Passover), 152–54,
    155, 156–58
Fruria, 93, 98

Gabat, 169, 170
Gallus, 171
Gamliel II, 17, 18, 21, 65, 74, 96,
    97, 112, 133, 137, 138, 146, 147,
    148, 232
Gamliel the Elder, 112, 138
Gedaliah, Fast of, 231
Geonic period, Geonim, 174, 175,
    243
Ger, 43, 44
Gerondi, Zerachiah b. Isaac
    Halevi, 51, 150, 175, 177
Gezer calendar, 18
Gideon, 120
Golden calf, 7, 44, 105
Gombiner, Abraham, 187
Great Sanhedrin, The (Hoenig), 69,
    207
Gunta, Ivan, 257

Hadrian, 168, 172, 210, 225
Hadrianic persecution, 168, 174,
    176, 187, 225, 244, 256
Haggadah, 97, 131, 132, 133, 134,
    138, 144, 145, 151, 152, 153,
    159, 163, 164
Haggai, 82, 125, 196, 201, 202
Hai Gaon, 46, 175, 176, 177, 243
Hakafot, 44, 46, 47
Hallel, 47, 124–25, 128, 133, 137,
    149, 150, 151
Haman, 70, 84, 86, 89, 159, 201
Hananiah, 70
Hannah, 35
Hasmonean dynasty, 50, 51, 174,
    194, 206, 217, 228
Hathach, 86
Havdalah, 125
Heliopolis, 205
Hellenism, 50, 156, 157, 158, 205
Hellenistic diaspora, 14, 35, 93,
    154. *See also* Alexandrian Jewry;
    Philo
Heller, Yom Tov, 257
Herod, 28, 217
Heseibah, 146
Hezekiah, 52, 90, 121, 122, 193,
    194, 195
High priest, 30, 32, 193, 194, 196,
    198, 217
Hillel, the Elder, 17, 61, 112, 125
Hillel II, 212
Historia shel Bayit Sheni
    (Klausner), 177, 248
Hitler, Adolf, 84, 167, 177, 258
Hodu, 80
Hoenig, Sidney B., 69, 207
Holocaust, 167, 168, 178, 253,
    255. *See also* Nazism
Holocaust Day, 254, 255, 257, 258
Horowitz, Israel S., 169, 207
Horowitz, Pinchas, 9
Hosea (king), 218
Hosea (prophet), 34, 36
Hoshana Rabba, 44–45, 47
Hoshea, R., 149
Huna, Rav, 146
Hyrcanus, John, 68, 208, 209
Hyrcanus II, 238, 239

Ibn Ezra, Abraham, 8, 9, 42, 84, 110, 112, 184
Idolatry, 15, 123
Iggeret Shabbat (Ibn Ezra), 9
India, 80, 222
Intercalation, 96, 193. *See also* Calendar, Jewish; Second Festival Day
Isaac, 25
Isaac b. Judah ibn Ghayyat, 175
Isaac b. Sheshet, 96
Isaac of Kenna, 75
Isaiah, 21, 29, 30
Ishmael, R., 23, 33, 158
Isserles, Moses, 244

Jacob, 40, 41, 42
Jacob bar Acha, 227, 229
Jacob b. Asher, 42, 59, 241
Jair, 81, 85
Jannaeus, Alexander. *See* Alexander Jannai
Jannai. *See* Alexander Jannai
Jason of Cyrene, 53
Jeconiah, 81, 87
Jehoiachin, 123
Jehoshaphat, 194
Jephthah, 85
Jeremiah, 163, 199–200, 246, 247
Jericho, 46
Jeroboam, 121
Jerusalem, 17, 28, 31, 43, 53, 95, 177, 204, 216
Jesus, 159, 160
Jochanan Maccabee, 54, 66, 68
John Hyrcanus, 68, 208, 209
Jonah, 36
Jonathan, 194
Jonathan Maccabee, 54, 68
Jose, R., 37, 250
Jose, R. (2d cent.), 186, 187
Jose, Haglili, 189
Joseph, 47
Joseph, R., 188
Joseph b. Gorion, 236
Josephus, Flavius, 28, 31, 35, 53, 63, 136, 169, 203, 208, 236, 239
    on Rosh HaShanah, 14, 16, 18
    on Sukkot, 16

on Chanukah, 51, 54, 60–61, 63–64, 67
on Purim, 87, 93
on Passover, 112, 113
on Shavuot, 186
on Xylophory, 217
on Fifteenth of Av, 216, 217
on Nikanor Day, 223
on destruction of Jerusalem, 237, 244, 248
Joshua, 46, 119, 249
Joshua (high priest), 201
Joshua, R., 21, 76
Joshua b. Chananiah, 125, 129
Joshua b. Levi, 59, 98, 149, 151, 227
Joshua b. Prachyah, 54
Josiah, 120, 121, 122, 123, 124
Josippon, 56, 75, 236, 238
Jubilees, Book of, 10, 14, 40, 41, 186, 187, 188, 194, 195
Judah, R., 1, 37
Judah b. Beteira, 148
Judah b. Illai, 149
Judah b. Shamua, 226
Judah b. Tabbai, 54
Judah HaChasid, 244
Judah HaNasi, 37, 75, 76, 95, 97, 210, 211, 226
Judah Maccabee, 51, 52, 53, 54, 55, 60, 64, 66, 67, 68, 69
Judeo-Christianity, 159, 161, 163, 165

Kaparot, 38
Karaites, 9, 10, 14, 42, 234, 247
Karban Chagigah, 101
Karban Tamid, 51, 52, 62, 101, 238, 240, 244
Kennedy, John F., 253
Kiddush, 125, 128, 129, 130, 131, 133
Kielce, 257
Kish, 81, 83, 84, 85
Klausner, Joseph, 177, 248
K'neged arbaa banim. See Four Sons
Knesset (Israel), 254, 255, 256
Kohanim, 6, 14, 17, 30, 34, 101, 119, 121

Kol Nidre, 38
Koresh, 79
Kovno, 257
Kush, 80
Kushi, 80

Laban, 40
Lag B'Omer, 167–78 passim
  historical basis, 168, 169, 170,
    171, 172–74, 177
  post-talmudic development,
    175–76
  as possible date for Holocaust
    commemoration, 168, 177,
    178, 258
Lcha Dodi, 88
Lechem oni, 111–12
Leslau, Wolf, 23
"Letter of Rabban Yochanan b.
  Zaccai," 160
Levi, R., 86, 87, 238, 240
Levinsky, Yom Tov, 256
Levites, 121, 124
Lulav, 44, 45, 47, 181
Lydda, 76, 98
Lydia, 205
Lysias, 55

Maccabee family, 249. *See names of
  members;* Hasmonean dynasty
Maccabee revolt, 50, 60, 64, 66,
  67, 68
Maccabees, First Book of, 51–53
Maccabees, Second Book of, 42,
  53–55, 182
Magen Avraham, 187
Maharsha, 75
Mah nishtanah. See Four
  Questions
Maimonides, Moses, 51, 70, 71,
  76, 106, 128, 129, 141, 145, 146,
  148, 191, 192, 236, 241, 242
Malachi, 82, 87, 196, 202
Mannah, 1
Manasseh, 122
Mandelkorn, Solomon, 5
Manual of Discipline, 33, 165
Marah, 1, 2, 3, 8
Marranos, 171

Mattathias, 66, 67, 68, 69, 70, 71
Matzah, matzot, 101, 111, 112,
  113, 118, 124, 131, 133, 134,
  138, 140, 141, 142, 147
Mechilta, 153
Megillah. See Esther, Book of
Megillat Antiochus, 51, 57, 63,
  64–69, 71, 72, 73, 75
Megillat Esther. See Esther, Book
  of
Megillat Taanit, 51, 53, 64, 70, 71, 66
  72, 76, 219, 222, 223, 224, 225,
  226, 227, 228, 229, 249, 250,
  253
Meir, R., 37, 96, 187, 188, 226, 232
Meiri, Menachem b. Solomon,
  175
Memorial lamps, 38
Men of the Great Assembly
  (Synagogue), 84, 91, 92, 126
Mereimar, 146
Messiah, messianism, 45, 173,
  249
Mezuzah, 107–8
Midrash Masseh Chanukah, 63, 70
Minor Passover, 207
Miriam, 250
Mishael, 70
Mohlin, Jacob b. Moses Halevi,
  175, 176
Mordecai, 35, 70, 81, 82, 83, 84,
  85, 87, 88, 90, 91, 201, 202, 221
Mordecai Day, 93, 98
Moses, 7, 28, 36, 40–41, 47, 48,
  62, 102, 103, 116, 119, 139, 186,
  189, 215, 250
Musaf, 14

Nachman, Rav, 87, 169, 172, 227,
  229
Nahmanides, Moses, 42, 113,
  114, 141, 142
Nathan, R., 24
Nazism, 84, 167, 177, 255
Nebuchadnezzar, 81, 159, 199,
  237, 246
Nebuzaradan, 237, 246, 248
Nehardea, 173

Nehemiah, 43, 55–56, 81, 83, 197,
   217
Nehemiah, R., 86, 88
Nemirov, 254
New Year. See Rosh HaShanah
New Year, Babylonian, 20
Nicolaus of Damascus, 208
Nikanor, 53, 55, 223, 224
Nikanor Day, 53, 93, 221, 222,
   223, 224, 229, 230
Nimrod, 159
Ninth of Av. See Tisha B'Av
Noachite Laws, 1, 2, 3
Noah, 116, 186

Omer, 45, 114, 115, 180, 186, 187,
   191.See also Sefirah
Onias IV, 54, 56, 73, 135, 205
Ovin, R., 45

Paganism, 121
Papa, Rav, 232, 236
Parents, honor of, 1, 3, 6–7
Parthian Empire, 67, 168, 171
Paschal lamb, 101, 103, 104, 105,
   106, 107, 108, 109, 111, 118,
   125, 131, 133, 134, 135, 138,
   140, 141, 142, 149, 184
Passover, 43, 101–66 passim, 168,
   169, 172, 188, 239
   sacrificial and Temple rites, 27,
      101, 102–3, 104, 105, 106,
      120–22, 123, 135–36, 137, 149
   paschal lamb, 101, 103, 104,
      105, 106, 107, 108, 109, 111,
      119, 125, 131, 133, 134, 135,
      138, 140, 141, 142, 149, 184
   date, 42, 101, 108, 191, 193,
      195, 207
   second day, 45, 192
   seasonal aspect, 19, 77, 182, 183
   redemptive-commemorative
      aspect, 6, 22, 44, 94, 102, 103,
      104, 105, 107, 108, 109, 111,
      112, 113, 117, 118, 130, 132,
      133, 137, 139, 145, 181
   analogies with Sukkot, 180,
      181, 182, 183

   relation to Shavuot, 27, 179,
      180, 181, 183
   Biblical mandate of, 102, 103,
      106, 108, 111, 113, 114, 140,
      145, 180
   uniqueness of, 101, 102
   in Philo, 102, 110, 112, 113, 135
   in Josephus, 112, 113
   Josiah's, 122–23
   postbiblical development, 119,
      120
   Seder service, 18, 30, 73,
      124–25, 128, 130–48 passim.
      See also Haggadah; Hallel
   matzah, 101, 111, 112, 113, 118,
      124, 131, 133, 134, 138, 140,
      141, 142, 147
   charoset, 125, 133
   maror, 101, 111, 118, 131, 133,
      134, 138, 147
   Kiddush, 125, 128, 129, 130,
      133, 151
   Reclining, 147
   Four Questions, 130, 133, 138,
      147, 149, 151
   Four Cups, 148–51
   Four Sons, 152–54, 155, 156–58
   Shfoch chamatcha, 144
   Minor (Second) Passover, 207
Paul, Paulinism, 155, 160, 162,
   163
Pentecost. See Shavuot
Pesach. See Passover
Pharisees, 16, 33, 50, 51, 54, 62,
   68, 127, 194, 209
Pharaoh, 102, 103, 116, 117, 132
Philo
   on Rosh HaShanah, 14, 16, 18,
      24
   on Yom Kippur, 28, 29, 35
   on Sukkot, 39, 58
   on Chanukah, 50
   on Passover, 102, 110, 112, 113,
      135
   on Shavuot, 186
   as diaspora spokesman, 14, 154
   use of allegory, 154
Phrygia, 205
Pilgrimage Festivals, 14, 30, 31,

77, 185, 189, 216. *See also names of festivals*
Podolya, 257
Pompey, 28, 50, 53, 236, 238, 239, 240
Post-Biblical History of the Jews (Raphall), 67
Prayer, in Judaism, 34–35, 185
Priests. *See* Kohanim
Prozbul, 128
Psamtik, 199
Pseudo-Smerdis, 79
Ptolemaic dynasty, 204
Ptolemy I, 204
Purim, 65, 74, 76, 79–99 passim, 167, 202, 207, 222, 223, 224, 230
 origins and background, 77, 80, 81, 82, 88, 89, 91
 initial opposition to, 50, 90, 91
 Mikra Megillah ritual, 92, 93, 94, 95, 97, 98, 99
 giving of gifts, 93
 See also Ahaseurus; Esther; Esther, Book of; Haman; Mordecai
Puritans, 11

Qumran sect, 23, 33, 155, 165, 166, 186, 194, 195

Raabad, 150, 151
Raphall, Morris J., 67
Rasha, 153
Rashi, 115, 116, 221, 229
Rashbam, 9, 40
Rav, 86, 143, 149, 153, 211, 212, 226
Rava, 87, 140, 141, 171, 172
Reclining, 146
Red Sea, crossing of, 1, 8, 94, 112, 113, 132, 144, 182
Rehoboam, 121
Reish Shata, 20
Resh Lakish, 127
Restoration and return, 15, 19, 31, 43
Rise and Fall of the Judean State, The (Zeitlin), 52
Rish Shattin, 20

Ritva, 63, 71
Rokeach, 59
Rome, Romans, 52, 53, 58, 67, 68, 98, 151, 157, 168, 170, 171, 173, 175, 176, 186, 208, 210, 217, 218, 227; 229, 239, 240
Rosh Chodesh, 192, 193, 195, 196, 197, 202, 206, 209
Rosh HaShanah, 13–25 passim, 27, 28, 182
 status in Jewish calendar, 13
 in Bible, 13
 as New Year, 13, 14, 18, 19, 20
 as Day of Judgment, 13, 14, 21, 23–24, 27, 40
 solemnity of, 13, 16, 21
 date, 13, 15, 18, 19, 24–25, 193, 203, 207
 second day, 196, 197
 as occasion for remembrance, 22
 sacrificial rites of, 13, 15, 16
 in Temple, 13, 14, 17
 universalist aspects, 14, 24
 in Philo, 14, 16, 24
 Shofar ritual. *See* Shofar
 during restoration and exile, 15, 16
 in Josephus, 14, 16, 18
 in Ezekiel, 20
 synagogue ritual, 16, 17
 in Talmud, 17–18, 20, 21, 22, 23–24
 names of, 18, 19, 20
 in Falasha tradition, 23

Saadia Gaon, 47, 236, 243
Sabbath, 1–11 passim, 13, 114, 125, 188
 as day of rest, 1, 3–4
 biblical commandment of, 1, 4, 7, 8
 socio-ethical aspects, 3–4, 5, 7
 holiness aspects, 5, 6, 7, 8,
 date of first, 8, 9
 and marital relations, 9–11
 in Talmud, 10, 11, 76, 125, 128
 blowing of Shofar on, 17

in Ezekiel, 123
    Kiddush, 128, 129
Sabbath Chazon, 218
Sabbath, Christian, 11
Sabbath Nachamu, 218
Sacrificial rituals, 6, 27, 29, 30, 37,
    45, 62, 101, 103, 123. *See also
    names of sacrifices*
Sadducees, 14, 16, 33, 50, 62, 127,
    155, 163, 164, 194, 209
Salome Alexandra, 50, 126
Samaritans, 9, 14, 208
Samuel, 120, 121
Samuel (amora), 143, 149, 211,
    212
Samuel b. Judah, 88
Sanhedrin, 191, 194, 206, 207,
    208, 209, 210, 215
Sanhedrin of Usha, 218
Sargon, 198, 222
Saul, 85
Second Festival Day, 191–213
    passim
Seder, 18, 30, 73, 124, 125, 126,
    128, 130–48 passim
Seder Olam, 8, 187, 250
Sefer HaMoadim (Levinsky), 256
Sefirah, 168, 175, 256. *See also
    Omer*
Seleucid dynasty, 50, 204, 206
Septuagint, 93, 95, 98
Seventeenth of Tammuz, 52, 231,
    234–36, 244
Shabaton, 13
Shavuot, 24, 78, 168, 169, 172,
    179–89 passim
    seasonal aspect, 77, 180, 181,
        182, 183
    historical aspect, 180
    anniversary of giving of Torah,
        186, 187
    names, 179, 180, 181, 182
    date, 179, 180, 186, 187, 188,
        189, 193, 195
    second day, 191, 192
    relation to Passover, 27, 179,
        180, 181, 183
    relation to Sukkot, 180, 181,
        182, 183

First Fruits, 77–78, 145, 179,
    183, 184. *See also Bikkurim*
    in Bible, 179
Shammai, 61, 127
Shapur II, 171
Shema, 132
Shfoch chamatcha, 144
Shila San, 222
Shimei, 81, 85
Shira, 94
Shiva-Asar b'Tammuz.
    See Seventeenth of Tammuz
Shmayah, 61, 125
Shmini Atzeret, 13, 48, 181
Shofar, 13, 14, 15, 17, 21, 23, 24,
    25, 121
Shrira Gaon, 175, 177
Shushan, 88
Simchat Be HaShoavah, 61–63,
    127
Simchat Torah, 48
Simon, R., 158, 231, 233
Simon b. Gamliel I, 94, 96, 188,
    215, 216, 217, 218, 225, 226
Simon b. Gamliel II, 97
Simon b. Shatach, 61, 127, 129,
    194, 209
Simon b. Yochai, 176
Simon Chasida, 236
Simon Maccabee. *See* Simon the
    Hasmonean
Simon the Hasmonean, 54, 58,
    68, 207
Simon the Just, 32, 69, 70
Sinai, revelation at, 1, 2, 3, 9, 21,
    102, 186
    date, 186–87, 189
    See also Shavuot; Sinaitic
        covenant; Torah, giving of
Sinaitic covenant, 2, 3
Sin-offering, 27
Sodom, 41
Solomon, 35, 48, 56, 88, 90, 120,
    121
Sossius, 28
Sukkah, 39–40, 41, 43, 45, 59, 145
Sukkot, 13, 15, 16, 31, 39–48
    passim, 78, 145, 195
    national-historical aspect, 39,

42, 43, 180, 181, 183
seasonal aspect, 19, 39, 77, 180,
   182, 183
date, 40–41, 42, 193
second day, 191
in Philo, 39, 58
and Chanukah, 42, 55, 57–58,
   182
and Exodus, 42, 43
and judgment period, 24, 40,
   45
analogies with Shavuot, 180,
   181, 182, 183
analogies with Passover, 180,
   181, 182, 183
See also Etrog; Hoshana Rabba;
   Lulav; Sukkah
Synagogue, 16, 17, 95

Taanit Esther. See Fast of Esther
Tabernacles. See Sukkot
Tam, 153
Tam, Rabbenu, 253
Tamid. See Karban Tamid
Tattenai, 86
Temple (Jerusalem), 37, 177, 194,
   207, 217
   First Temple, 30, 31, 33, 35, 56,
      88, 90, 120–21, 122, 129, 194,
      195, 216
   Second Temple, 31–33, 34, 35,
      56, 88, 120–21, 124
   Destruction, 34, 50, 52, 53, 68,
      73, 95, 126, 185, 195. See also
      Tisha B'Av
Temple of Onias, 53, 56, 73, 135,
   205
Ten Commandments. See
   Decalogue
Ten Days of Penitence, 28
Ten lost tribes, 198
Tenth of Tevet, 167, 254
Tineius Rufus, 168
Tisha B'Av, 97, 218, 222, 227, 233,
   236, 243, 245–51 passim
   in Bible, 231, 232, 247
   and Temple destruction, 235,
      245–46

date of numerous tragedies,
   245, 248, 258
as possible Holocaust
   commemoration, 257–58
and Shabtai Tzvi, 249–50
Titus, 159, 160, 238
Torah, giving of, 186, 187. See also
   Shavuot; Sinaitic revelation
Trajan, 210
Trajan Day, 229
Tzvi, Shabtai, 249, 250, 251

Usha, 218
Ushpizin, 41

Vaad HaL'umi, 254
Vashti, 89
Vespasian, 170
Vital, Chaim, 176

War of the Sons of Light and the
   Sons of Darkness, 23
Warsaw Ghetto Uprising, 253,
   254, 255
Weeks. See Shavuot

Xantem, 257
Xerxes I, 80, 82, 87
Xylophory, 217

Yadin, Yigal, 186
Yavneh, 17, 18
Yeb, 200
Yehuda, R., 115
Yehudi, Yehudim, 83
Yerucham, Rabbenu, 175
Yochanan, R., 24, 149, 191, 192,
   211, 212, 226, 243, 245, 247
Yochanan b. Hyrcanus, 194
Yochanan b. Nuri, 97
Yochanah b. Zaccai, 17, 114, 115,
   160, 163, 172
Yochanan Kohen Gadol, 70
Yoma, 27–28
Yom HaAtzmaut, 49
Yom Kippur, 13, 20, 27–38
   passim, 44, 182
   spiritual-judgmental aspects,
      24, 27, 32, 34, 36, 37, 38, 40

sacrificial and Temple rites, 27,
    29, 30, 31, 32, 33, 34, 37
  names, 27–28
  date, 28, 29, 193, 202
  in Bible, 27
  in Philo, 28, 29, 35
  in Josephus, 28, 31
Yom tov sheni shel galuyot. See
  Second Festival Day
Yosi, R., 226

Zebadiah, 194

Zechariah, 21, 43, 82, 196, 201,
    202, 231, 236, 242, 244, 247
Zedekiah, 237
Zeira, R., 227
Zeitlin, Solomon, 52
Zeresh, 84
Zerubbabel, 15, 83, 197, 201
Zhelyeznyk, Maxim, 257
Zichron, 22, 24
Zikaron, 22, 24
Zipporah, 80, 250
Zugot, 170–71, 172